LISTENING TO FEAR

LISTENING
TO FEAR

■

HELPING KIDS COPE, from
NIGHTMARES to the NIGHTLY NEWS

■

STEVEN MARANS, Ph.D.

AN OWL BOOK ■ Henry Holt and Company ■ New York

To Wendy, Alex, and Adam, who teach me every day
and whose love supports everything I do

HENRY HOLT AND COMPANY, LLC
Publishers since 1866
115 West 18th Street
New York, New York 10011

Henry Holt® is a registered trademark of
Henry Holt and Company, LLC.

**This book is for informational purposes only. It is not intended to take the
place of individualized advice from a trained medical or mental health professional.** Readers are advised to consult a physician, psychologist, or other
qualified health or mental health professional before acting on any of the information or advice in this book. Other than matters of public record, case
studies, and personal anecdotes, the persons described in this book are com-
posites rather than particular individuals. The names and identifying characteristics of persons, dates, places, and other details of events have been changed
with respect to all case studies and personal anecdotes described in this book.

Library of Congress Cataloging-in-Publication Data
Marans, Steven.
    Listening to fear : helping kids cope, from nightmares to the nightly
news / Steven Marans.—1st ed.
        p.   cm.
Includes index.
ISBN-13: 978-0-8050-7604-2
ISBN-10: 0-8050-7604-2
    1. Fear in children.   2. Child rearing.   I. Title.
BF723.F4M37 2005
155.4'1246—dc22   2004057553

Henry Holt books are available for special promotions and
premiums. For details contact: Director, Special Markets.

FIRST EDITION 2005

Designed by Gretchen Achilles

Printed in the United States of America
1   3   5   7   9   10   8   6   4   2

CONTENTS

APPENDIX B

QUESTIONS PARENTS ASK ABOUT

WAR AND TERRORISM

235

LISTENING TO FEAR

INTRODUCTION

Lord save little children! Because for every child born of woman's womb there is a time of running through a shadowed place, an alley with no doors, and a hunter whose footsteps ring brightly along the bricks behind him. With every child—rich or poor—however favored, however warm and safe the nursery, there is this time of echoing and vast aloneness, when there is no one to come nor to hear, and dry leaves scurrying past along a street become the rustle of Dread and the ticking of the old house is the cocking of the hunter's gun.

—From *THE NIGHT OF THE HUNTER* BY DAVIS GRUBB

I was driving into Manhattan with a van full of teenage boys. The attacks of September 11 were nineteen months behind us. The war in Iraq continued, but we were once again back to Code Yellow. As we turned into Midtown, the conversation changed. The boys' observations suddenly betrayed the anxiety that lay behind their attempts to convey hip indifference. As we passed an unattended golf bag on the sidewalk, one of the 16-year-olds laughingly pointed it out to the rest of us. "We'd better pick up speed—it's probably a terrorist bomb."

Similar scenarios unfolded as we made our way through the city. A group of Sikh men standing on a street corner became an al-Qaeda cell ready to spring into action. The mention of a visit to Chinatown elicited advice about where to buy surgical masks. The boys, all of them bright and well informed about the news of the world, laughed with every comment of this unfolding travelogue. But there was no laughter when we reached the site of the World Trade Center. The boys walked slowly, deliberate in their silence. A block away, I couldn't restrain myself from asking, "That was the first time you guys were here, right? What was it like, seeing the site?"

My 13-year-old son answered. He couldn't look at me and sounded a little choked up. "Dad, there are some things that words can't get at . . . some things you just have to feel inside, on your own."

What a time this is to be growing up. I heard my son's description and knew what he meant about silence and quietly bearing the unbearable. But at the same time I wanted to hug him, to talk the feelings of horror, loss, and fear out of him. At that moment and at so many other moments, I wished the world were not so ready to prove that the worst of our children's nightmares can in fact come true. What a time this is to be a parent.

It isn't as though the world of my childhood was free of brutality and danger. Snarling dogs and men attacking other men, women, and children remain horrifically etched in my memory. In 1962, the howling sirens of A-bomb drills represented an abstract threat to my 8-year-old imagination. It was an entirely different matter only a year later. With news of our president's assassination, it was impossible to ignore or avoid the upset and fear of my parents and teachers—of everyone. We were stricken and assaulted again as we watched the first live telecast of an assassin's murder.

When I was a teenager, as never before, the nightly news brought the toll of deaths from a seemingly never-ending war into all our homes. Fresh images of racial strife were regular television fare as American cities smoldered and burned. The violent death by assassination of Dr. Martin Luther King, Jr., inspired a deep sense of loss. It seemed the spiral of fear and chaos that can often lead to further violence and further loss could only continue.

There has never been a time when children were isolated from events demonstrating that our worst nightmares can come true. Every generation feels they have known the best and the worst that life can throw their way—and they're all correct. But things also change.

Over the last years there has been a progression in both the sources and the frequency of dangers that affect all of us. Drive-by and school shootings, massive terrorist attacks, threats of further terror violence, and war have significantly increased uncertainty about the world for my sons. And they are not alone.

Studies before and after 9/11 indicate that too many children today not only experience their worlds as unsafe but pay the price for their uncertainty and fear in symptoms that interfere with learning, relating, and feeling. For some, sleeping, eating, and toilet habits are disrupted; for others, worries emerge as complaints about aches and pains. For children and adults alike, concerns about sudden death, loss, physical danger, and loss of control leave us feeling vulnerable. At these times we may find it particularly difficult to concentrate. We may feel unable to enjoy our relationships and the pleasures of daily life.

Clearly, children who are closest, both physically and psychologically, to events of violence, destruction, and sudden loss are at the greatest risk for subsequent emotional difficulties. However, children whose parents are deeply affected by events are also especially susceptible to anxiety, depression, or trauma. When moms and dads aren't in control of themselves and their families, the world looks like a very dangerous place to their children. Similarly, when day-to-day life is regularly disrupted by overwhelming events, our kids are more likely to develop problems. These may recede as life returns to normal or, alternatively, have an enduring impact over the course of their development. Even when we do not experience or transmit our own preoccupation with the violence of war, terrorism, and other unexpected dangers, we may unwittingly make ourselves less available to our children. When this occurs, even in the absence of dramatic, immediate symptoms, kids are left alone with their fears.

In a group discussion a colleague led in a New York City neighborhood several weeks after the 2001 terrorist attacks, 11-year-old Cheri described watching the towers go down. She said it was horrible. Cheri did not want to elaborate on what she saw but volunteered that, since September 11, she had been frightened to be outside or go to school. She reported having frequent nightmares and was especially worried about burglars coming into her house. When asked what connections Cheri thought there might be between her new worries and the attack on the World Trade Center, her explanation surprised her parents and perhaps everyone else in the room. "Well, the CIA, FBI, and police kept all their evidence in the towers. When the towers were wrecked, all the evidence was destroyed and they had to let all the criminals go." Now, according to this 11-year-old, criminals roamed free on her neighborhood streets.

The chaos of terror for this young girl was located in a distortion of facts that were most accessible and closest to home. Because of all they had heard in the news about psychological trauma, her parents had assumed that their daughter's symptoms were related to 9/11. However, until this meeting, they had by their own account been so preoccupied with their own distress and worry that they hadn't inquired about the specific nature of Cheri's beliefs. For the first time since the attacks they began to listen to their daughter and to learn what forms her fears were taking and how they might help her.

As all parents know, children's fear may be prompted by circumstances far less dramatic than war news, terror threats, or school or community violence. At every stage of development, children demonstrate a vast repertoire of personal versions of terror. Infants can be overwhelmed by an unfamiliar face or by being alone at night in a darkened room. For toddlers, being separated from a parent evokes anxiety and dread. Who hasn't looked under the bed with a panicked 3-year-old who begs not to be left alone because of the monster that will emerge as soon as we leave? And what about the first days of day care and school that are so often marked by protest, tears, and complaints of aches and pains that should rightly keep them at home? Dogs or other animals do not have to pose any real threats in order for school-age kids to be terrified of them. Most kids have bouts of great concern about burglars, whether their house has been broken into or not. Even when there hasn't been a death in the family, many children have transient fears about their parents' safety and possible loss. While adolescents may at times profess indifference to the relationships among family members, the sounds of parents arguing may arouse just as much anxiety about divorce as it did when they were younger—even when the parents view their occasional struggles as a normal part of marriage, not a prelude to the end.

Throughout our development, our bodies are alternately the source of enormous pleasure and concern. From the earliest years, the feeling that the body is vulnerable, broken, or inadequate can lead to disproportionate fears. That doesn't stop the toddler or preschooler from melting down over the smallest of scrapes, or the school-age child from being so afraid of getting hurt that he or she will refuse to take part in a pickup soccer game.

All the sex education in the world won't halt preoccupying worries about bodies and sex brought on by menstruation and puberty. If losing control over our own bodies is the leading edge of our fears in early adolescence, losing control of our sexual feelings takes its place a few years later.

While there may never be an end to developmental sources of fear, there is a progression in the forms they take and in the strategies we have available to cope with them. Parents are instrumental in this process, at our best lending support to the maturing minds and bodies of our children. But for both parents and children there are times throughout life when our strategies are inadequate and a sense of danger dwarfs our most adaptive and productive resources.

It is tough enough to grapple with the fears fed by our developing minds and imaginations. It is an even harder struggle when the most normal developmental sources of fear are complicated by real events that reinforce and confirm our worst feelings and ideas. When events echo our most nightmarish fantasies, we often can't wrap our minds around them or cope with the overwhelming emotions they arouse.

As director of the National Center for Children Exposed to Violence, and in my years as a child and adult psychoanalyst, I have listened to and observed countless numbers of children and parents as they struggle with dangerous and frightening events. As a parent my-self, I know how difficult it is to find the words to say to our children in the midst of the real dangers that confront us all. I am aware that that my wish to protect my sons from being overburdened is made all the more difficult when dangers old and new are broadcast into our lives 24/7. Turning off our televisions cannot guarantee that our chil-dren are protected from the reality of violence and brutality that punctuates even the most peaceful and secure homes.

I also know from my own experiences and those of other parents that our attempts to reassure can often sound hollow even to our own ears. Just as bad are those times when we force our preoccupying wor-ries onto our children, as Cheri's parents did, before we have learned whether they share our fear—or have their own concerns about local, national, or global events.

In our wish to help our children, we need to remind ourselves that our own fear and uncertainty can prevent us from providing them with the most immediate and essential forms of comfort that we have to offer: paying attention and listening. Rather than feeling help-less, we can educate ourselves about the ways our children think, feel, and communicate their experience of an unpredictable and dangerous world. When we better understand how our children's minds work, we are in a better position to live up to our role as their protectors.

It's not always easy to listen to our children. And when we do, it's not always easy to make sense of what we are hearing. We've forgotten the language that children use to communicate worries and anxiety, and we often assume that what is most frightening to us is most fright-ening to them. We may unwittingly leave our children alone with their unique fears and, as a result, put them at greater risk of developing symptoms of distress that further erode their sense of competence and connection to the world.

Many difficulties lie in the path of listening to our children and understanding the specific sources of their anxiety. What is clear is that unless we are able to recognize our children's concerns and the sometimes-veiled ways they communicate them to us, we are in no position to reassure them or offer the kind of comfort and support they need most.

How can we reassure our children when they can't tell us the exact source and nature of their fears? How do we know when our children are distressed by the news? When real events seem to make our nightmares come true, how can we best support our children in ways that are consistent with who they are and what they need? How do we learn to listen?

I wrote this book to answer these and other questions so that parents will feel better equipped to help each other and their children deal with the uncertainty and fear that are an inevitable part of being alive. Beginning with a focus on how we register and respond to fear as adults, we will move through the phases of children's lives, from infancy to adolescence, exploring sources of danger and fear that emerge in each period of development. There is no way to shield our children entirely from violence, destruction, and loss, whether it is broadcast on television or touches them personally. But we can learn to understand and respond to our children's fears. In my years as a professional, and as a parent, I have learned that the journey to that place of understanding begins within ourselves.

■

CHAPTER ONE

IT WAS A DARK AND STORMY AFTERNOON: FACING OUR FEARS

The fort we had built with blankets, sofa pillows, and chairs was collapsing. Bored on a cold rainy Saturday in my family's basement, my brother, sister, and I flipped through the full range of the four channels on our black-and-white television. Maybe it was something about the music that played as the titles scrolled: melodic but with a threatening edge. It announced that something big and awful was about to happen. Or maybe it was the opening that grabbed us, the scene behind the credits where a bright summer sun beat down on a dry dusty road as police sirens grew louder in the background.

Whatever it was, we were hooked and would be completely captured by the most frightening film we had ever seen. *The Night of the Hunter,* the only film ever directed by Charles Laughton, had a fine cast that included Robert Mitchum, Lillian Gish, Shelley Winters, and Peter Graves. Their powerful depictions of love and loss, evil and danger, devotion and courage—and, finally, of salvation and safety—were incredibly compelling.

The story, set during the Great Depression, is about a psychopathic preacher who marries Willa, mother of John and Pearl. She has been widowed by a husband who, before being caught and hanged for bank robbery and murder, manages to stash his stolen cash in Pearl's doll. In pursuit of the hidden loot, the preacher murders Willa and then chases the children down the Ohio River until they are taken under the wing of Rachel, a kind but tough shotgun-wielding older woman, who stands up to the preacher, protects the children, and offers them a new home.

When the movie ended, we were no longer bored. We were scared speechless. For many nights, I anticipated dreams in which a disembodied voice, sounding very much like the preacher's, would wake me with a feeling of dread. Many years later I would find the book, written by Davis Grubb, on which the screenplay was based. There I found a passage that vividly described the troubled nights that followed our rainy-day viewing.

And in the shadow of the branch beneath the moon a child sees a tiger and the old ones say: There is no tiger! Go to sleep! And when they sleep it is a tiger's sleep and a tiger's night and a tiger's breathing at the windowpane. Lord save little children! For each of them has his Preacher to hound him down the dark river of fear and tonguelessness and never-a-door. Each one is mute and alone because there is no word for a child's fear and no ear to heed it and no one to understand it if heard. Lord save little children! They abide and they endure.

The film was like watching, alert and wide-eyed, the worst parts of a nightmare. It had captured so many of my worst fears that I felt as though I had grabbed hold of a live wire and simply couldn't let go. In time, the movie images no longer intruded on my waking thoughts or directly on the scenarios that filled my dreams. I suppose I was like the children described in Grubb's passage who have been fortunate enough to experience fear and move on.

Over the years I have watched *The Night of the Hunter*—and while I can still recall how scared I was at the first screening, like the memories of bad dreams, the strength of the fear has diminished. As

I began to work with children as an analyst and psychotherapist and, later, as a father to my own sons, I realized that while there were obvious advantages to distancing myself from the original and most intense reaction to it, the very distance I sought kept me from understanding the experiences of the children I wanted to help.

It comes as no surprise that we adults try to avoid recalling or living out memories of our worst, most uncomfortable feelings. We relegate them to the depths of unconscious life and deny them when they attempt to rear their ugly heads. As parents, we are confronted with a real dilemma. We want to know what frightens our children so we can reassure and soothe them, but at the same time we avoid revisiting one of the best sources of information we have: our own childhood experiences of fear. As a result, when we try to come to their aid, we may also feel an enormous distance from them. As we seek to provide comfort, we fumble with words that simply don't reach them.

Even when children are able to tell us directly what is frightening them, our reassuring statements that it's all going to be okay have little effect. This is the case whether the dangers that terrify our kids are imagined or real. It is hard to remember what that fear felt like, but for our kids' sake we need to try.

BARRIERS TO UNDERSTANDING CHILDREN'S FEARS

If we are unable to pin down or acknowledge the sources of our own fears, we will have a tough time knowing what makes our children so frightened. If we rely on them to tell us, we may be left as alone in the dark as they feel.

While our children can tell us they are scared, they are often unable to tell us why. When they are able to identify the immediate source of their alarm, we may not be as able to see or hear it so clearly. Other times, their behavior is the only way that they can communicate—or we can know—that they are afraid. We do our best to understand and extinguish our children's fears, but often our best is not good enough. At those moments, we are as confused and helpless as they are.

We speak the same language, but as parents we may feel that we've forgotten or never learned the magic words that might bring us closer to understanding what our children are trying to tell us. This mystery of meaning is especially striking and confusing because we too were once children. Why is it so hard? We had our own experiences of fear and terror, the same trouble communicating with our parents. We should know better. But we don't. In the midst of our children's struggles to tell us what's wrong, too often we just can't remember what it was like to be their age. Even if we can remember to walk past a certain dilapidated house in our neighborhood that once terrified us, from our perspective as adults we may now find it hard to imagine why.

In fact, we may chuckle or feel embarrassed about having such silly and irrational worries. Our disbelief and chagrin may be a convenient alternative to remembering how alone we felt when there was no immediate escape from the sense of helplessness our fear aroused.

OUR NIGHTMARES

We can get closer to the experience of our children's fear by finding a manageable way to acknowledge our own terrors. For example, try to recall what it was like to wake up from a childhood nightmare. Take a minute. Think back to a time when you were somewhere between the ages of 8 and 12. Recall as best as you can a dream frightening enough to wake you. Was it about falling or being chased? Was there a monster attacking you, or were parents and other family members being injured or killed? Did you ever dream that you were the monster who injures and kills? Was the nightmare that came to mind just now about injuries to your body or about being trapped, lost, and on your own? Did you ever have an overwhelmingly embarrassing dream about arriving to class naked or being yelled at by teachers and others for minor infractions? Do you remember bad dreams about burglars and kidnappers?

Now that you have conjured up the content of an old nightmare, can you remember what it felt like at the moment you woke up?

Many of us can recall springing from sleep with racing hearts. We couldn't seem to get enough oxygen. Clammy with sweat, our bodies were tense and frozen with fear. We remember feeling confused and disoriented as we desperately scanned every inch of the dark bedroom. At these moments, we searched for the boundaries of experience, trying to determine if the threat was real. Remember how carefully you listened for every creak in the house? Did absolute silence seem only to increase the likelihood that bad things lurked in the shadows, ready to pounce? Your terror might have propelled you from your bedroom, sending you either inching or scrambling down the hallway in search of a safe haven.

Facing our parents or older brothers and sisters, looking and feeling stricken, we were often speechless. If it wasn't too late at night, our sources of refuge and safety might still be awake and may have had the patience to ask solicitously about the bad dream before sending us back to bed.

BRAINS, BODIES, AND FEELINGS

Our bodies express the terror of nightmares dramatically. Our hearts pound and we gulp for air. We sweat. We are keenly aware of each new sound or flickering shadow that might signal danger. The disruption of our sleep and the feelings that follow reflect changes in brain activity that occur when we feel our safety is threatened. When dangers are real, these same responses prepare us for action and are essential to our survival. In the moments immediately following a nightmare, they may also contribute to the experience that we are indeed out of control.

What happens? First, our brains react by producing norepinephrine (adrenaline). Norepinephrine focuses us on the danger. We need to do this, because in situations of real or perceived threat we need to make quick decisions about how to protect ourselves. Next, norepinephrine causes our hearts to beat faster and increases our breathing rate. Both reactions provide our muscles with the additional oxygen and energy they need to fight or to run. Norepinephrine also prompts the release into our bloodstreams of a steroid called cortisol. Cortisol makes additional sugar stores available to our muscles. Cortisol also prevents us from thinking too much. This is important, because if we are convinced that danger is imminent, thinking for too long without acting can be fatal.

In the wake of a nightmare, the initial immobilization that you might feel is required for two mutually beneficial purposes. First, you collect yourself, allowing your overactive physical response to calm as you assess the nature and extent of the threat. Waking up to the sight of a real burglar in your path would have a significant impact on the next move you made! Second, these waking moments provide time for discriminating between what is real and what is not real. By conjuring up our long-forgotten nightmares, we remember that confusion and disorientation were central to the experience. In that twilight waking state, our bodies and minds conspired in a powerful way to convince us that, if we felt terror, danger could not be far behind.

It stands to reason that once we are fully awake we can look around and determine that perceived dangers aren't real. These nightmares, powerful enough to wake us up, pose no immediate threats. We have a good chuckle about our vivid imaginations and go back to sleep, right? Ah, if only! The problem is that we put greater stock in what we feel and imagine than we would like.

Perhaps the most important aspect of the fear aroused by our childhood nightmares was the feeling that we were not in control—that we couldn't predict, prepare, or defend against the threat to our safety. The immediate sense of terror helped us move beyond that initial state of disorientation. We sprang into action, seeking safety in the presence of parents or others whose strength and capacity to protect us from danger seemed greater than our own. They would not let us be harmed by the threatening characters of our dreams.

Being in our parents' presence served another crucial function.

Making contact with them through sight, sound, and touch helped us break free from clutches of our imagination and create a bridge back to the safer world of our daily lives. Like turning on the lights, being with parents helped to reorient us, to make more vivid the distinction between dreaming and waking states.

But the power of the imagination is strong, sometimes overpowering our capacity to return quickly to our ordinary daytime ability to check reality—to distinguish between real and unreal. The level of arousal created by the dangers in a nightmare inhibit the very functions of the brain that are in charge of quickly assessing that difference. So contact with the protective reality of our parents often offered only partial and temporary reassurance. Before we could sound the internal all-clear signal that would allow us to return to sleep, we would perform multiple maneuvers to ensure that our perimeters were secure or that a well-established warning system was in place so that we would not be caught unaware and unprepared again.

Most of us remember that no matter how short the hallway was that led back to our bedroom, it felt like a very long walk. With thoughts still disorganized and with few other words available, we may have repeated, mantralike, "It was only a dream." We did the best we could to establish safety zones. We clutched old cuddly toys we had previously cast aside as too babyish. In the wake of the nightmare, these toys that had earlier provided the surrogate warmth of parents were pressed into service again. Or we held on to family pets or baseball bats, or left the lights on and stayed awake as long as we could, watching and listening carefully for telltale signs of danger.

It's a nice idea, this "it's only a dream" business. But if you remember, the mantra didn't stand up to the feelings those dreams conjured up. Some of us found toys could indeed substitute for the comfort of our parents. Or we slept close to brothers and sisters and were comforted by the thought that the danger would get them before us—or, better, instead of us! We sought solutions to counteract feelings of being alone and insecure by turning to substitutes and talismans that reminded us of being held, comforted, and safe.

Those of us who remember the details of the nightmare experience will not forget how important it was to hold on to any hopeful reminders of reality while remaining vigilant to the threats that derived from the nightmare realms of our imagination. Uncertain that perceived threats were really only in our minds, we did whatever we could to protect ourselves, including staving off a return to sleep and dreams where our terror reigned. Alternatively, we did everything we could to disable the instant replay, change channels, and alter the script of the original dreams. Whatever the specific, most reliable solution that any of us found, each of these efforts attempted to reverse a central aspect of our nightmare. In its aftermath we would engineer any means possible to take charge, to reverse the experience of surprise and helplessness. As best as we could, we would not be endangered by our own ignorance and passivity again. Instead, we would now anticipate and prepare, ready to respond.

However long and varied the list of subjects for our worst nightmares might have been, if we were fortunate enough they did not ever come true or mirror real events. Most people are never chased by monsters and ghosts. Your house did not have to be burglarized for you to have bad dreams about burglars. You did not have to dive out of an airplane without a parachute to dream about falling. Similarly, dreams about being lost or about losing people we loved could occur with all the associated pain and horror as if we had in fact experienced the loss of a parent.

In short, even in the absence of real danger in our personal worlds, dreams could feel dangerous and terrifying enough to temporarily alter our brain chemistry, bodily sensations, and perceptions of reality.

THE STUFF OF NIGHTMARES

We actually know more than we would like to about the nature of fears powerful enough to leave us, as children, feeling unsafe in our own imagination and in the real world of daily life. We know about these dangers because, as adults, we have never been able fully to escape them. The same fears that generated our childhood nightmares fuel the most significant of our adult anxieties as well.

When we think about the broad categories of fear that we and our childhood selves share we recognize how familiar they are:

- Fear of losing control of our urges, feelings, and rational thoughts

- Fear of losing the love of others and the love of ourselves

- Fear of damage to our bodies and loss of functioning

- Fear of our own death and the deaths of those we love and depend on

- Fear of losing the order and structure in our world that provides the basis for anticipating, planning, and responding to new challenges

The fears that are the source of nightmare also lurk in the background of our waking lives. While we may not be hit over the head with the kinds of graphic, terrifying images that appear in dreams, we continually respond to signals of anxiety and concern that alert, prepare, and enable us to take protective action.

Think for a moment about each of the categories of fear just listed. Imagine, for example, your own death or the death of your spouse, your parent, or your child. Being left suddenly by someone you love, or feeling utterly ashamed and unworthy of your own love. Being in an accident that leaves you permanently disfigured or impaired. Going crazy, tormented by hallucinations and unable to control impulsive wild behavior. Or imagine a personal world disrupted by the disaster of a hurricane or warfare or terrorist attack. If you have slowed down in your reading long enough to conjure any of these situations, you will be aware of how difficult it is to stay with any of them for very long. We don't like to think about these fearful ideas, especially when we cast ourselves or our loved ones in the central roles.

The only thing worse than having to experience the feelings associated with these situations is to experience their full assault when they manifest themselves in real life. At these times, our immediate and subsequent reactions, both psychological and physical, are different from what we experience in the aftermath of a nightmare only by degree and intensity.

CONNECTING ADULT AND CHILDHOOD FEARS

It should be easy to appreciate our children's versions of danger and fear when our own experiences are derived from the same sources. Even though our worst fears have been with us since the beginning, our long experience does not necessarily translate into greater comfort with them. In fact, as we grow older, our fears grow increasingly more sophisticated and disguised.

The coping strategies we've learned to keep our earliest fears at bay also keep us from seeing and recognizing how our children struggle. To do our job as parents, to understand and respond to our children, we need to remember what it felt like to be a kid. To do this, especially when it comes to fear, we also need to appreciate the ways we learned to forget.

CHAPTER TWO

BUMPS IN THE NIGHT: UNDERSTANDING ADULT FEAR

You wake at the darkest hour of the night with your heart pounding. Did you hear a crash downstairs? Did someone rattle your window? You get up and inspect the house. Nothing. Yet when you get back in bed, sleep eludes you. Your heart pounds as you think about an upcoming airplane trip, an important presentation you must make to colleagues, or a routine medical test you have scheduled. In the darkness your daytime fears loom larger and larger and threaten to overwhelm you. Finally, near dawn, you manage to drift off. The next morning, in the clear light of day, your fears assume normal and manageable proportions.

When we are upset—as you were when you woke suddenly in the night—our minds don't work as well as we would like. In fact, at the height of anxiety, frustration, rage, or sadness, we'll often say we're "losing it." It's not that we have become completely incoherent and out of control but that we are keenly aware we're just not thinking clearly. The intensity of our feelings and our jumbled thoughts make us uncomfortable precisely because we can't put the brakes on and regroup as quickly as we would like. The "it" that we feel we're losing is control, perspective, grounding.

If our adult feelings are this intense, imagine how much more sinister and threatening nighttime fears can seem to small children. Before we enter their world, however, it's important for us to explore our own experience of fear. Only by recognizing our own worries can we turn to our children and offer them the guidance and comfort they need. So in this chapter we will walk in the world of adult fear and examine adult ways of meeting and managing it.

Understanding the ways our minds work can be a crucial step in taking back control over ourselves. This understanding is the frame of reference we need when our thoughts, emotions, and behaviors seem to have no bounds. Similarly, having some awareness of what lies behind the agitated emotions and behaviors of others—especially spouses and partners—can be useful in resisting the temptation to respond in an equally unbounded fashion.

LOSING CONTROL

We are, at times, so overcome by anxiety, frustration, rage, or grief that we simply may not know what to do with ourselves. At these moments we can't sit still or focus on any one thing. We're filled with so much emotion that we feel we will literally burst. The one and only thing we can zero in on is the upsetting thought or image itself, which replays over and over in our minds. When we can't think straight and feel unable to escape uncontrollable feelings or dangerous urges, we often describe the situation in language that both articulates and amplifies our fears: we're going crazy, we're falling apart, we're losing our minds.

This sense of losing control signals danger and vulnerability on two fronts. On the first we are unable to navigate our internal world with its dangerous desires and wishes, as frightening as they are conflicted. As a result, we feel our problem-solving skills are out of order and we can't turn down the volume on our most unpleasant feelings. As if that isn't enough, we are terrified that this awful state of affairs will never end.

Knowing our minds are working poorly, we feel that the normal challenges of everyday life are just too complicated to meet.

At worst, we may be unable to distinguish accurately between internal and external sources of danger. Feeling disoriented and confused can be enormously worrying on its own because we feel incapable of predicting what might happen next. When impulses connected to the emotions of love and hate are unregulated and out of control and we are unable to anticipate our own actions or the actions of others, the world can feel like a very dangerous place. Will we blurt out words of love, lust, or rage that are entirely inappropriate and lead to rejection and humiliation? Will we act on thoughts of excitement or revenge that invite rebuke or punishment? Or do we wind up believing that the words and actions of others are just as unpredictable, making every social interaction a source of potential danger?

As we attempt to reduce our discomfort and straighten out our thinking, we desperately try to identify where the danger lies, if only to give shape to what feels so distressing. If we could just organize and shape the nature of our disturbance in the real world, we would no longer feel so helpless and overwhelmed.

Consider phobias, things we have identified as so dangerous and frightening that we have developed specific strategies to avoid them. For some, encountering the much-feared thing produces an exaggerated startle, an accelerated heart rate, and general terror. For others, phobic responses aren't terribly dramatic; avoidant strategies are well rehearsed and reliable, especially when the sense of danger has been assigned to things that do not crop up in daily life. There are lots of phobias—snakes, the ocean, the dark, enclosed spaces—that are easily avoided with little cost to general functioning. Alternatively, there are many phobias requiring patterns of evasion that may have a much more profound and sometimes crippling impact on our lives. A healthy respect for rules of hygiene becomes a terror of life-threatening germs lurking in every handshake. A fear of flying means a grandmother cannot visit her family in another country. A fear of elevators restricts a worker to jobs in single-story buildings.

When these and other fears are constant, they become preoccupying obsessions that require equally constant or compulsive solutions. Regardless of the balance between biological and psychological contributions to phobias or to illnesses such as obsessive-compulsive disorder, these conditions are accompanied by feelings dramatically disproportionate to the perceived threats. Once a source of danger has been identified, feeling frightened by direct confrontation with it is no longer the only option. The simple possibility of contact with the thing you fear sends a loud and clear signal that action needs to be taken. However irrational the fear and whatever the price of the elaborate techniques of decreasing it are, the primary goal is to avoid feeling helpless.

DISPLACING OUR FEELINGS

Those of us who can't put ourselves in the phobic's shoes may be more familiar with the experience of generalized anxiety. When we are so nervous that we can't think straight, we do our best to decrease those feelings. Daily exercise that lasts just a bit longer and is done with more intensity than usual may help us burn off uncomfortable revved-up feelings. Making lists may help anchor our minds, ordering the racing thoughts that are distracting us.

At times of high unfocused anxiety, we don't have to have irrational fears of germs to launch into frenzies of household cleaning or reorganizing. And action is not the only way we try to avoid feelings of anxiety and vulnerability. At times of distress, eating, drinking, napping, or watching television more than usual may be preferred approaches. In whatever way that works, each of us seeks to order and control our mind, our emotions, and our world.

Think about it. In daily life, what are the sources of your discontent and angst? Is it the dishes that have once again been left in the sink? They've been left there before, but when your nerves are stretched and raw, the sight of them takes on increased value and importance. You have momentarily not only found *the* reason for your bad feelings but a solution as well. If only everyone in the family fulfilled their clear well-established household responsibilities, you wouldn't feel so burdened. Or maybe you walk in the door after a long day of work and your wife begins to bellyache about her day. Now, in addition to feeling tired, you feel burdened by her implicit request for sympathy. You know how the rest of the evening will go. Your wife will accuse you of being insensitive and unavailable or will withdraw into cold silence. This only fuels your anger and frustration. Your children's requests for attention sound like unreasonable demands when you don't have an iota of energy to deal with them. Add to that the creeping nagging feeling that you are overreacting and somehow failing them.

In scenarios like these, you have successfully displaced onto ready targets the anxiety and unhappiness that you felt long before coming home. Even if you were aware of what stirred up those uncomfortable feelings in the first place, by foisting the blame onto your family you push away the original offending thoughts. You lose sight of the fact that you were feeling anxious or needy in the first place.

PUTTING A LID ON IT

Because we don't like feeling anxious and out of control, acknowledging those feelings is something we go to great lengths to avoid. We protect ourselves as mightily as we can. Say you are behind on an assignment at work. For the moment, let's leave out whether or not the delay is objectively justified. Your boss or a colleague has asked for a status update or, worse, has been openly critical of what you have or haven't done. In a heartbeat, the context of your generally good or better-than-good performance seems to vanish. You have screwed up, and it doesn't feel good. Even if the question or critique is delivered in the most benign way, your conscience goes into overdrive. You screwed up! There are no immediate solutions to magically alter your boss's opinion or your own self-assessment. You feel incompetent, small—you have failed.

What if the criticism is totally unjustified? What if your immediate reaction was to feel enraged? Did you yell at your colleague? No? Why not? Maybe because to do so would reveal the extent of your hurt and your sense that you were the victim of an injustice. Perhaps whenever you feel justifiably angry the emotion is so intense that you worry that expressing it will appear irrational and potentially destructive. You don't want to come across as hypersensitive or weak; nor do you want to suffer the consequences of appearing insubordinate, irrational, and out of control.

In either case you may show an embarrassingly childish side of yourself in a professional setting. The very prospect of this kind of self-revelation makes you cringe just to think about it. However successful you were at sucking them up, the feelings do not just go away. In fact, you've added to the mix; self-doubt and self-loathing join your feelings of being misunderstood or maligned because you didn't stand up for yourself. What a mess.

SPOILING FOR A FIGHT

Even when we know what interaction, piece of news, or event has kicked off our strong and uncomfortable feelings, we may not know why they are so strong or why we feel so uncomfortable. We recognize that our feelings of anxiety and dread are disproportionate, whatever triggered them. Sometimes, the same feelings seem to come out of nowhere. If we can't even identify a threat, how can we defend ourselves against it? When there is no tangible danger, when it originates in our own minds, we still look to situations in daily life that can explain or justify why we feel the way we do.

People at home and at work don't need to be terribly critical for us to perceive them as harsh and attacking. The pain and anxiety we feel is just as real and perhaps more powerful if our "attackers" are in fact convenient external hooks for criticism that we also dish out to ourselves. After the fact, we may be able to recognize that we externalized, or cast onto others, the critical views that were really our own. Even though the cost may be great, we attempt to protect ourselves from the most painful and overbearing aspects of our consciences by assigning their harsh judgments to other people. Whether we do this on a temporary basis or as an unfortunate part of our personality, we take this evasive action for good reason.

We all know the feeling of shadowboxing with our own consciences. When we start giving ourselves grief, whether in the form of shame, guilt, or self-loathing, it is hard to escape—especially when we believe wholeheartedly that we deserve the beating. This feels so bad we go to extremes to avoid it, assigning our own worst views of ourselves to others. The process is far from pleasant for everyone involved.

Anticipating and experiencing attacks that we are now convinced are coming from folks out in the real world means that we perceive anything and everything they say as hostile. At worst, we will provoke the very criticism we at first only imagined, as well as the battle that so often follows. At these times, when we are literally spoiling for a fight, we may be totally unaware of this or why we are doing it. But there are also those times when, even as we defend ourselves against an imagined slight, we hear a little voice asking, "Why are you making such a big deal about this?" Somehow, we manage either to silence or ignore this voice of reason and self-reflection. We feel the world is against us, and our supposed critics soon find themselves embroiled in a fight that seems to come out of left field.

A friend of mine, Carol, told me the following story:

"I had taken leadership of a team in my firm that was working on a huge project negotiating with a number of other companies who were interested in a collaborative business venture. We had been researching all angles of this very complex proposal for weeks. As I reviewed the power-point presentation I was to give the next day, I realized a specific piece of information was missing that my team members had assured me was included. Each member of the team had assumed that someone else had covered it, or that its absence from the presentation meant it was no longer needed. To make matters worse, by the end of the day it was clear that there was not enough time to fill the gap. I was enraged. More important, I felt like a complete and utter fool. I was the leader of the project, and I had failed.

"There was no way to postpone the meeting the next day. I barely slept that night. I could not stop thinking about all the points at which I should have caught the problem. I tried to be angry about what my team had failed to do, but an unbearable weight of responsibility rested on my shoulders. My images of the next day's meeting ranged from outright rage from the assembled participants to their sniggering disdain for my incompetence. The scenarios always ended with me handing in my resignation by the end of the day. As the sleepless hours wore on, I became increasingly indignant about the anticipated attacks. I reviewed defensively all the work I had accomplished over the years and the sacrifices I had made for other projects.

"By the time I arrived at the meeting, I was not only incredibly anxious but also loaded for bear. I made the presentation. The first question raised was benign and had nothing to do with the missing data. But I was ready to hear any question as hypercritical. Before I could stop myself, I launched into an impassioned statement about the amount of work that had been done and how no one could be expected to anticipate or know the answers to absolutely every detail of how the project would unfold! The group looked stunned. My boss looked at me with some surprise and then quickly made a joke about how exhaustion could clearly impact the most brilliant of minds. Everyone chuckled with relief, including me. By the end of the meeting we had identified what further work was needed, including research into the area that had been left out of the presentation. The amazing thing was that in addition to the round of applause for our work, many of the participants approached me with compliments about my presentation and hard work.

"My boss later asked, 'What was up with that first response? For a few minutes there, I thought I was going to have to call the men in the white coats.' I explained how I had messed up and the resulting lack of sleep the previous night. He was amazed. 'You thought I would want the resignation of one of the most able and hard-working members of this firm? I wasn't joking when I said you had a brilliant mind. Do you really not know how valuable you are?'

"My head was swimming, and not just from fatigue. I realized at that moment the enormous discrepancy between my view of myself and the views others had of me. I also realized that my expectation of a hostile reception had overnight become such a firm conviction that I'd been primed for battle. Had my boss not stepped in, I might have gone on to crazed eruptions of defensive attacks, bringing me closer to my nightmare fantasy of resigning! The fact that eventually the deal went through was only further proof of the huge distance between the reality and my self-denigration. Now, when I find myself veering toward similar versions of this intense self-loathing, I try to remind myself of my boss's words. With the right mix of gravity and warmth, he said simply, 'You are too hard on yourself. You deserve to be kind to yourself—don't ever forget that.' "

Getting into unnecessary fights with imagined foes seldom resolves our pain or insecurity. Yet, however unpleasant it is, going back into the locked room with our harsh opinions of ourselves feels much worse. Instead, we locate the enemy and decide, with a vengeance, that the enemy is not us! Suddenly, we are no longer doing battle with an elusive foe but with a real live human being from whom we can protect ourselves. At these moments, when we judge ourselves as having sinned in thought, feeling, or deed, we are less able to love ourselves or feel the love of others. Even when we are not looking for "relieving" chances to fights, we find other ways to keep our offending thoughts hidden, not only from ourselves but from those others who, we believe, will surely share our harsh judgments.

I HAD IT COMING

There are many ways we try to soften the blows of our own judgments. Rather than looking for fights as a way of dispatching our guilt, we may seek criticism and attack because we feel we deserve punishment—sometimes for crimes that are hard to define. A friend of mine describes driving on the highway and feeling so anxious every time she sees a police car that she breaks into a sweat. "It doesn't matter that I'm driving at or even below the speed limit. I always worry that I will be pulled over and ticketed."

Later, she added to the story. "Each time that happens," she admitted, "the strangest memory comes to mind. I was five years old and stole the most beautiful pastels that I had ever seen from my classroom. It was so exciting, and it may me feel so bad!"

I fought off the temptation to interpret her childhood motivations and why this particular memory leaps so readily to mind when she sees a trooper in her rearview mirror.

"I have my own ideas about the multitude of sins those pastels may represent," she added. "I guess I prefer the brief elevation of my heart rate to recalling a catalog of guilt-producing ideas."

Real external consequences are not the only reason we feel frightened by the force and intensity of our own impulses and feelings. Feeling rage toward someone we love also evokes powerful signals of danger from the conscience. We register the anger as unacceptable and dangerous and fear that somehow it will wipe out our pleasurable feelings of affection, trust, and reliance that are the basis for important relationships. We are then in a real bind. We may not be able to dismiss the strong hostile feelings, but we also don't want to let loose with their expression in ways we fear may jeopardize the relationship. We may not be able to escape enormous guilt and shame over having destructive feelings and fantasies about someone we love. Unfortunately, we are rarely able consciously to choose the solutions to these dilemmas.

Compounding the problem, while we may succeed in pushing away and literally forgetting the angry, disappointed, and critical thoughts about the person we love, this change in focus decreases our anxiety and shifts our thoughts away from the original target. "Turning aggression against the self" is one way of describing this understandable but unfortunate way we have of juggling what feel like competing emotions of love and hate toward the spouses, children, parents, or friends upon whom we depend.

These psychological acrobatics are attempts to avoid several primal fears: loss of love of the person we love and upon whom we rely, loss of love of ourselves when feelings and impulses contradict our highest values and aspirations, and loss of control of emotions and impulses that, if put into action, would be as powerful, explosive, and dangerous as they feel. When we feel pressed on any of these fronts, we do what we can to minimize the imagined and real potential dangers.

Our efforts to keep dangerous thoughts and feelings at bay by displacing, projecting, and externalizing them cause problems of their own. As we try to disown unacceptable feelings, we run the risk of creating distortions and finding ourselves in an inhospitable and dangerous world. Alternatively, if we seek safety by withdrawing from the world, we are bereft of our connections with the very people whom we feel we need to protect from our own most frightening feelings and urges.

WHEN THE THREAT IS REAL

If you have ever had a serious brush with death or suffered serious injury, you most likely experienced an otherworldly sense that the disaster was happening to someone else. This dislocation reflects a disconnect that occurs between the brain's emotional regulation and executive functioning centers. It also explains the apparent calm (and absence of tears, screaming, and teeth gnashing) that observers of an emergency often find surprising and strange.

We don't have to be facing imminent death to experience the terror of losing control. Receiving news that you've tested positive for a chronic illness or witnessing a serious accident can dramatically raise heart rates, create a flood of perspiration, and cloud thinking. When we are confronted with illness and injury, we may be immediately overwhelmed with fear and panic. The loss of control of our bodies can lead not only to physical pain but also to the sense that there has been a breach in our armor, that we are now unprotected from further danger. Our self-image may be dramatically altered; we are no longer as robust and competent as we once thought. This kind of preoccupation with the body can be lasting. The physical discomfort and the real or imagined changes in the way our bodies function make it difficult to shake persistent thoughts and feelings about our vulnerability. This preoccupation distracts us and robs us of the pleasures associated with ordinary life.

But we don't have to be severely threatened to experience preoccupying fear. Even mundane events can trigger measurable anxiety. Studies have shown that "white-coat" phenomenon, the angst we may feel simply by seeing a doctor for a routine physical, is substantial enough to increase blood pressure. Often, if we happen to see people whose bodies are in any way altered by illness or accident, we may involuntarily turn away or consciously resist the urge to do so. This aversion may not reflect insensitivity but rather a set of fears that we harbor about our own bodies. When we don't look away but instead feel transfixed by someone else's infirmity, we may wince in what feels like sympathetic pain and grief. In either case, our response is related to personal nightmare fantasies about what might happen to *us*. We see someone in a wheelchair and we instantly find ourselves struggling with a host of troubling fears about our own competence, attractiveness, and mastery.

Each of us has an ideal view of ourselves. We feel at our best when we experience the closest possible match between that ideal and the lives we are leading. Our most immediate and important form of control is the control we have over our own bodies. Our bodies are the most fundamental representation of who we are as individuals, the vehicle through which we experience life with others, giving expression to thoughts, emotions, and urges. The beating of our hearts, our movements, sensations, perceptions, and thoughts, are physical capacities that define life itself. Working in concert, each organ and body part serves an essential function, enabling us to fulfill our deepest longings and aspirations.

As adults, we are most consciously aware of our bodies when we experience physical pleasures or when the minor aches, pains, and fatigue associated with physical achievement also signal mastery and prowess. At these moments—following sexual intimacy, hard work, childbearing, athletic achievement, or long hours of caring for our children—we celebrate our capacities and competence. We are so invested in these good feelings that early in life we imagine adjustments to our bodies—slimmer, more athletic, more attractive—that might enhance our pleasure. We do our best to keep threats to our bodies at bay in the way we take care of ourselves physically and by the lengths we will go to avert conscious reminders of our worst fears. We are blessed with the pleasure and satisfaction that our bodies deliver and burdened with the understanding that injury or cumulative life experience can dramatically diminish or end those good feelings.

There are times when we are especially sensitive about our bodies and the way they work. At those times, how they look and feel becomes a source of intense preoccupation. At the most benign end of the spectrum, these concerns may accompany the physical changes that occur with pregnancy or aging. We notice the differences between the ideal images of our bodies and the way we look in the mirror. We compare ourselves to others who are younger or more shapely. In the face of our dissatisfaction, we may go on a diet, increase our exercise, or color our hair. Alternatively, a sporty new car or wardrobe may serve as a proxy for attempts to defy aging and may temporarily revitalize sagging, youthful spirits. Our children and their accomplishments can also create a sense of reflected glory when we have passed the peak of our own physical achievements. A telltale sign of these phenomena can be spotted when the emotional, competitive intensity of our investment in our children's academic, artistic, or athletic pursuits is greater than theirs is! At the other end of the spectrum, there are times when our bodies do not work the way we would like because of aging, illness, or injury. Regardless of their source, physical limitations can either be accepted and integrated as an aspect of our identity or be defied and rejected as unwanted and hated. When we are unable to tolerate or revise our self-image in response to real circumstances, we may be less forgiving of ourselves and waste a great deal of energy in anger and disappointment. Paradoxically, our entire experience of who we are may be defined by who we are not. When our gauges are set to unrealistic, unobtainable standards, we struggle to find pleasure and satisfaction in our lives.

LOSING SOMEONE WE LOVE

The only thing more frightening than threats to our own bodies are threats to the lives of those we love. The death of a parent, a spouse, or a friend, or, perhaps most painful, the death of a child, not only marks the end of one of the most crucial and integral relationships of our lives but also the end of a connection that has gone from past to present and into an anticipated future together. Perhaps the best way of appreciating the intensity and importance of our closest relationships is to consider what it would be like to lose them. News of the unexpected death of a loved one produces physical changes along with a sense of disorientation, numbness, and chaotic feelings. In the face of this kind of news, we often we find ourselves saying that it's like a bad dream. This sense of shock accompanies the death of a loved one whether or not the news is sudden and unexpected. And that enormous sense that the world is suddenly a different place is consistent with the facts. The world *is* a different place when a person we love is no longer part of it.

The dazed, dislocated sense of disbelief that may, in varying degrees, last days, weeks, or months reflects how jarring the death of a loved one is to our entire experience. Whether we have lost a parent or a spouse, a child, a friend, or a mentor, there is a void. Once anchored to the reality of a loved one's presence, we are suddenly without a mooring. The huge cargo of current experiences, memories, needs, and feelings involving this special person is adrift and without bearings.

For a time, we feel and act differently. We find little if any pleasure in eating, our sleep may be disrupted, and even our waking hours feel like sleepwalking. We take little genuine interest in the events of daily life and often feel less invested in the people around us. The withdrawal we feel is involuntary as we invest our emotional energy in reorienting our internal world to the new external one. We are not yet ready to accept the reality of our loss.

Our attention focuses not only on our pain but also on the images, memories, places, and things so intimately connected to the person we have loved and lost. We may even find ourselves using their favorite sayings and mannerisms to keep loved ones we have lost close in our minds. However complicated or straightforward the relationship, however much love, resentment, or ambivalence we felt toward the person who died, the loss is powerful. We will miss all the wonderful things about the relationship and mourn the possibility of repairing the things that weren't so great.

While mourning the death of someone whose life and relationship with us has been central in helping to shape who we are is never easy, for some it can be much more complicated. The degree to which we have been able to resolve the difference between what we wanted and what we got from these important relationships can play a crucial role in how well we adapt. When our expectations were high and unrealized, we are often left with an even more profound and complicated sense of loss. This may also occur in situations of sudden or premature death, particularly with the death of a spouse or a child. Disbelief is compounded by a sense of being cruelly cheated. In these situations, mourning may develop into depression if our sense of the lost opportunity to "get it right" or our rage about being robbed of someone we love leads to a defiant refusal to accept the loss itself. Remaining entirely fixed on the devastation and deprivation of the loss for a prolonged period may be one way of maintaining a more intense feeling of connection to the person we have lost.

With a powerful unconscious determination, some are unable to give up this exclusive investment. They avoid reconnecting with the world and the people around them. For most of us, however, the sad, empty, disconnected feelings gradually give way. Over time, the intensity of the pain recedes, while we maintain a rich set of memories, values, and feelings. In this way we can integrate a relationship that is now part of the past into the life we live in the present. In identifying with the people we have loved and lost—not only by adopting their mannerisms but also by applying the values, skills, and knowledge we learned from them in daily life—we can remain connected to them at no expense to our connection with the world of the living. Our lost loved ones become part of us. In small and often unconscious ways, they remain with us forever.

WHEN SYMPTOMS SPEAK LOUDLY OF OUR FEARS

Even in the absence of real external threats, none of us is entirely free from anxiety or from the side effects of our efforts to locate and defend against the sources of our discomfort. For some, though, psychological difficulties produce a sense of anxiety and danger that is constant. For them, eternal vigilance and defense can produce symptoms that dramatically interfere with their ability to lead normal lives. They just can't let their guard down; they feel it's essential to deflect dangers associated with even more disturbing thoughts and feelings. When the dangers are no longer lurking in the shadows but are clear, present, and real, no one can avoid the clobbering that their full weight delivers.

On the other hand, we are all vulnerable when our most powerful internal fears converge with reality, when our normal capacity to think straight and maintain a sense of emotional order is overwhelmed. It was Sigmund Freud who decades ago referred to the traumatic situation as one in which we are unable to rely on ordinary coping strategies or to recognize our helplessness in the face of it. There are many problems that result from this state of affairs, but chief among them is that we hate feeling helpless.

Whether we struggle with the transient anxieties of daily life, the chronic anxieties of a lifetime, or the sudden overwhelming realization of nightmare themes, we do our best to take control of the thoughts and feelings that accompany them. The greater the danger, the more determined and dramatic our efforts may be to avoid the original source. When we are successful in avoiding the full force of feelings of helplessness, we may no longer be able to see or recognize their true origins. When that happens, we find other ways to express our anxiety. These include:

- Interference with sleep

- Significant changes in appetite: overeating or not eating enough

- Increased bodily complaints and unrealistic concerns about health

- Changes in emotional states: increased irritability, depressive sadness, hopelessness and withdrawal, persistent feelings of dread, worry, and jumpiness

- Panic attacks

- Preoccupying conscious thoughts involving loss, loss of love, self-loathing, bodily damage, and impending disaster or, ultimately, a more wholesale inability to distinguish between fantasy and reality

- Decreased feelings of intimacy and affection in interactions with loved ones, decreased sexual interest, and withdrawal from social situations

- Decreased concentration and increased distractibility

- Increased complaints about others or ease in entering into arguments, especially with friends and associates

- New, ritualistic behaviors that accompany obsessive self-doubt, such as compulsive hand washing and cleaning or compulsive checking on issues involving the physical safety of self and others

- Increased smoking and drinking, or reliance on drugs not prescribed by a physician

Whether these symptoms seem to be connected to events that arouse our fears or indicate new problems, it's difficult to recognize them as signals of distress when we are in the thick of them. We are in a no-win situation when our defenses against fundamental human fears are compounded by shame over any of these symptoms. Let's hope that we are able to remember an essential truth (or are reminded by people who care for us): we are all vulnerable to the same fears.

Recognizing and appreciating that we are indeed symptomatic may require a great deal of courage. It's also the first step to recovery. When we have physical ailments that do not respond to home remedies, we seek the help of medical professionals. If we deny the need for medical care because of our need to avoid fears about bodily damage, compromised views of our strength and competence, or, ultimately, thoughts of death, we threaten our own well-being and that of every person who depends on us. The same can be said about our mental health. When, as a result of our struggles, we can't communicate that we feel isolated and scared, or that we are hurting and feel small and ashamed, we will remain alone and stuck.

When someone isn't able to reach out for needed help, loved ones must insist on it. Taking such actions is both appropriate and necessary. Confronting the people we love, sensitively but firmly, with the impact that their symptoms are having both on themselves and others, is a fearsome responsibility all its own. When we are unable to help our partners take the first steps to taking control of their lives, we need to seek out those who can guide us. Talking with professionals we can trust—primary care physicians, mental health professionals, clergy with whom we have existing relationships—can be just the opportunity that opens the door to getting our spouses the help they need.

If we can't tolerate knowing our own fears, how can we know them in our children? If our greatest fears are the ones that left us feeling alone as children and, now, as adults, will our continued efforts to push them away keep us from listening to our own children? Or in our wish to spare them, will we inadvertently ignore the specific ways that they are afraid as we reassure them that there is nothing to be afraid of?

Violent tragedies have drawn international attention over the last years; perhaps we have found a curious kind of strength in numbers. We've looked together at things that do far more than go bump in the night. Perhaps, in the face of a hunter who has made a rustling on any street in our country the rustle of dread, we are prepared to examine, together, the fears that too often interfere with the strengths, hopes, and aspirations we also share.

If we can tolerate knowing what we are all so afraid of, maybe we will be better able to help our children feel strength in numbers as they find their greatest source of support in us. If we can come closer to understanding the language of our children's fears, we will be in a much better position to translate our wish to reassure them into words and actions that they will understand. Our children will feel protected by us only when we are able to recognize that they are afraid, and that their fears are reflections of our own.

CHAPTER THREE

■

BEING SCARED TOGETHER: OUR YOUNGEST CHILDREN (BIRTH TO 18 MONTHS)

I'm just going to look one more time," said the friend we were visiting. I hadn't counted, but I think this new mother had left the living room at least a dozen times in the course of our half-hour visit. Her baby was sleeping peacefully, but I could see she was terrified that if she didn't remain vigilant he might stop breathing. The baby monitor at her side was a talisman against disaster. But she would only trust the evidence of her own eyes that her infant was still safe.

Remember all the trips you made to the room where your newborn was sleeping to check that the baby was still breathing? That soft spot on the head was always another wonderfully intrusive thought, guaranteed to make any new parent cringe with anxiety. While we're cringing, remember the first time your baby had a low-grade fever? At times, no amount of factual information could convince you that your baby wasn't battling a life-threatening illness.

In this chapter, we will look not only at fears for our babies but also at our babies' own experiences of fear. As we will see, the two are closely intertwined.

Friends tell the story of their fussy first baby, Tony, and how anxious they became when they couldn't calm him as quickly as they thought they should. Both parents describe the unpleasant autonomic responses (increased heart rates and breathing and wrenching of the gut) that were instantly triggered by their 6-week-old's high-pitched shrieking. The father told me later, "I don't know what was worse, the sound of his wailing—it reminded me of the uninterrupted high end of an ambulance siren—or the horror that he would stop breathing in his effort to sustain it. We were both wrecks."

Several years later, my friends could smile about their frantic efforts to comfort Tony. They recalled that their rocking, back patting, and pacing was more jarring than calming. Fortunately for this couple, the wife's mother knew as much about parents as she did about babies, and she was visiting during one of these angst-filled crying jags. As distressed as she was to see these new parents struggling, she knew not to volunteer advice.

Then, in tears, the young mother told her mother how awful she felt about her inability to comfort her own child. In response, the mother asked a very simple question. "No matter how silly you think it might be, what is it that you are afraid of?"

Between sobs, my friend confessed. "That I'm a terrible mother, that something is terribly wrong, the baby will die, and if he doesn't he'll always be miserable and hate me."

This went on for a few minutes, until my friend's mother replied, "No wonder, with all these terrible thoughts, it's so hard to feel calm as you try to comfort your baby."

My friends remember that Tony remained very fussy for another couple of months—not all the time, but when it happened they realized that reacting anxiously was of no service either to the baby or to themselves. They were also able to recognize the signs of their own exhaustion and frustration and devise a tag-team approach. At 6 months, Tony was sleeping and eating well and was an alert, engaged, and much more readily comforted baby. My friends began to forget what those earliest panicky evenings had felt like.

But that changed at 8 months, when Tony screamed as if terrified and enraged whenever his parents left his room after saying good night. One or the other parent would rush back into the room and find Tony on his feet, clinging to the rails of his crib, tears streaming down a face that seemed melted with anguish. The parents began to struggle with each other about the amount of time that Tony's demands were taking away from their time together. They argued about whether to let Tony cry himself to sleep or hold and rock him before returning him to his crib. Neither parent could stand to hear or see his deep distress. "It made us feel terrible—we had to help him—but it was also incredibly frustrating to lose that wonderful time in the evening that wasn't completely centered on him!" my friend recalls.

The problem was that falling asleep was getting no easier for Tony. His parents had read the books about establishing sleep schedules, but they just couldn't put any of their eminently reasonable plans into action. In their discussions with me, both parents described a split between what they knew—that spending hours with Tony every night was not a good idea for anyone—and what they felt— that to deny his agonized demands for attention was hurtful and cruel.

They came to realize that their inability to tolerate Tony's upset responses confirmed what might have been the baby's own worst fear: "I can't feel comfortable, I can't survive without them!" The reality was that Tony, like all other babies, would in fact survive without their immediate presence, but his parents were giving him no opportunities to discover this for himself. Their own anxiety robbed Tony of the chance to strengthen his internal resources, help him to master his fear of being alone, and contribute to his feelings of self-reliance. Realizing that their "help" was actually depriving their son of what he really needed went a long way. The howling, they now understood, was necessary and temporary. Moreover, Tony's parents were able to recognize that they were trying to achieve a well-intentioned but impossible goal: to shield their son from all fear.

Over the course of seven nights, these parents were able gradually to decrease the frequency of the visits they made to Tony's room and the amount of time they spent with him. They took turns responding and fought the urge to pick him up and cuddle him. It was especially hard to resist those little outstretched arms! Instead, they stood by his crib, stroking his head and back as they spoke soothingly about going to sleep and seeing him in the morning. Gradually, the nightly howls of protest stopped. It wasn't the last time that fear would interrupt Tony's sleep. But it was the last time that his parents would feel so certain that he was unable to master his fear or that they were incapable of helping him in that process.

Alongside the joys and excitement about being new parents are concerns about anything that might mar our children's physical perfection, absolute happiness, safety, and freedom from fear. Infancy is a powerful introduction to our awesome responsibilities as parents. It is the beginning of a lifetime of learning that there are huge differences between our fears and those of our children. Locating and appreciating the distinctions can help us to respond more specifically to the needs and concerns of our kids.

We will not always get it right. At times we might undermine our children's mastery. We may soothe our own anxieties by overindulging theirs. Alternatively, we may deprive our children of the assistance that they need out of concern that we are spoiling them. At these times we may aspire to some adult version of competence in our youngest children, failing to recognize that their resources for toughness and self-reliance are still developing. In the midst of the physical and emotional exhaustion that is part of being a new parent, we may feel guilty when we finally get the quiet adult time we need as the baby sleeps. Instead of enjoying these blessed moments, we may find ourselves worrying that the baby is sleeping so much that something must be wrong.

As parents, knowing the difference between our fears and concerns and those of our young children is not always easy. It is made all the more difficult when we are unable to recognize, understand, or tolerate our own anxiety and distress, let alone communicate our most vulnerable feelings to the spouses or partners with whom we share our parenting responsibilities. Sometimes it seems easier to displace our fears onto worries about our babies than it is to recognize and explore the source of our concerns. For a couple, arguing the finer points of child care may be easier than facing the challenges of feeling uncertain together. We are perhaps at our best and most available to learning about our children's needs and how to meet them when we acknowledge that our limited understanding is a virtue, not an admission of incompetence.

LEARNING TO UNDERSTAND

As parents and caregivers, we have perhaps no greater challenge than trying to understand what it is our kids need from us. Getting to know our children in each phase of their development involves observing and translating what we see and hear into our best approximations of their experiences. In each developmental stage we learn new idioms of the evolving language of behavior and words that our children use to communicate their needs. With many missteps and bruises along the way, we become better at interpreting and responding to those needs.

Infancy introduces a dance between parent and child—both partners simultaneously acting and reacting, teaching and learning—that continues over the life of the relationship. There is perhaps no more uncertain phase of parenting than infancy. Without a common language, each partner is learning the most fundamental of steps. For parents, instruction manuals and advice from family, friends, and pediatricians can never completely decode the full range of their baby's highly individualized set of shifting signals and cues.

The earliest pattern of interactions between caregiver and baby provides a foundation for understanding the earliest experiences of distress and fear. It is our job to deal with our babies' distress in ways they can internalize and increasingly rely upon in our absence.

For infants and caregivers, the most prevalent forms of distress are located and communicated via the body. Before we can talk about the subjective fears of childhood, we need to understand the earliest basis for the experience of distress and the ways parents and infants deal with it.

BUILDING BLOCKS

In the earliest period of development, biological processes are central in establishing a baby's rudimentary sense of self as distinct from other. This is built on sensations that contribute to an internal psychological "self " that both experiences the body and guides its actions. For example, the mouth plays a leading role in shaping the baby's earliest self-images in the context of the world. The mouth is not only crucial in its role of eating to sustain life but also in activities such as sucking, licking, and biting. It is also a central organ of perceiving, regulating, and altering sensations.

In the absence of hunger, the baby mouths fingers, toes, toys, pacifiers, and the mother's breast. This instinctual mouthing and sucking is a way to self-soothe; it decreases tension and distress and is one way the baby begins to explore the outside world. Similarly, through crying when uncomfortable or making high-pitched squeals to attract the mother's attention, the baby learns about the mouth's power to communicate.

While central, the mouth is not the only source of pleasure and self-soothing. A broader range of inborn processes involving sight, hearing, reflexes, muscle tone, and more also influence the infant's earliest experience of the body and the emergence of a self. Variations in sleep and wake cycles, quiet and alert periods, gazing into the caregiver's face, and patterns of withdrawal from or responsiveness to comforting also play a central role in the baby's development of a sense of the world outside.

From the beginning of life, parents' and caregivers' interactions help to organize and shape the ways in which a baby expresses needs. The mother or primary caregiver's involvement and intimate contact with the infant's body—feeding, cleaning, holding, cooing—are basic and essential ingredients of this earliest relationship, this "primary attachment." Their enormous investment in and attention to the baby's most basic bodily needs sensitizes parents to the ways that they can diminish the baby's discomfort.

Along the way parents also learn the "language" of an infant's cues. They recognize the baby's array of specific sources of pleasure ("Oh, she likes it when I tickle her tummy!") and distress ("He hates loud noises!"). They also attribute emotional meaning to dramatic and subtle changes in their baby's behavior. A baby's inborn sensitivities to various stimuli—touch, sound, stomach upsets—complicate the caregiver's task of learning how to understand and establish reliable means of responding to the baby's needs. Parents of fussy babies often feel hopeless and incompetent (not to mention exhausted) when their attempts to soothe prove unsuccessful. These feelings of inadequacy have less to do with poor skills as parents than with the frustration of their natural intense wish to protect their infant from pain and discomfort.

These feelings are all the more burdensome when parents feel deprived by the baby of the earliest experiences of reciprocal love. After hours of trying to relieve the baby's discomfort—walking, rocking, stroking, trying new formulas—parents may resent a baby who doesn't offer the rewards of contentment, pleasure, and peace. The associated frustration and anger we may feel toward the baby at these times can make us feel especially guilty and uncomfortable.

It is hard to admit that we can hate someone we love, that they are driving us crazy. Brace yourselves, because you will experience similar levels of frustration and rage with your children at many different points in their lives. But it's particularly troublesome to have these feelings toward babies, those utterly dependent and vulnerable objects of our adoration.

It is not uncommon for one parent to feel more defeated and per-haps angrier than the other. Particularly when we are feeling most stretched, there is a greater likelihood of feelings being displaced from baby to partner. It was always in the middle of the longest nights of our child's inconsolable discomfort that my wife and I would get most irri-tated with each other. Ah, those first few colic-ridden months! When our son's howling kept both of us awake, whoever wasn't holding or at-tempting to soothe the baby always had a better idea about how it should be done. Fortunately—and not at three in the morning—we re-alized that arguing robbed us of the support we needed from each other precisely at the time in our infant's life when the power of his biology outmatched the power and effectiveness of our efforts to relieve his dis-comfort. When we realized how limited our control was (and with fre-quent reminders to each other that colic would not last forever), my wife and I were much better able to comfort each other. Our distress and fatigue did not disappear until our son's colic did. However, we stopped directing each other's comforting efforts and stopped displac-ing our angst when these efforts inevitably failed.

In the midst of these difficult early months, it is easy to imagine that the parent-child relationship is headed down a rocky road. But colic does abate, babies eventually startle less easily, and sudden noises don't distress them forever. And parents learn from experience to off-set these early obstacles. It is often only after things have smoothed out and parents are able to experience their baby's comforted re-sponses that they begin to believe both in their own effectiveness and in a shared and deepening bond with their child.

It will be a hard-won but important achievement when, at each phase of development, you are able to recognize the limits of your controls and appreciate that differing temperaments, qualities, and characteristics are powerful influences on our children's strengths and vulnerabilities—as powerful as our efforts to help and guide them along the way.

ME AND NOT ME

While diminishing physical tension (between need and gratification) and maximizing pleasure appear to be essential tasks during this early period of development, the baby's experiences of frustration and discomfort play equally significant roles in maturation and development. In fact, because discomfort followed by relief is so often connected to parental absence and reappearance, the repetition of this drama actually contributes to the infant's growing capacity to differentiate "me" from "not me."

The discrepancies between need and satisfaction may include nuances of parent-infant interactions: failure to elicit a smile, a cuddle, a soothing or playful tone of voice, or physical proximity, as well as hunger or the discomfort of a soiled diaper. Similarly, beginning with the mouth as a literal juncture between inner and outer reality, the sensations associated with repeated sequences of coordinated activity—sucking, biting, licking, swallowing, looking, listening, touching—foster the infant's capacity to locate and identify where sensations come from and thus contributes further to his or her definition of body boundaries.

While infants recognize their mother's face in the earliest weeks of life, by the middle of the first year their response to her is no longer dominated by the satisfaction of bodily needs alone. With an increased appreciation of physical separateness, the infant can now clearly associate the pleasures of care with their most important sources—parents and the most significant caregivers. As at no other time, the very presence of parents is itself an enormous source of pleasure and satisfaction. Equally, our absence becomes a huge source of anxiety and distress. By the middle of the first year and beyond, infants will look to us for the meaning of new situations, watching our faces for signs of calm or agitation. Our older babies appreciate the details of our responses and learn about our specific ways of responding (muted or exaggerated, calm or fearful), including how we deal with closeness and separation.

WHERE DID THEY GO?

Our 8-month-old's protests about being "abandoned" at night, or other children's protests about being held by others or separated from parents at the day-care center, stem from the infant's feeling that a parent who is "not here" is "gone forever." With the delineation of boundaries, the infant views the parent or central caregiver as the bridge between himself or herself and the rest of the world. When the ambassadors are unavailable, the older baby may appear panic-stricken, looking around wildly, as if disoriented, having temporarily lost the organizing connection to the broader world. Whether the parent leaves and returns with anguish and anxiety or with pleasure and calm will exacerbate or diminish the intensity of the baby's distress.

Games of peek-a-boo, play involving hiding and finding objects, and the repetition of real experiences of Mommy and Daddy coming and going help the infant on the way to establishing the idea of *object permanence*. This is the ability to conceive that things continue to exist even when hidden, that "not here is maybe there" applies to parents as well. When they are mentally able to hold their parents in mind, or represent internally their images even when they're not in sight, babies can "take parents along" as they explore the world beyond the lap and crawl, stand, and take the first of many independent steps.

I'M HERE FOR YOU

Sitting in the airport recently, I watched a very new walker testing his skills as his parents grabbed a bite at McDonald's. The place was crowded and noisy, but the baby didn't seem to mind. He toddled away from his dad, looking very pleased with himself. "Tyler, come back here," his dad would say, when Tyler got more than a few yards away. And Tyler did. He would lean into his dad's lap for a hug and then take off again. Soon many people in the restaurant were watching and appreciating this baby's exploration of his newfound independence. When one stranger's encouragement got a little too enthusiastic, Tyler toddled back to Dad for another check-in.

There is something greatly reassuring to both child and parents when the scrambling or darting away is accompanied by periodic returns as a toddling infant refuels. When the anchoring relationship is reliable and secure, these safe explorations broaden the scope of independence by providing young children with demonstrations of what their bodies can do. Increased dexterity, language acquisition, and rudimentary cause-and-effect thinking provide a burgeoning set of tools for exploration and mastery that feels wonderful and can be a joy to watch, as Tyler's walks in McDonald's demonstrates.

A child's achievement of psychological differentiation and separation from parents is not without challenges and is often accompanied by times of increased tension, anger, sadness, and anxiety. But anxiety and fear are necessary ingredients in the process of progressive development and mastery. Every baby develops unique methods for coping with new sources of discomfort that are based on self-soothing behaviors and those learned from comforting caregivers. Cognitive development allows toddlers to be more aware of the outside world, and they begin to consider in advance the consequences of their actions— the beginning of mature thought. This ability to predict can lead to greater trepidation, and a temporary retreat to "babyish" behaviors, or to daring attempts at greater self-reliance—like Tyler's.

I'LL ALWAYS HAVE BLANKIE

The explorer-researcher toddler may also experience walking away, or being walked away from, as painful. At these moments of worrisome separation, when the internal images of parents just don't give enough reassurance, a young child often turns to a specific soft blanket or cuddly toy for comfort.

These items are available to children to smell, hold, and fondle in the absence of the primary caregiver until the real thing is once again within reach. These "transitional objects," a phenomenon described by British pediatrician and psychoanalyst D. W. Winnicott, are fundamentally different from the real parent, whose comings and goings are unpredictable and upsetting. Why? Because, unlike the adult in question, cuddly toys and soft blankets are completely under the young child's control.

WHEN THINGS GO WRONG

Young children can best tackle and master the challenges of development in the context of a generally secure, reliable, and loving relationship with the adults who care for them. When there are major disruptions in those relationships, such as prolonged separations that extend into weeks and months, a parent's emotional unavailability (due, for example, to severe depression), grossly inconsistent handling that alternates between overindulgence and neglect, or physical abuse, the toddler infant may develop very early forms of psychological difficulties. In the extreme, these include failure to thrive (significantly decreased rate of weight gain and growth), depression (a preponderance of lethargy, withdrawal, and an absence of pleasure or interest in others), hypersensitivity to stimulation (with a low threshold for startle, arousal, and ease of upset), and extreme wariness and fearfulness in interactions with others.

When these conditions and the family circumstances that lead to them go unrecognized and untreated, emotional, social, and intellectual development may be seriously compromised. When the world of infancy remains unpredictable and scary, feelings of pleasure and mastery normally associated with exploration and engagement can be replaced by experiences of fearfulness and defeat that may lead to a retreat and withdrawal for years to come.

REFLECTING ON YOU

In many ways, the size of our young children's world is defined by the range of close relationships they rely on. Similarly, their sense of safety is most immediately determined by the degree to which they can rely on those closest to them to let them know when a new situation is safe to explore, provide comfort from frightening feelings, and protect them in situations where there is real danger. For young children, whether danger is imagined or real, the degree to which we respond calmly or anxiously has an enormous impact, both immediately and in the long term, on how they will respond to scary situations.

Kids recover quickly from the fear and indignity of a fall when we attend to them evenly, treating any injury with a bandage or a kiss and simple words of reassurance about their well-being. On the other hand, we fuel their fears when we gasp and run over to them and express horror by urgently examining every inch of their bodies as we repeatedly ask if they're all right. This alarmist approach conveys that their bodies are not safe and that exploration of the world is fraught with danger. Rather than reflecting confidence in them, we communicate how frightened we are about them and how distressing we find the inevitable bumps and bruises that are the price of childhood achievement.

When we respond to our children's concerns or fears about losing us by never being out of their sight, we deprive them of opportunities for experimenting and learning that we won't disappear forever. We also confirm, by our own behavior, that we too believe that they cannot survive without us, no matter how short the separation. One of the most painful examples of this counterproductive dance will occur dramatically in the next phase of development, as preschool or out-of-home day care introduces new versions of old emotional challenges for both parents and children.

Older parents will remember how hard it was to leave our children in day-care programs, no matter how much confidence we had (intellectually) in either the programs or in our children's abilities to adapt to them? We may have felt guilty, imagining that we were aban-doning our responsibilities and our children or convinced that they would be emotionally overwhelmed and unable to recover.

Those early days of trying to leave for work as our child clung weeping to one leg may have only confirmed our fears about the devas-tation we were inflicting on them. In addition to ambivalence inspired by guilt, we also felt a kind of pain that is old and oh, so familiar. We know loss and abandonment. We know what it feels like to imagine that "gone for now" really means "lost forever." In our identification with the real and imagined anguish of our children, we may succumb to the wish to eliminate all our own fears in ways that only extend them. And so we stay, or we stand outside waving and waving. It is sometimes so hard to hold on to the facts that are reported to us by the child-care providers, those reassurances that once we have gone our children stop crying and get on with their day. Their tears, we are told, dry up. They engage in a range of activities that they would never have experienced as fully at home. In short, they are doing fine.

Experienced preschool and day-care providers know how scary separations can be for both parent and child. They recognize that if they don't interrupt the dance, they too will be confirming that the worst feelings of fear and desperation—for both child and parent—are justified. They know that the longer it takes to close the first door of the day, the longer it will take to open other doors to many new and stimulating activities that will help increase the child's compe-tence and broaden the scope of his or her world.

■

CHAPTER FOUR

FACING THE NEW IN THE WIDER WORLD: TODDLING AND BEYOND (18 TO 36 MONTHS)

I was on the deck of an evening ferry. It was dark and we were sailing through a dense fog. Suddenly a door opened, and a two-year-old ran out and slipped on the mist-coated deck. His mother was quicker than his flailing limbs. She swooped him into her arms. Recovering from the unexpected loss of control, the toddler replaced his surprised, almost insulted expression with a warm, adoring smile for his rescuer. Then the foghorn blared suddenly. Out on deck it was more than loud. It surrounded us with a roaring version of the foggy mist.

The young subject of my observations had not taken in the ferry captain's explanation that on nights like this the regular sounding of the foghorn was standard operating procedure, not an indication of imminent danger. His body went rigid as he arched away from his form-fitting cuddle against his mother's body. His eyes were wide, his warm smile replaced by horrified tension. He jerked his head, scanning left to right before throwing it back and letting out a howl accompanied by a flood of tears that spilled from clenched-tight eyes. Then he pressed his hands to his ears, blocking out whatever might be out there that could create such a terrifying sound, and buried his face into his mother's chest and sobbed.

His mother knew what had frightened him. She held him closer, stroked his head, and put the obvious into words. "You were scared by that big loud noise. You didn't know what it was . . . there, there, you're okay and Mommy is here . . . you heard a noise the boat makes . . . you're okay. . . ." And still holding him close, she took him inside.

What was it about the foghorn that was so frightening? The unfamiliarity of the noise triggered a physiological response in the toddler. All hands on deck! High alert! Better to assume the worst and be prepared!

The little boy had quickly surveyed his surroundings as if to locate the source of potential danger, a crucial step in taking evasive or protective action. But he did not yet have the internal repertoire of experience to compare the sound he was hearing with a set of associations and memories. He could not understand what he was hearing and dismiss it as a loud but harmless noise. The absence of these points of comparison was compounded by the suddenness of the noise, his automatic startle response, and his increased heart rate—physiological responses that many adults on board that night might also have experienced the first time the foghorn sounded! The less-than-calm seas and the cover of fog probably had stimulated thoughts of maritime disasters among many of the passengers.

The difference for the toddler was that he was little. He had as few methods of protecting himself as he had memories of foghorn sounds. At that critical moment, the familiar arms of his mother were not enough. He was overwhelmed when the potential danger surpassed his capacity to meet it. He fell apart before he could accept, let alone be reassured by, the next best thing to fending for himself—being protected by his mother.

There was a great match, though, between what this mother knew of her child and how she responded. She deftly stepped in at two moments when her son was unable to rely totally on his own devices. When she caught him in his fall on the slippery deck, she interrupted what might have been a fuller loss of control. He was clearly surprised by the discrepancy between his sense of being able to walk independently and slipping on the wet, unfamiliar surface.

It's likely that when the foghorn sounded he was even more fearful and vulnerable to danger because he'd lost his balance only moments before. But at both points his mother took charge and physically protected him, as well as containing and controlling his sense of emotional disarray. She embraced him while soothing him with words that explained his experience of being overwhelmed. Providing her son with a connection between feelings and ideas helped him replace a shocking assault of frightening and humiliating feelings with words to order the experience. In addition, this mother was able to lend to her son the most important signal of safety—her own calm. She demonstrated that she had heard the captain's advisory that there was no imminent danger at hand and showed her son that his most reliable gauge of safety, his mother, was in control.

The foghorn continued to sound periodically throughout the rest of the crossing. When I saw this little boy again, he was no longer in his mother's arms. He was outside on deck again but now walked very closely sandwiched between both parents. Watching from behind, I couldn't see his expression, but when the horn sounded he didn't shriek or scramble to be held. However, he did reach quickly to take hold of the hand that each parent offered; after a few moments he let go and continued his exploration.

Let's put this story in a developmental context. In this chapter, we will see children begin to interact with the world in new ways. As their physical, social, and emotional skills develop, they begin explorations that are full of excitement. But exploration can sometimes lead to unexpected and shocking things. It can be frightening and disorienting. As they move through toddlerhood, children—with the help of parents and caregivers who must know when to step in and when to step back—learn to face and assimilate these experiences and use them to make sense of the wider world.

"I CAN DO IT!"

Accompanying every advance in physical development is a broader array of challenges. Neat how that works, isn't it? Rapid maturation of the brain and the rest of the body in toddlerhood, that period between 18 and 36 months, allows children to experience all the pleasures associated with four little words: "I can do it!" Walking and running independently, talking, being able to declare ideas and direct fantasy play all confer on exploring toddlers a degree of control and mastery of themselves and the wider world.

Significant advances in capabilities and control—for example, in neuromusculature and attendant motor coordination, as well as in cognitive and communicative potential—are central to the child's developing mind. With new capacities come new demands and new struggles.

Toilet training is often described as a crucial component of this period of development. But its meaning and significance go well beyond the establishment of civilized habits. As with the mouth's earlier role, the skin, eyes and ears, and the process of elimination now help children to increase their recognition of what is inside the body and what is outside. This enhances the developing sense of where the boundaries of their own bodies begin and end. In this, as in all other phases of development, the maturing capacities of the body are prerequisites for meeting new demands and expectations. Regardless of complicated feelings about complying with parents' wishes, before toddlers can give up diapers in favor of the toilet, they have to achieve control of the sphincter muscles, and that occurs only with maturation of the central nervous system.

Recognizing the distinctions between self and others and between what is inside and outside the body is a complicated business for toddlers. It's not possible for us to remember all the details of what's involved as we engage our small children in toilet training. We may not fully appreciate, for example, that it may take young children awhile—and a leap of faith—to believe that even if what comes out of them gets flushed down the toilet, their own bodies will remain intact. With their limited appreciation for spatial orientation, relative sizes, and physical properties, the opening in the toilet seems like a hazardously perfect fit for a small body, especially when the accompanying flushing action and noise looks and sounds so powerful and fierce. Until experience, experimentation, and parental reminders about the facts combine to reassure young children about the essential integrity and safety of their bodies, struggles with parents over control may not be the only source of resistance to using the toilet.

"I ENJOY BEING A GIRL!"

As the young child's appreciation of boundaries and sense of a separate self increases, so does the natural tendency to compare his or her body with that of others. Comparing leads to the child's appreciation of anatomical differences between the sexes and between children's and adults' bodies. This recognition of differences arouses curiosity and concerns about bodily integrity and safety as parents help their children learn that the parts of boys' and girls' bodies that make them different were parts they were born with and ones that they keep.

During a period when what is and isn't part of the body is so central and when children's ideas are based on the most concrete of their observations, it's not surprising that both boys and girls share fears that their bodies can be damaged, that precious parts can be lost. Listening carefully to their comments and questions is the first and most important step in being able to give our children information that not only responds to their specific concerns but also provides the basis for pleasure in their bodies. If we want our children to feel good about who they are, simply telling them to be proud is not enough. We also need to pay attention to the normal concerns and distortions that young children have about bodies and anatomical differences, which can interfere with the pride they feel about themselves as boys and as girls.

Achieving this can be a delicate business. As part of an effort to introduce and welcome new participants in a child-care program, families and staff gathered for a late summer picnic. A bold and precociously verbal 2½-year-old girl took the intent of the picnic seriously as she made the rounds to each cluster of children and adults. "Hi," she announced. "My name is Ingrid. I am a girl and I have a vagina. I like my vagina, and I like being a big girl."

Her dumbfounded listeners didn't have time to come up with a suitable reply before Ingrid was off to the next group. Ingrid also frequently repeated versions of this statement to her new playmates when she began attending the program, raising questions in staffers' minds about why these topics were preoccupying her. In discussions with the child-care program director, Ingrid's parents acknowledged that in their hopes and concerns about raising a daughter who would always feel good about her body they might have gone too far.

While both parents and program staff supported the good feelings that Ingrid professed, they also gently convinced her that everyone really did know and like the fact that she was a girl. Telling her name to new people she met and simply joining or asking her new playmates to play would suffice. Ingrid was also invited to bring any questions that she had about her body or about the differences between boys and girls to her parents and teachers. The adults in Ingrid's life agreed that before repeatedly volunteering information about these topics they would listen carefully to the specific nature of her questions.

The questions that Ingrid did raise over time were not so different from the ones many children ask as they struggle with the concerns and possible fears aroused by anatomical differences. Ian was also around 2½ when he first verbalized, with considerable anxiety, his observations about very young children in various states of undress at a pool party at the house of family friends. As Ian's mother was helping him out of his wet bathing suit, a naked little girl who was trying to escape the clutches of her own mother captured his attention. After looking down at his penis, he pointed at the girl and loudly and repeatedly demanded,

"Mommy, where's her pee-pee?" Ian's mom felt a bit embarrassed but wanted to use this opportunity to help teach her son almost as much as she wanted him to lower the volume of his inquiry.

The explanation that she gave him was one that she and Ian's dad would repeat over the next months in response to the different elaborations of the original question—"Mommy, did you have a pee-pee?" "What happened to that girl's?" and so on. Before answering, Ian's parents would listen to his ideas. They were often surprised by how specific their son's theories were, but they came to understand why his questions were so important and why he needed them to remind him of the facts. On one occasion, Ian stated quite simply, "Girls used to be boys until they lost their penis." *Lost* their penis? "It fell off and they couldn't find it anymore," Ian added. Ian's parents offered simple statements of facts that attempted to address the most basic of his concerns. They would say, "Boys' and girls' bodies are different because boys were born with penises and girls were born with vaginas. Girls will always have vaginas; boys will always have penises. When they grow up their bodies will be bigger and be like the bodies of their mommies and daddies."

While a onetime answer did not immediately resolve Ian's curiosity and concern, his questions eventually abated. Several months after the pool party, Ian's mom casually asked her son if there were any more questions he might have. "No," Ian confidently responded, "I know all about bodies."

RELATIVE POWER

As with independent mobility, language, and imagination, achieving toilet training is an important activity that supports the young child's developing sense of control over a body whose boundaries are now better defined and experienced as more clearly separate from the bodies of others. Pleasing parents goes hand in hand with the young child's own pleasure in adding yet another accomplishment to a growing list that signals mastery and control—the "I can do it" spirit that is so central in this phase of development.

One of the great things about children's early sense of diffuse boundaries between themselves and others is that they are able to experience the powers and capacities of parents as extensions of their own. But with an increasingly separate sense of self, toddlers begin to recognize that they are not as big and as powerful as they once may have imagined. They are much clearer about the fact that many things that are physically and emotionally gratifying—being fed, cuddled, praised, played with, and kept warm—do not always occur simply because they want them to. Being separate means just that. And being separate means that if you, the little kid, are not in control of when and how every one of your greatest needs and most immediately important whims is satisfied, then someone else is.

As parents we reinforce their burgeoning recognition—*re-cognition*, or new way of knowing—of the distribution of relative power and skills by introducing new demands that are based, as closely as possible, on the child's new capacities for meeting them. We ask our kids to wait longer, because they *can* wait longer. With achievements in mobility, manipulation, and imaginative thought, our toddlers are better equipped to wait or to distract themselves when we can't devote our attention to them as fully or as swiftly as they might like. Similarly, the ability to hold in mind the memory of many previous situations in which their needs were ultimately met is an enormous boon as toddlers learn from experience that *later* does not mean *never*.

These accomplishments develop over time through a process of natural experimentation. There is nothing like experience to lay the groundwork for the reality of how the wider world works, and there is no better opportunity for confronting reality than when we defy our children's immediate wishes and say no. New parental requirements for bigger behaviors introduce specific contingencies for pleasure and satisfaction. Winning our approval becomes a crucial incentive for our kids to comply with expectations in ways that were not on the radar screen in the days of go-anytime diapers or on-demand feedings.

As parents, we are usually more than ready to say goodbye to dirty wet diapers. We may also be ready for uninterrupted stretches of time when our young children do not need us. But for many reasons, our children may not readily embrace this new world order. In their uncertainty, the combination of feeling an intense need and having to wait and rely on parents for the need to be met reminds them of just how small and powerless they really are. And this can be scary.

Toddlers continue to develop their ideas about boundaries and about the permanence of things and people in various ways. Along with using the toilet come experiments that involve endless games of pouring, filling, and emptying containers of toys, sand, and water. These games help the young child confirm hypotheses about what is inside and outside different spaces. More elaborate peek-a-boo and chase-me games with parents support the idea that going away does not mean never coming back.

LEARNING TO WAIT

By 18 months, most children have mastered the notion that the block they saw a few seconds ago has not disappeared simply because it has been hidden under a piece of fabric. Does the same rule apply to people? Well, yes, so where's the problem? The answer is that toddlers haven't fully conquered the emotional realities of delaying gratification of their most immediate wishes. Waiting is hard, especially when it's waiting for a parent to help you do something you want to do *right now*.

Our children's increased recognition of separateness and of the differences between adult and child capabilities is crucial to their developing capacity to test reality. This greater appreciation of the way things "really are" in the world is a major advance in development and a source of considerable conflict and anxiety. Our toddlers' greater awareness of their own dependency is at stark odds with their wish for autonomy and omnipotent controls—especially at those crucial moments when the fact that they do not share in their parents' power is so clear.

All too frequently, we are confronted with an inconsolable toddler who has been unable to accomplish a given task or satisfy a need. The child may loudly protest the very activity or goal that he or she can't accomplish alone and bitterly refuse all our efforts to help. A young child crumpling to the floor in tears is a poignant illustration of the frightening and overwhelming struggle between the competing aims of independence and dependence, between the pride of personal achievement and the humiliation of defeat.

THE GROCERY STORE MELTDOWN

My older son was 2½. We were in a supermarket, and I had a very small window of opportunity to pick up essential ingredients for a dinner party that was only hours away. We'd planned well, but the execution was hampered by the unscheduled needs of our two boys, toddler and infant. My wife and I decided to divide and conquer. Taking Alex with me seemed like a good idea. But the problem became frustratingly apparent within minutes of parking the car at the store. You see, Alex and I had two completely separate timetables and agendas. I was racing; he was not.

I was unfastening him from his car seat when I heard the first in what would be a long series of declarations of intent. Alex had been looking at a book. "No!" he howled. "Not done!" he screamed as he clutched the book and braced himself rigidly in his seat. Still calm, I told him, "No problem. We can bring the book, and you can look at it while you're sitting in the shopping cart."

"No! Finish it here!"

My calm was slipping with each attempt at firm explanation

about needing to get home quickly, helping Mommy, greeting the dinner guests. . . . You get the picture. Alex was having none of it.

I finally just pulled him briskly from his seat. You won't be surprised that taking the book along did not seem to help. However, once inside he remembered that being at the store was a great opportunity to find his favorite cereal. With the promise of getting something he wanted, Alex could now enjoy the game of racing around the aisles in the shopping cart. Ignoring my frenzy, he was gleeful as his chariot picked up speed and made one of many sharp turns. We got the cereal. He was a happy camper. And then I made a fatal error.

In a reasonable voice, Alex told me that he would like to get out of the cart and walk with me so he could help. I told him the final thing on the list was sour cream, and he could help me find it. Tearing along the dairy section, clock ticking, we zeroed in on this last item. I spotted the container, on a shelf beyond Alex's reach. He insisted on putting it into the cart himself so I began to pick him up so he could reach it.

All hell broke lose. "Want to do it *myself*!" he protested, in a voice everyone in the store could hear—or at least so it seemed to me.

I tried calmly to explain that he would need my help, but the logic of space, size, and reach were as far over his head as the sour cream container. Alex threw himself down and screamed. "I want to do it myself!" Over and over and over, his rage now accompanied by tears that poured down his cheeks and feet and fists that hammered on the aisle floor.

It only took me only seconds to recognize that the success of our dinner party was at odds with what I knew I needed to do with my son. I could give him a chance to calm himself down, or I could pick him up and beat a hasty retreat. Did I mention that the supermarket was more crowded than I could ever remember and by now the entire community seemed to hover around the dairy section? I cracked a strained smile. I issued tight, angry instructions to stop this behavior at once, as I imagined the opinions of everyone around me, let alone the headlines in the next day's local paper. I avoided looking around, determined not to add to the pressure I felt by seeing in the faces of imagined observers the confirmation of my own ignominious defeat at the hands of a 2½-year-old. How many in this vast crowd were my patients or members of the public who had heard me lecture on children and parenting? I wondered.

I was down to the wire, emotionally and practically. I needed to act. So I swooped my screaming son into my arms and threw the container of sour cream into the cart. I struggled only momentarily to angle his stiff, unyielding legs into the shopping cart seat and then gave up and tucked him under one arm, his legs and arms flailing, while I pushed the cart with my other hand as fast as I could to the checkout counter. As Alex's screaming chorus alternated between "Nooooo!" and "You're hurting me!" I experienced the only good piece of luck in the entire mission. There was only one person ahead of us in line, an older woman who gave me her place with what I hoped was a sympathetic smile. And while my little scene was not the first or last such event that the cashier would see on this or any other day, I could only barely hear her jovial comment about how tough toddlers can be. I wanted to protest that I knew all about toddlers and their development, but at that moment I just needed to go home. Really, I knew nothing of practical value about young children at all.

There are good reasons for giving the term *terrible twos* to toddlerhood. Why is a period known for such a rush of new physical and cognitive acquisitions also so explosive? In the middle of your young child's meltdown—whether it happens in a supermarket aisle or a new friend's living room—it may be impossible to remember that fear and anxiety have anything to do with your child's dramatic display. Only in the absence of such intensity—either with distance from my own experience or as an observer or listener—could I consider the anatomy of a tantrum or truly appreciate the high stakes involved in my toddler's struggle to tolerate his relatively lowly place in the larger world and negotiate the distance between his desires and his power, size, and capacity.

Young children do eventually get better at delaying immediate gratification of their wishes, in part because they are developing and improving the emotional equipment that helps them tolerate frustration. During this period in development, children's language and communication abilities increase dramatically, as do physical abilities and the capacity for independent navigation. There are also important advances in capacities for making connections between their own actions and reactions. They also learn to rely on previous patterns and memories. They will get the snack they've been promised *after* the trip to the park.

At this stage:

- Words can substitute for actions (Molly can ask for her doll rather than wandering around trying to find it).

- Remembering simple sequences of events can help the child anticipate the immediate future ("My blankie will come out of the dryer—it's not gone forever—and when it comes out, it will be nice and warm").

- Increased coordination can broaden the range of pleasurable physical activities (Tom can climb in and out of the baby pool and splash water over the side to cool off his little brother, who can't climb yet).

These capacities promote young children's sense of effectiveness and can divert them from the intensity of needs and impulses that were previously only satisfied when Mom or Dad jumped in to offer an immediate and satisfactory response. It is a major achievement for everyone involved when your daughter can tell you that she's hungry instead of crying to let you know. Now, when we suggest that our son needs to wait a few minutes, he may be able to mobilize internal defenses against feeling hurt and sustain the wait by rolling cars on the floor because he knows that "a few minutes" means "not too long." Or he may use language to beg us to hurry up or loudly crash his cars to deflect the anger he feels because we're not responding to his needs more quickly.

DANGERS OF LOVING AND HATING

As our young children continue to develop, they are also in a better position to understand the connection between their own behavior and the praise and love they crave from us. But those scenes in the supermarket are dramatic reminders that fulfilling our wishes is not uppermost in our toddlers' minds! The tug-of-war that so often occurs between toddlers and their parents is a demonstration of the enormous struggle children feel about competing aims: wanting what they want *now* and wanting to please the parents they love.

It is not easy for parents to see that there is any such internal struggle when rage, not love, is the most prominent feeling the tantrum expresses. But it is this battle between the loving wish to please and the hatred that follows frustration of their wishes that creates so much anxiety and fear for toddlers. And unpleasant as they can be, these conflicts and the accompanying uncomfortable feelings are not only inevitable parts of development but essential ingredients for moving forward into a more civilized social world. Kids begin to discover that they feel better when they don't fall apart. And relief from the anxiety and fear that comes with hating the parents you love is a wonderful incentive that tips the balance in favor of complying with parental demands and expectations.

Struggles about control that are played out around things like cleanliness, waiting for what you want, and following directions diminish significantly as young children take on, or internalize, their parents' expectations. Achieving aims at first set by parents now becomes a source of pride of their own. It feels good to remember to brush your teeth, instead of needing Mom to remind you several times to get it done. (This feeling of pride in complying with and sharing parental values is uneven throughout development, of course. The wish to please and to share parental ideals can be antithetical to adolescents, whose sense of independence is for a time based on noncompliance and overt rejection of anything their parents seem to want.)

OF FACT AND FANTASY

Young children's language development, their capacity to understand symbols and object permanence, and cause-and-effect thinking set the stage for them to construct what has been called the "representational world." This inner world is one that each of us builds. It is populated by a variety of composite images of ourselves and others, based on our experiences, urges, and feelings.

This inner world begins to take greater shape during the toddler phase of development. Although the youngest children may not have a sense of their own imagination or of internal thought processes, their inner life of representations begins to express itself in their changing fantasies, as well as in their attitudes and behavior toward us. Sometimes our kids comply with our requests because they are locked into internal views of us as wonderful and all-giving. Alternatively, their tirades against us seem to reflect the idea that we are frustrating figures set on earth to deprive them of pleasure. Their internal reference points are variable and confusing. They can just as easily see us as sources of safety and comfort at one moment and as obstacles in their path to independence at another. And of course we are both.

We are not the only victims of our toddlers' shifting images and changing points of view. Our fickle young children have equally rapid shifts in feelings about themselves. As they struggle with the frustrations of daily life, and in the face of balancing their loving and destructive urges, they can feel victorious and capable at one moment and frightened and helpless the next.

With their growing capacity for imagination, fighting with parents is no longer the only way that children resolve internal struggles between competing urges and wishes. The richness and flexibility of their representational worlds and the inner life of fantasy begin to support self-reliance. Now children can call loving images of their parents to mind in their absence, which allows for longer periods of independent activity. They are sustained not only by their memory of

Mommy and Daddy but also by the confident expectation that their needs will ultimately be satisfied.

As kids internalize family standards, they better understand the consequences of their actions. Good behavior no longer requires our constant presence and repeated reminders when our child takes on our standards and expectations as his or her own. The negative and positive feelings connected with actions are now part of a developing capacity for judgment. If we could hear this child's internal discussion at times of temptation it might sound something like this: "I shouldn't paint on the walls because Mommy and Daddy don't like me to" or "I feel very proud when I use the toilet like a big kid."

In the absence of real gratification of wishes, impulses, and feelings, our children can find expression and, to some degree, a substitute for satisfaction through fantasies in which they get to manipulate and control the activities and outcomes of interactions between themselves and others over whom they have no control in the disappointing aspects of real life—especially us. For example, a little girl might continue to talk to her mommy after she gets dropped off at day care—but now "Mommy" is a doll or a stuffed animal. "Mommy's staying at day care today," she makes the doll say.

The ability to fantasize on purpose—to alter or entirely replace real experiences with more gratifying wish-fulfilling imaginative scenarios—is an enormous achievement. With this incredible advance in mental operations, young children in the later part of toddlerhood can now hold on to a variety of internal images and play with them; they can pretend. Using their increasingly rich imaginations, they can temporarily escape the toughest of real-world disappointments and frustrations. Fantasies take the edge off a frustrating experience and help them plan and rehearse different outcomes.

Throughout development and in adult life, fantasies not only are intentionally engineered but also can develop at an unconscious level. There, our deepest longings or feelings of conflict aroused by unacceptable wishes can be played out beneath our conscious awareness. As adults, we know that fantasies can provide hidden relief and pleasure.

Alternatively, they may generate a burden of anxiety and fear whose origins are not easily or consciously recognized. When unconscious fantasies give form to unacceptable impulses and wishes, we employ a range of internal defensive operations to disguise them before they find expression in conscious thought.

As parents and caregivers, we can begin to observe identifiable aspects of fantasies in our toddlers. Fantasies can diminish anxiety when a child's urges are at odds with our expectations or with the beginnings of the child's own internalized standards. For example, young kids who have achieved toilet training often abhor messiness and disorder. Their protests and upset about getting dirty may reflect an active repudiation of the pleasure of the very messy, smearing activities that we so vehemently discouraged.

Two-year-old Sean was visiting my house with his father. He was gleeful as he sat on the floor to play with the toy truck, stuffed animals, and ball that I offered him. After a few moments of rolling the truck and the ball, Sean got a worried look on his face, looked at his hands, and came toward me with his arms extended as I stood by the kitchen sink. He said one word: "Wash." I wiped his hands with a wet paper towel, and Sean returned to his joyful play on the floor. Several moments later, the worried expression returned, and again Sean interrupted his play so that we could get rid of the offending dirt on his hands. This time Sean shot his dad an anxious look as he approached me. His dad said, "Don't be silly. You're fine. Just play."

When Sean returned to his truck-rolling game, his dad told me, with a note of slight irritation and some confusion, that his son had been very concerned about being clean lately, frequently requesting that his hands be washed. I asked about how things had been going in general. With great pride, his dad reported that his son had recently begun to use the toilet.

When I suggested that Sean's concerns about staying clean might be connected to this latest achievement, his dad looked incredulous. "You know, I hadn't thought of that. But it makes sense, especially since we talked so much to Sean about how big boys stop wearing diapers and use the toilet so they can be nice and clean. I guess he's taking cleanliness pretty seriously!"

Sean was. On his last trip to the sink, it was Dad who responded. As he wiped his son's hands, he said, in a softer tone, "You know, when you finish playing and before you leave we can wash because I know how much big boys like to have nice clean hands." Giving the child a hug, his dad added, "And you're my big boy!" Before racing back to push the truck across the floor, Sean looked at his dad and beamed.

This strategy of turning away from one set of highly pleasurable but equally problematic feelings (the wish to get really dirty) by adopting opposite ones (the wish to be clean) can require a dramatic or even hostile response to the original longings. In my business, these determined efforts at disavowal are referred to as *reaction formations*. On the way to taking on external demands as fully their own, a young child gets crucial support from clear communication of expectations as well as the satisfaction of parents' approval and pleasure when the goals are successfully met. That's what Sean's dad was up to at my kitchen sink.

While there will be opportunities throughout life for externalizing and displacing conflicts onto parents, siblings, friends, teachers, girl-friends or boyfriends, spouses or partners, colleagues, and telemarketers, in this phase conflicts among competing urges, wishes, thoughts, and feelings can be internal and belong to the child alone. The anxiety aroused by the conflict between loving and hating and by dangers asso-ciated with destructive or aggressive wishes and feelings require solu-tions in fantasy and action that are part of growing up.

FEARS OF SEPARATION AND LOSS

At times it can be hard to figure out what's scaring our toddlers, or know how to respond when there are no obvious external sources for their fears. Something that has been a standard part of our child's

routine can suddenly emerge as a new focal point for terror and struggle. We are so relieved to have navigated those nights of angry, tearful
protests that surfaced at bedtime with our 8-to-12-month-old that revisiting them with our big boy of 18 to 36 months can feel like a
setback when he develops bedtime fears. As he moves into his much-
prized big-kid bed, crib railings no longer provide the useful restraint that allowed us to leave the room—if not emotionally, then
at least physically.

One of a parent's most important tasks is to help the toddler learn
about the difference between fantasy and reality, and nighttime is the
most crucial testing ground of this skill. As adults, we know that it is
necessary to let go of our connections to the details and reality of
waking life to get to sleep. Most of us have an easier time getting to
sleep when there is a minimum of intruding reminders of the real
world—no unusual noise, light, or movement. In the absence of stimulation from our immediate surroundings, peace, quiet, and fatigue
allow our bodies and minds to disconnect and fall into sleep. But we
also know that our senses can be kept on high alert by internal sources
of stimulation.

When we are anxious and unhappy, it is hard to shake a repetitive
review of the most troubling aspects of the day or break our circular
attempts at problem-solving, whose revolutions seem to gain in speed
and intensity. We can't switch gears and find relief in fantasies that
take us a million miles away from the troubling feelings at hand. Instead, we are locked in a present world of problems that rely on the
very order, reason, and logic that our minds need a break from for our
bodies to slide into sleep.

However tough we may find it to get to sleep at night, particularly
at difficult moments in our lives, for most of us sleep is a welcome
event. But for toddlers and young children, sleep can feel like surrender
to their most dangerous ideas, images, and feelings, which are at best
only loosely distinguished from reality. Routine is central in helping
our young children to master anxieties, but as our toddlers reach a new
threshold of worry about separation, even well-established patterns of

bathing, tooth brushing, cuddling, and stories may not be a sufficient hedge against anxiety. Instead, these bedtime rituals come to signal the interruption of contact with us that they dread.

THE BOSS OF BEDTIME

A father told me about the urgency of his daughter's demands for un-interrupted contact at bedtime. Suzy was almost three years old and thrilled about having moved into her big-girl bed six months earlier. She knew exactly which mermaid sheet patterns she wanted, insisting that they had to be different from the ones on her 5-year-old sister's bed. She was so proud. Even months after the change, Suzy would arrange her favorite stuffed animals around her and announce, "I love my bed," her dad told me.

"We would finish the last of three stories, give her a hug and kiss, negotiate how wide a stream of light would come through her door-way, and say good night." But then, according to my friend, "Sleep-time paradise was lost!" Over the next several nights, Suzy would pop out after she had snuggled down in her big-girl bed.

"One night, we didn't even notice that Suzy was with us in the living room," Suzy's dad recalled. "We were both reading, and one of us looked up and there she was: silent, a solemn expression on her face, with her favorite teddy bear under her arm. I asked her what the matter was, and she replied that she wasn't sleepy and wanted to be downstairs. I told her it was late, picked her up, and took her back to bed. There was no protest as I tucked her in and again adjusted the door to the right amount of hallway light. Ten minutes later, there she was again: same stance, same teddy bear. Again, I took her upstairs and asked if she was feeling okay. I only realized after several nights of this what an unfortunate question that would turn out to be."

Once again, Suzy simply stated that she wasn't tired and wanted to be downstairs with her parents. That night she only came down once more, just as they were getting ready to go to bed themselves.

"That first night we both remained calm. We didn't even keep tally of whose turn it was to take her upstairs. After the second night we were no longer so calm. We argued about who had been doing the heavy lifting. Suzy now told us that her tummy hurt but the pain quickly migrated to her head. Her temperature was normal and the physical complaints either quickly shifted or miraculously disappeared if she was with us. We became emphatic: it was way past her bedtime and we were tired and needed time to ourselves. Our insistence that she stay in bed only seemed to fuel her insistence."

Suzy got in bed, but her parents soon found her clutching her teddy and sitting at the top of the stairs.

"With real irritation, we both went up this time and told her we had had enough. She needed to stay in her bed. Moments later, she was back, now with an angry scowl on her face, teddy at her side. When I picked her up, she kicked and screamed that she didn't want to go to bed. We were exhausted and feeling defeated. Her anger was the last thing that was going to elicit any sympathy or creative new strategies for achieving my objective. She would stay in bed and that was that!"

That, of course, was not that. Suzy reappeared at the top of the stairs.

"Racing upstairs, I grabbed her," her dad said, looking chagrined. "She went stiff and remained that way as I put her roughly back in bed. She didn't cry. She just squeezed her cuddly bear and looked at me with frozen disbelief. I left. She did not come down again that night. It was not one or our finer moments."

In their consultation with me, Suzy's parents eventually saw that that outburst achieved their aim. Suzy was now staying in bed, but she had lost her recently acquired ability to use the toilet and was in diapers again. She had become cranky and had started to dissolve into tantrums with any request, especially at bath time but also about getting dressed, eating, or following any schedule other than her own.

I suggested to these parents that they pick a quiet time well before Suzy's bedtime for a brief chat with her. While her older sister played in an adjoining room, they sat on a sofa with Suzy between them. Her father began by saying that sometimes big girls had big feelings that made it hard to go to sleep at night and that they wanted to help make bedtime nice again, without Suzy or Mommy and Daddy getting upset. Suzy's mother added that she knew Suzy was mad that they didn't let her stay with them when she couldn't sleep. Maybe there was something that made it hard for her to feel safe and comfortable in her room by herself. Suzy fidgeted. She protested that she *did* stay in her big-girl bed and that now she just wanted to play with her sister.

While we had all acknowledged that it was unlikely that Suzy would suddenly be able to articulate the meaning and motivation behind her recent difficulties, her parents had been hopeful. But they signaled each other not to press for a longer encounter that might move from sympathetic discussion to angry interrogation.

Helping children articulate feelings that are, at the moment, too big and hazy for words can be a very important step in their efforts to achieve mastery of the uncertain aspects of their worlds. However, when the feelings are too powerful and overwhelming, actions like Suzy's do speak louder than words. Her parents needed to take a different, more behavioral tack.

Putting aside their wish for a quick talking cure, Suzy's parents remained calm. When it was time to begin Suzy's formerly successful bedtime routine, her parents moved into the second part of the plan we discussed. Before a potential battle about bathing could begin, Suzy's mother told her that tonight they would have a special story in addition to the ones that Suzy chose. Suzy was excited about this treat and went easily into the tub at her mother's suggestion that they would only be able to get to the extra story if she had her bath and got ready for bed quickly enough. For the first time in days, there were no fights about beginning or ending the bath, and when Mommy got a bit wet in the process it did not seem to be the result of an angry, well-aimed splash.

Suzy arranged her cuddly toys, eagerly chose her books, and, after the second reading, said she wanted the special story. And so, armed with the list we had discussed, her mother began the story.

"Once upon a time, there was a family of rabbits. There was a mommy, a daddy, and two bunny girls named—"

Suzy interrupted with "Sarah and Wooly!"

"Wooly was younger than Sarah," her mother continued, "but she was learning to do new big-bunny things every day. She knew how to wash her face and how to eat with a bunny fork and to play nicely with other bunnies and even how to use the special bunny toilet instead of bunny diapers. She could hop very fast and jump very high, almost as fast and high as her big-bunny sister. She had gotten so big that her parents finally got her something very special that she had wanted—a big bunny's bed! It was the best bed that Wooly could have, and she picked all the things that she wanted on it.

"What do you think she wanted on her bed?" Suzy's mother asked.

Suzy quickly listed pretty mermaid sheets, a cozy pillow, and lots and lots of cuddle toys, so that Wooly wouldn't be alone.

"Wooly loved her new bed and loved being a big bunny. But one night, Wooly didn't want to stay in her bed. She felt so alone. She only wanted to be with her parents. They said, 'No, Wooly, it's your bedtime and you need to go back to sleep!' Well, Wooly didn't want to, so what do you think she did?"

Suzy chimed in with a giggle. "Wooly didn't go back to bed and just didn't!"

"Her parents kept putting Wooly back to bed, and Wooly kept getting up. Each time they put her back, Wooly got more and more mad. She didn't like being alone, but she also didn't like it that her parents were still up and just by themselves, with each other. That made Wooly mad and sad. She felt all alone and she wanted to be the big boss, not her parents! And so Wooly and her parents kept getting into fights about who was the boss of bedtimes. It made Wooly very unhappy and worried to be mad at her parents and to see them mad at her.

"But Wooly's parents understood that something must be bothering Wooly and they didn't want her to be worried. They told Wooly that they did want her to go to bed like a big bunny but they also told her something else that was very important. Do you know what they told her?"

Wide-eyed, Suzy mimicked an angry adult voice. "You go to bed *now!*"

Mommy winced inside but continued. "They had said that before. But now they said to Wooly, 'We love you very much . . . even when you are mad at us.' They told Wooly that maybe something had scared her and made it hard for her to feel safe in her room by herself. . . . Can you think of what might have scared Wooly?"

Suzy immediately said no and quickly ended the story. "And they lived happily after."

Suzy's mother took her cue from her daughter and did not press the investigation. She did, however, furnish her own ending to this first of many versions of similar stories.

"The mommy and daddy rabbit wanted to help Wooly feel like a big bunny again. They didn't want to have fights every night, and they didn't want her to feel afraid. And so, for a little while after they finished bedtime stories, they asked Wooly if she would like for them to stay, sitting next to her bed for just a few minutes while she got comfortable for sleep. And do you know what Wooly said?"

"Stay," said Suzy, in the voice of a very sleepy and very little girl. For the rest of the week, Suzy asked to be told the story of Wooly. She would alter the details, adding and subtracting elements of the story. As she continued to elaborate on the adventures of Wooly the bunny, she confronted dangerous animals and monsters, as well as burglars, whom she would vanquish with an increasing array of skills, strength, and magic. But for a while the ending of the original story remained the same. Her parents would sit by her bed for no more than ten minutes as she drifted off to sleep.

Over the next weeks, her parents reported that Suzy was back to her big-girl self. Her defiance didn't disappear completely, but it was clear that she had weathered a storm that had calmed for now. Over the next several months, her tolerance increased for being alone at night, engaged in solitary play or in activities with her older sister, as did her pleasure in being a big girl. Her list of accomplishments grew, as did the frequency with which she announced them to anyone who would listen. For Suzy, moving forward held far more appeal than regressing back to infancy. With her parents' help, she was able to turn down the volume on her worries about the meaning of being separated from them, about the consequences of their joint rage, and about the realities of being small.

While Suzy's parents were delighted to replace their own feelings of helplessness, rage, and guilt with a sense of their daughter's relief and pride in herself, they remained frustrated that they were never able to fulfill their Sigmund Freud fantasies of discovering the specific location of Suzy's disrupted bedtime routine. There had to be some concrete version of fear that Suzy just couldn't find words for. That might be true. But it might be that, at this stage in her development, Suzy just didn't possess the elaborate repertoire of protective responses she needed to allay her fears in her big unprotected bed. She fell back on the blanket presence of parents as her most reliable source of safety.

It's not clear to me whether Suzy's revelation many years later was a real and significant piece of the earlier puzzle or just a fulfillment of her parents' investigative wish. At age 12, Suzy had been babysitting a neighbor's two-year-old. She said that he "pitched a fit" when his parents left and then calmed down until bedtime. She read him story after story until she wound up falling asleep on his bed with him. As she reported this story to her parents, she remembered being frightened at night at about the same age as her charge.

"There was a long time when I was really scared to be alone at night," she said. "Do you remember the stuffed owl I used to have on my dresser? Well, every night, when the light from the hallway shown through the door, it cast a huge shadow on the wall next to my bed. It looked like some huge angry dragon that was flying straight at me, coming to hurt me or take me away. I thought no one would know and I would be gone forever."

In early separations, infants can be frightened and disoriented because they don't understand that when Mom and Dad leave the room, they aren't gone forever. In a later period of development, the child may believe that his or her voracious demands, anger, frustration, and moves toward independence will combine to make him or her the agent of the parents' destruction. Until reunited with Mommy and Daddy, a young child may imagine that they have gone away forever and feel completely alone, bereft, and guilty. That terror of permanent separation is what Suzy recalled so vividly some nine years later.

REMEMBER, WE'RE THE GROWN-UPS

If we forget that we react to our children's behavior, or pretend that we don't sometimes feel challenged or completely overwhelmed by their demands, our attempts to find new ways of helping them to address the most troubling sources of their needs will fall flat. If we feel badly about the frustration and even rage engendered by our toddlers' tantrums or temporary setbacks in potty training or bedtime routines, we will have a much harder time recognizing the difference between appropriate limit-setting that supports our children's growth and the fear- or humiliation-inducing tirades and rough physical handling that we may feel like delivering.

In part, toddlers' tantrums reflect rage and frustration because there are real limits to their own capacities to gratify themselves, and limits on their control over their parents' powers of gratification. Their fear may be about being small and, at times, helpless. This feeling is compounded by fear of their own intense actions and hateful emotions and of the frightening responses of parents.

Helping toddlers to see the distinction between themselves and others is part of the reality testing that allows them to learn to delay gratification and distinguish between their feelings, thoughts, and actions and those of other people. We often refer to tantrums as *meltdowns* because, as with nuclear reactors, when the operational controls slip, the power that is unleashed grows exponentially. Toddlers may be especially vulnerable to this cascade phenomenon and to fear it because their ability to control powerful feelings is still forming.

The capacity for delaying gratification is still shaky. Toddlers remain unconvinced by their limited experience that waiting will not be forever or that the anger and hatred aroused in them by waiting will not destroy the people they love. Of course, it turns out that parents do return, even when toddlers are very angry about their departure. It is equally difficult to hear the word *no* when it confirms how small and incapable they are in comparison to how big and powerful they imagine themselves to be. At these moments, disappointment and rage far outweigh the pleasures that accompany their very real new accomplishments.

When toddlers can't rely on their own controls at times of tantrums, parental brakes can help decrease the intensity and speed of a meltdown. When our children are at the height of their frustration and rage, we need to lend them a perspective to help them moderate the intensity of their feelings and the fears that often follow. After all, we're the grown-ups. We can do this by offering toddlers a more reassuring version of reality. The ideas we need to communicate are:

- You are not alone. We will not leave you, even when you are feeling most angry and out of control.

- You will not be allowed to remain out of control.

- We will not make you feel like a bad, horrible, unloved, and unlovable monster as you struggle and learn how to be the big-kid boss of your strongest feelings.

- We are here to help you as you learn.

- You can sometimes hate the people that you also love.

- You can control angry feelings and thoughts so they don't escalate into destructive and hurtful actions.

WE DO OUR BEST TO HELP

Of course, you can't say those things to toddlers in words. Too often, when parents recognize that their young children are about to lose it or have already gone into meltdown mode, they rely on verbal reasoning and intellectualization rather than on action. You've probably seen these phenomena as the flip side of the parent screaming at the screaming toddler in the grocery store. For what seems like an eternity, the parent stands patiently over the young child who is screaming, kicking, and spitting with rage, calmly repeating choice phrases like, "I can see that you're very angry."

These parents can be observed bending at the waist, frozen smile on their faces as they try to talk thoughtfully to their raging child about unhappy, sad, or angry feelings. "I know that you are feeling very angry with Mommy, but you can't behave like this." Or, when that gambit fails, they go to the two-choices option: that is, "You can choose between this cereal or that cereal, but you can't have both." Or, finally, as the smile loses its grip, "You know, Daddy is getting very angry that you are acting like this."

It's not that any of these statements are wrong in and of themselves. It's just that there is such a mismatch between the adult words and the toddler's emotions and behavior. Once children have crossed over into the language of action and unregulated emotion, words on their own are ineffective in helping them regain control and feel safe again. As your facial muscles strain with your public smile and you are flushed with a combination of indignation and embarrassment, your angry child will feel about as much of a sense of control as you do— that is, very little.

Our own sense of humiliation and rage often gets in the way of taking the necessary steps to interrupt our toddlers' tantrums. And issues of power, size, and capacity are ones we remain vulnerable to throughout our lives. Recognizing the power of the feelings that our young children can provoke in us, and forgiving ourselves for our vulnerability to them, can be the first step to taking charge of out-of-control behavior. Offering your child the chance to get off the floor and stop kicking and screaming—or, when at home, letting the child know that you will return to the room after he or she has calmed down—can be the very brief prelude to either removing your child from the scene of confrontation or sitting, holding, and distracting him or her.

Remember the little boy on the ferry? Physical contact with his mother was the most reassuring response when he felt overwhelmed and threatened by the loud unfamiliar noise of the foghorn. As he clung to her, his sobs decreased and his breathing returned to normal. It was only when he stopped gulping for air and lightened his grip that his mother began to add words to her attempts to comfort him. As if intuitively reading the balance between the emotional demands created by a frightening event and his capacity to regulate his feelings, this mother tailored her comments to what she could see of his experience. She responded naturally and automatically. Let's learn from her success by breaking it down into categories:

1. Identifying and putting words to emotions ("You got scared; you had a very big feeling")

2. Explaining the emotional reaction ("You got scared when you heard a big loud noise; you didn't know what it was")

3. Explaining the source of the upset ("You heard a noise the boat makes; the loud noise hurt your ears")

4. Repeating the child's reaction and simply stating the facts ("You got scared when you heard a big loud noise because you didn't know what it was")

5. Calmly reminding the child of your protective presence ("I'm right here; what you heard was the sound a boat makes to let the other boats know where it is; you're safe with me and the boat is safe")

By using these approaches, we help our toddlers and young children recover from acute episodes of intense and startling fear and help prepare them for dealing with similar situations in future. We also help establish basic cognitive and linguistic tools that will help them regulate their emotions and feel safer and in greater control of their world.

ORGANIZING WORLDS
AND GAUGING RISK

Your child's developing language affords him or her a larger set of tools for organizing and making sense of the world outside, as well as the internal world of ideas and feelings. One of the extraordinary aspects of development is that advances in language acquisition are accompanied by cognitive advances in simple reasoning. Toddlers possess not only an increased array of words to label things, actions, feelings, and experience but also the ability to string these word labels together to create the beginnings of cohesive theories about how their minds and the minds of others work. Recognizing and remembering the connection between a feeling that can be identified with words and a specific event or idea is the foundation for being able to expand their range of reactions to novel and potentially frightening experiences as well.

After being comforted by his mother, the little boy on the ferry may have continued to experience an elevated heart rate when he heard the foghorn. But the disorganizing impact of shock and novelty were gone. With experience, he could anticipate and guard against the unpleasant and upsetting fear by staying close to his parents and holding their hands. No longer unprepared, the little boy was also no longer helpless and overwhelmed as he took action against remembered unpleasant and uncomfortable feelings of fear and vulnerability. With his mother's assistance, he was able to use his toddler's language and cognitive skills to label, order, remember, anticipate, and protect against the impending blasts. "Bad noise hurts my ears," he said, when the foghorn blew again. "Yes, but it reminds us we're safe," his mom said.

Parents are the first and best reality-testers for toddlers and young children; they look to us to confirm or challenge their scary ideas about bad things that might happen to them. In the same way that they look directly to us for praise and appreciation, our children use us to gauge how much anxiety is warranted in any given situation that has raised anxiety in their own minds. A girl might view a dog in the park with trepidation, but if her mom says, "Look, this is a nice friendly dog. Let's pat him carefully on his back," the child feels safe to approach. If on the other hand a fierce dog appears in their path, the girl might realize that by taking her hand and calmly crossing to another part of the park, her mom is protecting her from potential harm.

As our children look to our faces for smiles and other indications of our pleasure, they also scan our faces for signs of distress and listen to our voices for notes of tension, anger, and fear. The difference between their reactions and ours to the same events helps them define an internal set of standards they will use to gauge the level of distress that is warranted the next time the event occurs. We can see this sequence vividly in the little boy's first and second encounters with the foghorn. Would he have been satisfied with holding his mother and father's hands if their behavior indicated that they shared his level of fear and agitation? Not likely. If he had seen panic in his mother's face and if, instead of calm, she had responded with urgency and desperation, this boy's worst feelings about imminent danger would have been confirmed by his most reliable barometer, his mother.

DISPLACEMENT, PLAY, AND MASTERY

As we saw in chapter 2, adults may displace feelings or attention from one set of anxious or distressful circumstances to unrelated ones. We have a bad day at work and blow up at home about a single dirty dish in the sink. Children use this same defensive maneuver—avoiding the weight of anxiety associated with conscious recognition of its original source—in enormously adaptive ways. When a little girl has been told she needs to wait, she doesn't have to worry about making Mommy mad by yelling at her to get off the phone. Instead, she goes to her toys in another corner of the room and repeatedly crashes a vehicle into blocks until the phone call ends.

There are many situations in which play about aggression or being aggressive in play is more beneficial in mastering aggressive urges and impulses than expressing them directly and suffering parental disapproval. In this phase there are additional processes that also become available to young children in the service of protecting themselves and others from unwanted or conflicting urges and feelings. These unconscious, automatic defensive mechanisms are the beginnings of processes that we will employ to varying degrees throughout our lives. They are:

- Denial, or disavowal of a particular feeling or aspect of reality

- Projection, or disowning an unwanted feeling about others by assigning to someone else

- Displacement, or shifting the target of our feelings about one person to another, or about one situation to another, or to a toy or other inanimate figure

The discomfort that hostile impulses stir up runs counter to the love children feel for their parents, but the impulses may be significantly diminished if they are disowned. The hostile feelings do not disappear, but their targets shift. Not hearing parents' instructions or protesting that the new baby brother belongs to the next-door neighbors, being fearful of others' hatred or frightened of monsters and noises in the night, or crashing blocks instead of bothering a mommy who is on the phone are all preferable to the destruction of loved ones that young kids imagine will occur when they are feeling angry with the people upon whom they depend. These defense mechanisms give growing kids opportunities to express competing feelings of love and hate without directing them at the parent. These new options for dealing with intense and conflicted feelings introduce a new set of challenges for us as parents. Our task is to pay attention and try to understand how our children's expressed fears may serve as necessary outlets for their own conflicted feelings of love and hate.

There is a huge difference between setting limits with our children, helping them put the brakes on their expressions of rage and frustration, and responding to them with an equally open and intense expression of our own similar feelings. I am not suggesting that children, even young children, should never know that their parents are angry or that their behavior has caused parental displeasure. I am suggesting that when we are able to modulate the intensity of our emotional responses to our children's anger, we are in a much better position to help them get control and learn about the real consequences of strong feelings. One of the most terrifying consequences of rage and hatred is to lose the love of the parent toward whom these feelings are directed.

When parents cannot tolerate the natural occurrence of their young children's strongest, negative feelings and recoil or counterattack in response, they confirm their children's worst and most primitive fears. When adults lose it, scream, or yell and hit in response to young children's defiant and angry behavior, they demonstrate that feelings and thoughts can destroy loving connections.

But when we are able to maintain order and restraint even in the face of the most maddening and exhausting challenges to our sanity and self-control that young children can throw our way, we demonstrate that feelings do not destroy bodies or connections between people who love each other. In our strength and in our capacities to contain *our* strongest, angriest emotions, we offer our children safety and security. We show them that their bad feelings are not powerful enough to dramatically disrupt our connection with them. We offer our young children models for how to tolerate their own hateful, angry feelings.

Young children's real competencies in communicating and acting on needs independently, and their continued experience of our consistent and tolerant availability, promote a growing resolution of struggles driven by their strongest feelings about themselves and their relationships with us. This psychological rapprochement, or renewal of more harmonious relations, occurs not only between children and parents over issues of control and compliance but also within the child between powerful and conflicting urges and feelings.

In the latter part of the toddler phase, children can begin to tolerate ambivalent attitudes toward themselves and their parents, between love and hate, and between conflicting desires for dependence and self-reliance. In this phase, our kids' ability to recognize others as separate entities and to own their strongest feelings about the most important people in their lives also extends their capacity for empathy. They begin to express concern for others and ask us questions about our moods. In late toddlerhood, your daughter may come over and give you a comforting pat when you are upset. Your son may help a playmate up when he falls down on the playground, pat the dust from his friend, and say, "You're okay." These children now understand when a parent or friend is happy or hurt. And they practice dealing with it by assigning such feelings to their stuffed animals and dolls.

PLAY TO THE RESCUE

Toddlers often use games and imaginative play to work on the basic ingredients of their concerns and fears. Earlier games of peek-a-boo or chase-me served important functions in helping toddlers to establish a sense that out of sight does not mean gone forever. These activities also supported the recognition of their growing capacities to be active and effective in their search for the person they desired—taking small but significant steps in the developmental trajectory toward mastery and increased autonomy. Similarly, filling and emptying containers of water, sand, blocks, and toys added to a wealth of knowledge about the conservation of things. These activities also provided additional opportunities to work on notions of proportion and size and were essential in dealing with fears about who or what can go down bathtub drains and toilets!

How does playing change as your child grows? Toward the end of the second year and into the third year of life, children will begin to use toys and other play items to replay and elaborate on their daily experiences and fantasies, as well as for the purpose of engaging in pleasurable interactions with parents and caregivers. Moving cars across the floor, carrying and feeding baby dolls, playing with puppets, and imitating day-to-day adult activities offer wonderful opportunities to rework old experiences, to rehearse new ones, and to try on new roles. They also set the stage for imaginative play in which the child will develop complex scripts and story lines in fantasy scenarios.

By age three, there is a gradual shift in the child's view of other children as well. Early on they may perceive peers as playthings or objects that get in the way of personal pursuits. As parents we are relieved when our young children no longer behave like little thugs (or their victims). Increasingly, our kids not only play side by side but also turn to one another as companions and partners in shared activities. These are fun precisely because there is more pleasure in cooperation than there is in unilateral action and bashing others.

The achievements a child moves through in toddlerhood expand our young children's range of possible pleasures. Their growth also increases the complexity of their internal sources of danger and fears. Among these, the struggle between dependence and independence is one that will reverberate throughout life. Your young children's burgeoning capacity for independent functioning is a source of pride to them, yet with that comes the knowledge that they are separate from their parents, and vulnerable.

As the central tasks of the toddler phase merge with subsequent stages, the groundwork is laid for more complex relationships both within the child's family and outside it. The most important people in children's lives will continue to populate their longings, fantasies, and preoccupations in the developmental phases to come. Often, these longings and fantasies will be sources of pleasure, safety, and security. At other times they will be the very focal points of risk, danger, and fear.

■

CHAPTER FIVE

OEDIPUS RISING
(AGES 3 TO 6)

Young children will go to remarkable lengths to diminish overwhelming fear as real events converge with internal, personal versions of danger. Listen to this story my friend Mark told me. He was doing research for a graduate school paper, reading about psychological development in children with severely impaired sight, when he found himself recalling a distant memory.

"I don't remember having any thoughts about the event, since it happened when I was a little kid," Mark told me. "One summer morning when I was about four and a half, I looked out the front window of our house, and there on top of the telephone pole was a big fat raccoon. I told my mother, and I guess she must have made phone calls, because later in the day a bunch of people came by to check out the raccoon, which had not moved over the course of many hours. I remember standing at the window almost all day, waiting anxiously to see what would happen to the poor, cuddly-looking, helpless raccoon that clearly needed saving.

"I know I couldn't have possibly stood there all day, but that's what I remember. By the end of the afternoon, the raccoon was still on top of the pole, but finally, to my great relief, help arrived. A huge red fire truck—a hook and ladder—showed up. It was very exciting, because they raised the ladder and a fireman went up and grabbed the raccoon and brought it down in his arms. The raccoon was finally safe."

That was Mark's story. He was amazed that a memory that had been locked away from consciousness for so long could suddenly emerge so vividly. "It was uncanny. I could remember every aspect of that day, how cloudy and bright, how warm it was, the view of the street, even the changing light over the course of the day."

Mark was so struck by the power of this resurfaced memory that several weeks later on a visit to his parents he told them the story. His parents listened intently, then looked at each other with a mixture of surprise, concern, and caution. An awkward silence developed.

"What's up, what's going on?" he asked his parents.

"Do you want to know what really happened?" Mark's father asked.

As it turned out, some of what Mark remembered was accurate— just not the important parts. What he could not have known was that, for weeks before this raccoon had perched on top of the telephone pole, it or its relatives had been making a mess of neighborhood garbage cans, leaving refuse everywhere in the wake of their marauding. And there was more.

There was no hook-and-ladder rescue mission. No firemen came. Earlier in the day, the Good Humor ice cream man had made his rounds and had also spotted the raccoon. This man lived nearby and decided to help rid the neighborhood of the troublesome creature. That afternoon, at the end of his rounds, the Good Humor man came back with his shotgun, stood on top of his truck, took aim, and shot the raccoon dead.

Mark was disbelieving at first. He couldn't square this story with his own memory. He was finally able to recall the Good Humor truck and to remember vaguely the white-uniformed man's role in the unfolding drama. But he has never been able to remember the shooting, a dead raccoon, or the feelings that must have accompanied them.

"I mean, there was this furry, cuddly raccoon. What does a

four-and-a-half-year-old know about a flea- and rabies-ridden trash-marauding vermin? To me he was a scared little thing that needed big people to take care of him," Mark said.

Obviously, something very different had happened. The friendly Good Humor man that everyone loved had turned out to be dangerous and scary. Could he turn on children just as easily as he had on the animal? Did the rest of the adults, including his parents, think shooting that cuddly creature was okay?

"Maybe, *my* version was better than believing that a world of warm and fuzzy feelings could be so easily blasted away. What could be *my* fate if I went where I didn't belong, did things I shouldn't do? Who knew? I guess my mind wasn't taking any chances."

Mark's parents couldn't remember if he had reacted to the raccoon execution. They thought he might have had more trouble sleeping, maybe had some nightmares, but they weren't sure. They were surprised by his revision of the event and amazed that he even remembered it. They said, "How could we have known?"

Indeed, who could have known? We cannot read our young children's minds, and there is much they don't tell us. Yet there is no better time to discover the distance between a child's experiences of real events and our assumptions about what they mean to him or her than during the preschool years. In this chapter we will see that, in this phase of development, kids are able to use words and pictures, to represent ideas and feelings and to create cohesive stories in their fantasies and play. When we watch and listen carefully enough, when we are able to take our children's lead, we can learn an enormous amount about what they find scariest and most exciting.

When we understand more about how the minds of 3-to-6-year-olds work, we are in a much better position to help them deal with their internal struggles. These emerge in the form of nighttime monsters, sleep difficulties, fights over family rules and expectations, and angry demands for our exclusive attention. And we can't easily quell their fears just by stating the facts.

Mark's parents, like most adults, did not know what it was like for their young child to watch as a story ended so violently. Nor did they know to be on the watch for difficulties that might follow. Had they known more about their little boy's mind and imagination, Mark's parents might well have tried to protect him from witnessing the shooting of the animal.

If our preschool kids witness scary things, there are several simple questions parents can pose to initiate a discussion that can help children deal with what they have seen:

1. What did you see or hear?

2. What do you feel about what happened?

3. Why do you think the event happened?

4. Do you have questions about what happened?

The point of the questions is to help children verbalize their thoughts. We need to give them time to respond. We need to respect that they may not wish to talk about scary things on our schedule. When children say they don't want to talk about frightening events, we need to listen. We tell them we realize that it may be hard to talk about upsetting events and we are ready to listen when they are ready to talk. Most important, we want to help them to feel safe again.

In Mark's case, in the absence of supervision and distraction from the unfolding drama that ended with the Good Humor man assuming a very different line of work, Mark's parents might have sat down with their son and asked him his ideas about what he had seen. They might have asked how he was feeling about what happened to the raccoon. Mark might or might not have mentioned his worries about the Good Humor man, but he might have expressed how sad and scary it was that any grown-up would hurt such a vulnerable, cuddly animal. This would have been an opportunity for Mark's parents to ask why he thought something like that would happen. Once they heard his theories, they would have been able to respond as factually as possible to his concerns. They might have put words to Mark's apparent distress, such as, "You had some big feelings about what you saw," or "You must have some ideas about what you saw." If Mark had not been able to put his obvious upset into words, his parents might have said, "It wasn't nice to see the raccoon killed," and then asked about his thoughts and questions. If Mark had raised his feelings of sympathy for the raccoon and asked specifically why it had been killed, they might first stress that animals are different from people. They might have added that sometimes animals that live in the woods can get so hurt or sick it is better for them to die. They would have responded with facts about any confusion Mark might have expressed about the shooter's motivation or about other reasons for the raccoon's death. "No, the Good Humor man wasn't angry . . . and the raccoon wasn't shot because it was bad." But the most important thing Mark's parents could have done for him if they had been unable to keep him from witnessing the raccoon's death would have been to listen.

MEETING CHILDREN
WHERE THEY ARE

The period from ages 3 to 6—sometimes referred to as the oedipal phase of development—is a time of mental integration involving biological urges, the direction of love and hate, and the relationship between unconscious and conscious thoughts and feelings in the realities of daily life. For a child to move successfully through the demands of the oedipal phase, he or she will call on overlapping and mutually supportive developmental achievements.

- In **social relations,** a child will have developed a primary relationship to his or her parents, internal representations of mother and father as separate, and a good sense of the self as an initiator of things (and a successful one at that), as well the capacity for empathizing with the feelings of others.

- In **cognition,** he or she will have developed the ability to flexibly apply personal knowledge and values—empathy, fairness, ambivalence—in a broadening social context and to call on this ability when assuming various social roles, taking the perspective of others, tolerating mixed feeling about the self and others, appreciating the rights and responsibilities of the self and others, and sensing that they can act and feel differently at different times.

- In the **moral arena,** the child will have a developing sense of right and wrong, good and bad, recognizing the link between actions and their consequences in relation to the parents (approval and pleasure versus disapproval and anger) and to the self (well-being and pride versus shame and guilt).

- In the **physical realm,** the child will develop the capacity for fine and gross motor coordination for pleasurable and playful activities such as running, jumping, and climbing, as well as self-care (toilet use, tooth brushing, hand washing) and imitating adult behavior in play (cooking, driving a car, caring for a baby, building things).

- In the **emotional arena,** the child will develop a wide range of feelings (including excitement, happiness, sadness, remorse, fear, disappointment, pride, anger, envy, love, and hate) that can be distinguished, expressed, and communicated to others.

- The child's **psychological integration** will include the capacity for remembering personal history, realizing that dreams and imagination come from within oneself, increasingly perceiving complex social situations involving the rudiments of cause and effect and time sequences, and developing narrative structures to make sense of inner and external experiences.

- In the **biological arena,** bodily changes unfold that determine and organize the child's physical capacities as well as establishing focal points for stimulation and pleasure. These maturational changes influence psychological development throughout a child's growth, most dramatically in puberty; in this phase they show up in intense emotions and longings (love) and in raw expressions of rivalry and aggression (hate). These feelings are directed to both same- and opposite-sex parents during the oedipal phase. Later, during adolescence, these powerful emotions will be directed toward peers.

These developmental achievements become integrated during this phase and determine how children experience the body, urges, relationships, and fears—as well as the way they navigate them.

THE JOY OF GETTING BIGGER AND BETTER

If, in our adult years, we could feel about our bodies the way our kids do when they are somewhere between 3 and 6 years old, we would be spending a lot less time, energy, and money on all the products, procedures, and exercises intended to make us look younger than we really are. The toddler's struggles and pride around a growing sense of separateness and control of basic bodily functions usher in the 3-to-6-year-olds' increasingly complicated love affair with their bodies and with the most important people in their lives.

By age 3, children generally are quite clear that they are either a girl or a boy and are aware of the types of play activities and dress expected of children of their sex. A sense of gender develops early in infancy and is the result of multiple interacting forces, including parents and others who treat boys and girls differently; anatomically distinctive sensations arising from the genitals in the course of parental care, toilet training, and self-stimulation (including penile erection, clitoral stimulation, and the sensations accompanying defecation and urination); and other biological factors, including genetic and endocrine influences on brain and behavior. During the first year of life and beyond, the internal psychological sense of gender is not simply an either-or issue. Both boys and girls desire some of the characteristics and opportunities of the opposite sex, and there are, of course, a broad range of attributes and experiences that both genders share.

Children take pleasure in the explosion of physical achievements that accompany their neuromuscular maturation. In this phase they are much more able to appreciate the specific sensations of their genitals. As they become progressively aware of this pleasure, their genitals not only define their anatomical identity but also contribute to a core gender identity about which they feel enormously proud. While normal masturbatory behavior is present from infancy in all children, during this phase both boys and girls engage in more focused masturbation and, much to the discomfort of many parents, may enjoy displaying their bodies and, at times, showing off their genitals.

During this 3-to-6-year-old phase, children are proud of what their bodies can do—whether in rough-and-tumble play, learning new skills on the playground, and displaying fine and gross motor skills and coordination, or in gaining parental attention through playing at adult roles, clowning, or performing new feats of skill and knowledge.

SCARY THINGS ABOUT
GETTING BIGGER

In each developmental phase, where there are achievements there will be dilemmas, sources of anxiety and fear. Not surprisingly, in a phase where physical ability and the pleasures of the body are so closely tied to feeling good about oneself, children may become especially vulnerable to feeling rejected, hurt, and enraged when their parents don't notice them or when they fail to master or perform some task for which they still may be too small or immature. While struggles about control dominated the toddler phase, this next phase is beset by rivalry and concerns about competence. When your 4-year-old son rejects your help with some new feat and declares, with substantial feeling, "I'll do it *myself*," remember that he does not want to recognize his own limitations—and doesn't want you to notice them either! Your child may chafe at rules he sees as demeaning or belittling of the authority he wishes he had.

Problems and frustrations on the road to mastery can also heighten sibling rivalry. For children with younger and older brothers and sisters, rivalry for Mommy and Daddy's attention can go in both developmental directions—resentment and longing for the kind of attention the younger sibling receives and envy of the achievements of the older ones. Susie might regress to wanting a bottle when her mom is breastfeeding a new baby; Jack might start trailing his older brother to the end of the block, saying that he too has to go to school. Competition with brothers and sisters can reach heated and hateful proportions that may lead to additional internal conflicts about love and hate and about the advantages and burdens of both moving forward and remaining small.

For toddlers, their greatest concerns about the body have to do with the dangers of being separate and no longer being able to view their parents' powers as their own. For the 3-to-6-year-old, fears about the body remain prominent, but the threats are organized specifically around damaging the body and losing the pleasure and pride it yields.

WHAT'S OEDIPUS GOT TO DO WITH IT?

One of the most crucial achievements for kids in the 3-to-6-year-old range is being able to recognize that in addition to the relationship parents have with them, they have a relationship with each other too. They also come to see that their parents' relationship has aspects that are separate from their role as parents. Now, giving up the belief that you are not the center of everyone's attention is not an easy task. This more realistic appraisal of family life is not, at least for the 3-to-6-year-old, the happiest aspect of getting bigger.

The very ingredients that allow children to establish richer, more complex, and empathetic relationships with others also helps them see that moms and dads have needs too, independent of their children. Unlike the earlier phases where parents were seen as either all good or all bad, depending on the child's state of frustration or satisfaction, kids now see parents as full people. Realizing not only that Mommy and Daddy are complete people, but also that they have strong, loving feelings for each other, can send our children on a vigorous campaign to recapture the central position, if only for a while, either by being *very* good, attractive, and clever or by being *very* naughty, destructive, and demanding.

During this stage, little Angela may say to her mother, "When I grow up, I'm going to marry Daddy." "And where will I be?" Mom asks. "Oh, you'll be dead," her daughter says matter-of-factly.

It is the jealousy, competition, and ultimate identification with the same-sex parent that led Freud to allude to the Greek myth of Oedipus in giving a name to this period. You'll recall from your high-school English class that Oedipus tragically murders his father and marries his mother. The name captures elements of this developmental drama but may oversimplify the real phenomenon of this phase. In fact, Oedipus didn't recognize that the man he murdered was his father or that his new wife was his mother. Knowledge and remorse only came later.

The real struggles for children in this period can be especially painful because they continue to love us even in the midst of powerful feelings of competition. Enormous imagined dangers come with these enormous conflicts, including fear of losing the rival parent you also love; losing the love of either parent because of your hostile wishes, and suffering retaliation for expressing these wishes. In the face of these conflicts, children work out possible compromises. To reach resolution, a child finds ways to be powerful and central, to feel proud of achievements, and at the same time to have the continuing secure presence and love of both parents. These solutions to the dangers of their competitive wishes are possible because of the child's advancing cognitive, emotional, social, and physical abilities. Successful resolution of the oedipal phase will provide a template for perceptions about the self and intimate relations with others well into the future.

Children in the earliest periods of development were explorers; 3-to-6-year-olds are best described as scientists. They're curious, developing hypotheses and experimenting in thought and play about relations with parents about relationships with other children, and about how their minds work. It may be a good thing that our children's preoccupations with a broad range of concerns about feelings toward the same- and opposite-sex parent happen in the context of consolidating important developing mental structures and capacities.

As adults, we can certainly identify with the challenge of accepting disappointing reality. We may be less able, though, to remember the nature of the central disappointments we experienced as very young kids—such as feeling excluded from important aspects of our parents' relationship. If you think about it long enough, and swallow the pride that may interfere with your memories, you can probably recall numerous times when you felt left out. Perhaps you were asked to leave the room during private discussions, or when your parents were having a conversation that had nothing to do with you, or when they stayed up later and went to bed together while you went to bed earlier by yourself. Being left out hurts! A friend recalls her fury when her father, home from a business trip, stopped to kiss her mom before he gave *her* the present he had brought. She was so furious, in fact, that she shattered the adorable toy china tea set he had carefully picked out for her.

BEHIND THE BEDROOM DOOR

As adults, we find it difficult to remember our own earliest theories about our parents' sexual lives. There's a good reason for this: they have gone underground. One of the most important achievements of the oedipal phase is that conscious aspects of our curiosity and preoccupation—and, let's face it, any thoughts about parents having sexual lives beyond their activities to produce *us*—get relegated to the unconscious part of our minds. It requires real effort for us to consider that our 3-to-6-year-old children may not have gotten there yet and are still in the throes of dealing with the complicated feelings involved in their ideas about their parents' sexual relationship.

Kids do not need to see their parents having intercourse to have their own ideas about what goes on behind closed bedroom doors. Children's fantasies of sexual intercourse can be confusing and frightening, based as they are on a combination of their observations of their parents' affection for each other, information they have been given about where babies come from, and the application of their own intense sexual and aggressive urges—imagining intercourse as something exciting, violent, and dangerous.

But there may be another reason for children's discomfort and fear. Because sexual intercourse represents the ultimate adult activity from which the child is excluded, children's notions about their parents' intimate lives may be a potent source of hurt and rage. This rage further fuels kids' notions that sexual activity is hurtful and dangerous.

When we shield our children from direct observations of adult sexuality we help them turn down the volume on the conflicted feelings that accompany their curiosity and developing theories about the origin of babies and about the special intimacy that exists between parents. When they aren't bombarded by seeing and hearing too much, kids are in a much better position to digest these complex issues over time and on their own schedules.

OVEREXPOSURE AND
OVERSTIMULATION

All young children are curious about their bodies and increasingly curious about the differences between boys and girls and between adults' and children's bodies. Frequently, regardless of the policies about privacy in the home and in day care, opportunities will come along to see bodies in varying stages of undress. This might be in the women's changing room at the pool, or when Joey accompanies Dad to the men's room at a ballgame—or simply by walking into an unlocked bathroom or bedroom at home.

Seeing the genitals of another child or the naked body of a parent will stimulate questions about body parts and anatomical differences. By responding matter-of-factly to a child's specific questions, parents provide vocabulary and knowledge that help contain excitement and reduce concerns about these issues.

When exposure to nudity is the primary source of early "education," young children learn very little. Don't leave your kids to contend with these dilemmas alone. When they are unable to contain the flood of feelings, they are left with a sense of being out of control, frightened, and small. By falling back on earlier ways of behaving and relating, children escape from overstimulation that creates discomfort and a sense of inadequacy. Retreating from areas of uncomfortable excitement may be quite dramatic and baffling to parents and may include increasing clinginess, loss of newly established toileting habits, fussy eating, and generally increased crankiness and tantrums.

There is *never* a time when it is useful or instructive for children to view parents having sex. For toddlers and preschoolers, viewing sexual activities between parents can be especially overwhelming as they struggle with normal confusion and efforts to integrate developing ideas about their own bodies and where babies come from. These efforts at mastery are further complicated by children's confused versions of the emotions involved in what they see and hear if they witness sex. Are they fighting? Are they hurting each other? Is that why they are making those noises?

Try to imagine how you might have felt if, as a toddler or preschooler, you had walked in on your parents when they were engaged in sexual activity. Makes you pretty uncomfortable to think about, right? The same discomfort that keeps you from lingering on that thought or memory for more than an instant can serve as an important reminder about the need to protect our children from experiences that are too much for them. I call this a live-wire issue, because it is dangerous and painful, yet almost impossible to let go of once it's touched.

Parents who come to me with concerns about their toddlers and preschoolers often are surprised when I ask about their policy on nudity and adult privacy in the home. Many are convinced that the best way to ensure that their kids grow up feeling comfortable about the human body is to not make a big deal about nudity—doors are often left open when parents are bathing, dressing, or using the toilet. Once I've introduced the topic, though, after some initial defensiveness, it is striking how often these same parents will make comments like, "Hmmm, now that you mention it, Erica does seem to like to watch us get dressed" or "Robert does seem to end up in the bathroom with us often," and so on.

Children are naturally curious about bodies, gender, and sexuality. That should never be cause for concern for parents. However, in order for children to really learn about and master the issues that make them most curious, they also have to be comfortable. For many children, seeing too much stimulates more excitement and curiosity than it satisfies. For some, the level of constant excitement connected with regular observations of nudity may not only lead to symptoms of retreat in the form of behavior but also, more generally, away from a spirit of curiosity. Such a loss is associated with overstimulation, discomfort, and unease. So listen to your children's comments and pay attention to behavior that demonstrates their interests about bodies.

Helping them find words to discuss their questions will encourage their continued research in a healthy way.

The same calm and ease that you convey when talking about bodies can be played out in the ways you deal with privacy. We do not need to register shame or harsh prohibitive stances as we ask our children to wait outside the bathroom. And while your nudity around the house may represent genuine ease with the human body that you hope your young children will share, they may instead experience a burden that you would never knowingly wish on them. When you are mindful of the balance they need to strike between excitement, curiosity, and pleasure and respect for your privacy, they will also feel encouraged to continue to seek you out as a trusted resource in their research efforts about this fascinating topic.

STICKS AND STONES: UNDERSTANDING AGGRESSION

We adults need to continue to think from the perspective of children when we consider the ways they may be affected by exposure to the aggression of others. Remember, we play a central role in helping our kids distinguish between imagined and real dangers. Demonstrating the limits between angry feelings and destructive action is crucial in helping children feel safe and secure.

When parents argue briefly and infrequently within the broader context of a close and loving relationship, their child will learn that when you love people, getting angry does not destroy them or lead to their disappearance. When, after a spat, parents return to the spirit of cooperation that characterizes their relationship, the child learns that disagreements can be resolved with words, that arguments end, and that problems can be solved. When your child expresses concern about the inevitable sights and sounds of your occasional arguments, explain that when people are very close and love each other they can, at times, also have disagreements and get angry with each other. Being angry doesn't mean that Mom and Dad stop loving each other. Because they love each other, they'll work out their disagreements. It is crucial to give children an opportunity to give voice to their concerns and fears. They may ask, "Are you getting divorced? Do you still love each other? Will you stay mad?"

While it is helpful to listen carefully and respond to our children's questions, it is not helpful to share the details of our arguments. Yes, they're curious and might even feel excluded, but in the end they'll be better off if they are not burdened by information that may invite them to take sides. In fact, children feel most reassured when you not only remind them that it's okay to have angry feelings in loving relationships but also demonstrate the strength of parental intimacy by reiterating that there are aspects of the adult partnership that are private.

The fact that children have something important to learn from their parents' occasional fights does not mean that children are free from fear when they hear Mom and Dad yell at each other. Toddlers and young children are actively engaged in testing the extent to which their own anger brings on dangerous consequences. They are equally unclear about whether anger between parents will produce similar outcomes. It is part of our jobs as parents to try to *limit,* not eliminate, our children's exposure to our marital struggles. Ensuring our own privacy helps us protect them from being overwhelmed by concerns about the general stability of family life.

If you find that all too frequently you can't turn down the intensity of angry and negative feelings and don't even notice where and in front of whom your fights happen, it's time to step back and ask some important questions. What is going on in your life and in your partner's life? What are the perceived points of irritation and the underlying experiences of hurt, frustration, and disappointment that you're playing out? What patterns of interaction are repeating and beginning to feel like automatic responses? Can you and your partner help each other turn down the volume of animosity and redirect arguments to focus on the source of problems and possible solutions? Can you consider the impact of frequent arguments on children and to recognize when arguments need to be interrupted, postponed, and relocated for their sake?

When you are unable to address these questions or find answers that move you forward in your relationship, you need help. It is time to consult a professional who is trained to assist individuals and couples in assessing the nature of their problems and charting an appropriate course of action.

MASTERS AND COMMANDERS

Visit a day-care center or play group of kids this age, and what do you see? Children playing at being mommies and daddies, teachers, truck drivers, store clerks, and other familiar grown-up roles. As they recognize that they are small and cannot enjoy the privileges and pleasures of grown-ups, children soften the blow by suspending disbelief and playing at imagining what cannot be in real life. By turning to fantasy and play, children turn from a passive role in which they might fall prey to dangers and disappointments to an active one in which they can feel as though they are masters of their own fate.

At play, children have greater access to wishes that don't have to be compromised too quickly by reality. In addition to helping to decrease frustration, the 3-to-6-year-old child's capacity for symbolic representation, imaginative thought, and play opens the door to broader, more elaborate forms of taking charge of fear. In a world where the child is author, director, and actor, play yields pleasure, reduces anxiety, and compensates for the inadequacy felt by comparisons with adults.

Watch and listen unobtrusively while your 3-to-6-year-old children are playing. Unless you are invited to join in, just observe. Don't ask questions. Resist all temptations to jump in or edit the storyline or action that emerges in your kids' play. If children don't feel intruded upon or don't bolt from the scene, you will see them move fluidly through a range of themes that are determined solely by the urgency of what is uppermost in their minds, whether it is exciting, pleasurable, or a source of fear.

The wonderful thing about young children's play is that it provides a parallel world completely under their control. Wishes come true and mastery is complete. Imaginative play allows kids to juggle the inconsistencies they perceive between fantasies and reality. Different themes, each of which is central to the world of the 3-to-6-year-old, can be played out at different times. At one moment, aggressive competition with a rival may be uppermost as the child assumes the role of the strongest, most attractive, and competent member of the family. That same role may simultaneously give expression to the child's exhibitionistic wish to be admired and the wish to protect and care for the object of his or her desire.

Play may easily and seamlessly shift from themes of power and strength to scenarios involving the production and feeding of babies. Repeated crashing of toy cars may at one moment express the child's concerns about aggression and bodily intactness and, at the next, the excitement of destructive power as a wonderful antidote to the fear of being small and helpless. With additional features and elaboration, the same scenario may play out the child's fantasies about sexual intercourse as violent and potentially dangerous. Similarly, play that expresses curiosity about activities behind closed dollhouse doors or in closets and bedrooms gives vent to sexual excitement and to disappointment at being excluded from parental activities. Interest in comparing physical attributes between sexes, and between small boys and men or small girls and women, all find expression and directorial control in the 3-to-6-year-old's play.

JOEY'S STORY: PLAYING FOR HEALTH

Joey was 4 when he took part in three interviews as part of a study about young children and their play. We invited parents and children from a local nursery school to participate and told them very simply that we wanted to learn about how they play. The analysts who conducted the interviews knew nothing about the backgrounds of the children; they were instructed after an initial introduction to invite the child to play, follow the child's lead, participate in the play as much as the child wished—and to observe. Other clinicians involved in the study interviewed parents about their children's developmental history and current functioning at home and asked nursery school teachers about social interactions and behavior in their classrooms.

Children and parents were told that the play meetings would be videotaped from behind a one-way mirror. Some children were especially curious to see how this setup worked; others, like Joey, simply wanted to play. On his first visit with Dr. C, he was told that his mother could stay in the playroom for as long as he wanted. After only a few minutes of exploring the dollhouse, toy figures, cars, building blocks, animal puppets, and drawing materials, Joey told his mother, "You can go now," and began to play.

Joey was a wonderful player. He used his new friend Dr. C more as an observer and narrator than as a full-fledged playmate. During his three sessions, Joey arranged props and set the scenes for elaborate and imaginative story lines that involved a mother, father, baby, brother and sister, and a "he-man" superhero. Powerful car and truck crashes were central to his play, as was the question of who would have the strength and power to protect or rescue the multiple victims from further injury. Joey alternated between the role of a small baby who required a great deal of care and who, if unattended, would be run over by one of the crashing cars, and the role of the invincible superhero who saves the day.

Joey introduced each segment of his play with the simple statement, "Let's pretend that . . ." He described each of the people, vehicles, and injuries in terms of "big and little," and at every point of his narration he connected the notions of size and strength to safety. When he wasn't bashing and crashing cars, tenderly feeding the baby doll, or completing his superhero rescue missions, Joey's talks with

Dr. C revolved around themes of size, capacity, and vulnerability. After one sequence in which there was an enormous pileup of cars on a bridge, Joey took a sudden break from making crashing sound effects. Looking quite somber, he told Dr. C, "You know, I was in a big accident with my mommy. Yes, the accident happened because my father was away. My mommy and I were very afraid. We screamed, but we weren't hurt. The cuts were only teeny-tiny."

However teeny-tiny the cuts, the impact of that accident was very big and had made Joey feel very small. As if to protest this feeling, Joey immediately told Dr. C about his new shoes that make him run "very fast." He turned from this interchange about "real" things to a play sequence about the baby, who first is struck by a car and killed and then, coming alive again, assumes the strengths and deep voice of a magical superhero, "so strong, it can bash houses and cars and break them!"

Next, Joey went back to his detailed care of the baby, feeding her "a trillion pounds of tuna fish so she would grow very strong." He was gentle with the baby and cautious about feeding her hot food because she might get hurt. He quickly interjected that, in real life, he likes very hot food but he *never* gets hurt.

At this point Dr. C asked Joey if he had any babies in his house. "Yes," he replied passionately. "I have one baby at home. My mother and I have one baby. Her name is Colette; she's just three months old!"

Joey returned to play involving care of a baby and suddenly introduced a mommy and daddy into the scene. "I know!" he said. "This puppet could be the mommy and this one could be the daddy." With great excitement he added, "Let's pretend they kiss!" He brought their faces together for the kiss and they both fell down.

Pointing, he told Dr. C, "Look at the bloods! She has bloods and even the father has bloods!"

By the time Dr. C could ask what should happen to help them, the imaginary ambulance was on its way. Joey supplied both the horsepower and the wailing siren. Then Joey introduced a brother and sister figure. They too kissed, fell down, and shed "bloods," requiring a trip to the hospital. But in this version the ambulance ran them both over. They are briefly killed until the baby, now equipped with super strength and a deep voice, announces, "I can help them!"

Before Joey said goodbye to Dr. C, the themes of danger, strength, and competence had been resolved. Lining the family figures up, Joey compared their sizes and announced, "The mother is a bit bigger than the father and the sister is just like the mommy and the brother is just like the daddy, and if the baby eats enough tuna fish, she'll get to be big and strong too!"

Facts that Dr. C could not possibly have known made observing the child's play instructive, both as to what was on Joey's mind and as a window into the ways children's minds work in general. Discussions with Joey's parents and his teachers helped place his play in the context of real life. First, there really had been a minor accident, and Joey's father had been away when it occurred. It was only a fender bender, and his mother had suffered a very small cut that an EMT treated at the scene. In the period immediately after the accident, Joey insisted that one of his parents sit with him as he went to sleep. He told them he was afraid, but he couldn't tell them why. They complied with his wishes, and after a week Joey was able to return to his usual easy bedtime routine.

It was only later that Joey's parents wondered about a connection between his nighttime worries and the accident. In the following weeks, they noticed a great deal of play involving crashing toy cars. They would have made nothing of it except that Joey also went over the details of the events with them repeatedly and always with great excitement. Joey's mom was surprised that the incident had had such an impact. After all, the damage to the car and themselves was so slight.

The accident had happened. But in contrast to Joey's account, he had no baby sister. Nor were there indications of any marital problems or of any opportunities for Joey to see dangerous consequences of kissing or for exposure to sexual activities between the parents. Joey's television watching was limited to PBS and almost always occurred in the presence of one of his parents. He had had no difficulties with eating, toileting, or relating and only the recent brief problem with sleeping. His parents and teachers viewed Joey as an exceptionally bright, sociable, even-tempered, and playful boy who was well liked by all the other children in the program.

Any suggestion that Joey's play reflected true and *nothing but true* versions of real events misses the beauty of his capacity to use imagination and play as a means of working on themes that were uppermost in his mind: his body and safety; comparisons of power, size, and capacity; relationships; babies; aggression; adult roles; and sexual curiosity. Joey's play and general functioning, like that of many other children, serves as a window into the internal and external challenges to the resources available to 3-to-6-year old children as they struggle to ensure their own sense of safety and security and growing adaptation to the world around them. Like so many other children engaged in similar play themes, the fact that Joey was not suffering any lasting symptoms and was functioning well at home and school was an important sign of his success in negotiating worrisome real-life events and age-appropriate concerns. Joey was able to use play to work out his concerns and manage his own emotional growth.

MANEUVERS OF THE MIND

As in earlier phases of development, from ages 3 to 6 a child's areas of achievement are also the greatest sources of vulnerability and fear. An investment in the pleasures of the body—both genital and general—heightens the risk that children experience about their prized possession. The notion that injury or impairment can hurt the body is of real concern for children in this phase of development. What we love most is the most painful to imagine losing. The threat of injury or impairment is powerful at this point because the body's growth provides very real opportunities for children to feel mastery of themselves and the world. That mastery is a basis for both pride and increased autonomy.

The oedipal conflicts we discussed earlier also add to a child's sense of danger as he or she feels both love and hate for the same-sex parent, seen as a competitor. For all of us, the superego, or conscience, is an onboard source of praise and self-love as well as the voice of denunciation and rebuke. But at this stage in children's lives, the punitive aspects of the superego are particularly strong; the line between good and bad is clearly drawn. Moral nuance is not the hallmark of this age group. To have wishes and feelings that run counter to internalized rules and values feels dangerous. Being "bad" means being pummeled by shame and guilt. Ultimately, the young child equates "bad" thoughts and feelings with being unworthy of love. This is the bad news. The good news is that the conflict between love and hate helps create opportunities for resolution.

Many of us can easily recall the cartoons we grew up with that featured a character struggling with whether or not to give in to an urge that could lead to a whole lot of pleasure and a whole lot of grief. In cartoons, this character was shown with a devil on one shoulder and an angel on the other, each whispering in an ear to give instruction. The cartoon was a vivid portrayal of the internal struggle between opposing wishes that becomes increasingly familiar during cartoon-watching days and well beyond.

During the 3-to-6-year-old phase, a child develops a much more sophisticated version of the infant's capacity for what psychologists call "signal anxiety." The idea of signal anxiety refers to the unpleasant taste of dread that serves as an early-warning system associated with impulses that feel dangerous and chaotic. This signal gives children the opportunity to avoid the full thrust of potentially dangerous thoughts, feelings, and actions by disguising them and finding ways to express them while flying under the radar of our own conscious awareness. However, signal anxiety may also lead to the development of symptoms.

An economic principle drives the multiple forms our imaginary fears take. The power of hostile and aggressive impulses or of longings for exclusive affectionate relationships do not simply disappear because they are offensive to the developing conscience of the young child or because the consequences of acting them out would be more disastrous than pleasurable. When they receive an anxious signal, young children unconsciously and automatically seek to disown the worst or most conflicted of their wishes. *They* are not the ones with the destructive feelings toward parents who insist on a bedtime that is so much earlier than their own. It's the ferocious monster under the bed that is really so angry! And the monster's intended victim is not the parents but the little boy or girl who so desperately needs their protection.

This may be a scary way to avoid angry feelings toward the parents you love, but there is secondary gain if the fear that you transferred to the monster also requires that your parents pay attention to you exactly at the point when their attention was directed elsewhere. This side benefit is particularly important when their attention was focused on each other—the major source of your envy and rage in the first place.

There is a range of other maneuvers of the mind that become available to help children in this phase of development to evade ownership of urges, wishes, and feelings that arouse their fears of internal dangers: shame, guilt, loss of love, bodily damage, and loss of control. These include moving away from their own developmental capabilities as a way of avoiding some of the longings and conflicts that accompany them. This set of *regressive* symptoms may include reversals in achievements in the area of toileting and self-care or be reflected in a return to thumb sucking or clinging behaviors with parents.

Alternatively, children may display the intensity of their neediness *and* of their opposition to their wishes by engaging parents in struggles about almost anything. The separation difficulties, nightmares, frequent battling with parents, and other symptoms that are so common in this period serve the child's attempts to withdraw from or displace the conflicts aroused by his or her powerful wishes for exclusive love, competition, and destructive power. Phobias—irrational fears of places and things such as school, dogs, spiders, and germs—also help to locate unwanted impulses outside the child. By shifting feelings of being trapped and helpless brought on by the intensity of their own aggression, phobic children relocate the source of danger to something outside themselves. While they come with a high price, phobias do provide children with the opportunity to take over some sense of control. Now they can *avoid* dangerous feelings of hatred and fantasies of hurting someone they love by avoiding the thing they're phobic about—and avoid being overwhelmed by the guilt, shame, and anxiety that accompanies those feelings.

Organized and regular group experiences offer a wider context in which to work through the conflicts and tasks of this phase of development. Engagement in a real world that is broader and goes beyond the intensity of family relationships can be an escape from the dangerous internal conflicts of the 3-to-6-year-old phase. School programs and group activities help children forge relationships with peers and with authoritative adults other than their parents, and this promotes their psychological independence. With more opportunities for role assignment, turn taking, and shared invention, play with other children broadens the range of fantasies and activities available for trying on new skills.

In addition, relationships that our children have with other kids and adults outside the family capitalize on and promote skills that allow them to feel increasingly in charge of their worlds and capable of quieting some of the internal sources of conflict that cause anxiety and fear. By age 6, children are better able to tolerate frustration, rely on their increased intellectual and physical capacities, and feel confident in their ability to function, with pleasure, in the absence of their parents. Moving into the world beyond the family affords the child a wider range of stimulation and opportunities for using new skills, such as reading, writing, and problem solving in the classroom setting. These also contribute to an overarching sense of achievement, mastery, and competence that will carry a child into the next developmental phase with confidence.

RESOLUTION AND
RELATIVE SAFETY

While not always free of anxiety, our children's experiments in thought and pretend play promote integration of evolving views of themselves and others. The conflict between loving and hating can now lead to further consolidation and integration of their images of "good" and "bad" parents into representations of us as whole, autonomous people who have relationships beyond our roles with them. In muting the intensity of longings of this oedipal phase, our children by age 6 now strive to live up to the ideal of being like their parents—rivals or not—and to identify with our rules and values. These achievements of internalization and the consolidation of the conscience, or superego, allow the child to pull back from overt rivalry with the same-sex parent. Instead, children can now feel that they haven't lost out in the struggles but have in fact taken on our roles as parents internally.

This process of joining what you can't beat, feeling allied with our ideals, expectations, and restraints, serves as a reparative alternative to the anxiety, frustration, and hurt that accompanied the earlier competition. Intense feelings of wounded pride and anxiety can now serve as signal feelings, or affects, that can alert the child to how he or she is feeling in response to specific thoughts and actions (in the past, present, and future). This capacity leads to the child's ability to observe himself or herself and to establish theories of how his or her mind works independent of us.

While our approval and praise as well as the admiration of other adults and peers will remain important throughout life, the introduction in this phase of children's ability to refer to internal theories about themselves—locating sources of pleasure, memories, ideals, positive and negative consequences of thoughts and actions—allows our children to give up a singular reliance on external sources of reward for the regulation of their self-esteem. Taking greater independent control of their inner lives helps our children to feel safer, more confident, and more secure—in themselves and in their negotiation of the essential and unavoidable tasks, challenges, and fears they will need to confront.

■

CHAPTER SIX

A GIANT LEAP INTO
THE WORLD OF SCHOOL
(AGES 7 TO 12)

Scott's parents lived in a wonderful, rambling old Victorian residence. The neighbors called it the Addams Family house. The whole family loved it, but every single time 8-year-old Scott's mother asked him to get something from the unfinished part of its basement, it ended in a fight. She asked, he did his best—and then the yelling began.

Here's how it would go: Scott's mom would ask him to bring up the toolbox. Scott would go, but once he got downstairs and stood on the threshold of the dark space on the other side of the door, he froze.

To avoid being sent downstairs, Scott would retreat to a part of the house where he would claim he couldn't hear his mom's requests. When she called, he wouldn't answer. Her reminders would intensify with repetition and reach a crescendo. Finally, another of Scott's brothers and sisters, or one of his parents, would fetch the needed item and Scott would be in the doghouse again.

Scott hated every detail of this scenario. But what he hated most, what made him feel like such a baby, was the fact that the dark dank storage room with its low unfinished ceiling, rough cement floor, and cold stone walls was scary enough to stop him. He didn't know why.

There was no logic to his hazy ideas about someone or something "getting him" if he went in there alone. The old part of the basement was actually a cool place to hang out in with friends and siblings, but not when he was on his own.

Scott's parents eventually noticed a pattern to their youngest son's behavior. Finally, after several months, when she asked him to fetch some paper towels, Scott's mother decided to investigate. He headed downstairs. After a few minutes, when he hadn't reappeared, she went after him.

There he stood, just outside the door to the small dark space. Scott didn't startle when he realized that his mother was standing quietly behind him. But he felt a terrible mix of shame and guilt, as if he had been caught defying the most sacred family rule. But his mom didn't yell at him. What she saw was a frightened boy who didn't want to feel little anymore. She asked gently what he thought the trouble was, but he could only shrug.

Scott's mom knew he didn't want to look at her, so she turned to the side and said, casually "It's amazing what our imaginations can come up with sometimes, isn't it? I mean, everyone has stories about the places in their homes they won't go to, and we know why they won't tell anybody else about it. Everybody's got a place at some time in their life that our imaginations fill with all sorts of things. But Scott, do you know why people really have such a hard time getting themselves into those places, those rooms where they don't want to go?"

Scott glanced briefly at his mom and shook his head.

"Because they forget they can turn on the lights. They can check out the room before they go in, and they can find out whether the stuff of their imagination is really in there."

After a few moments, Scott's mom added, "Just this once, let's you and I turn on the light and have a look together. Let's see what we see and what we don't." And so they did.

Scott and his mom didn't find any real dangers lurking in the basement that day, but it would take a lot more practice and tentative play with the light switch before Scott could master his fear. His mom recognized that he was well on his way when, several months later, Scott, one of his older brothers, and some friends turned the basement into a haunted house and charged other neighborhood kids fifty cents to experience the exciting side of temporarily being afraid. Now, instead of feeling frightened of what he couldn't see, Scott was the stage manager—able, like a younger child at play, to manipulate and control the images of his imagination. As he moved from the passive feeling of being frozen with fear to the active role of inducing terror in others, his fear was leavened with the excitement that relief from tension can bring.

LEAPING TOWARD MASTERY

During the period between ages 6 and 11, children make tremendous advances in intellectual capacities and physical and social skills. They also encounter greatly increased opportunities to help them move into the broader world beyond family life. School-age children develop new abilities to appreciate the relationship between cause and effect and engage in more complex problem solving. Their increased awareness of other people's perspectives enriches and deepens their capacity to learn and to develop friendships with peers. In addition, their increased physical strength, dexterity, and coordination offer greater control and command of their bodies.

This phase offers a widening array of settings for experimentation: in the classroom, on playing fields, in music and art classes, and in the homes of other children. School-age children can test their abilities and discover that they are capable of mastering a larger slice of the world than "when they were little." Friendship begins to serve as an alternative to the exclusive, much closer, and more dependent connection to parents of younger children. School-age kids find new partners with whom they explore the world outside the family.

Similarly, earlier intense interests and curiosity about sexuality, the origins of babies, the intimate life of parents, and the mysteries of anatomical differences between boys and girls can now fuel and be shaped by new learning challenges at school and in extracurricular activities. The feelings of competition and rivalry that were so central to the previous phase of development are now enthusiastically expressed in games and in relationships with peers. There's a broader audience that still includes parents but now goes well beyond them. Children are able to demonstrate their prowess and attractiveness in a broader range of activities, including intellectual tasks and mastery of athletic and creative pursuits.

In addition, the demands and rewards associated with a relatively stable conscience, or superego, are now regularly exercised in the school-age child's interests and activities, although exceptions such as cheating at games or being mean to peers and family members do come up. But in this phase kids usually insist on following the "rules of the game"— including the golden rule of treating others as you would like them to treat you— and they operate from a very definite sense of right and wrong.

At this stage, children still feel internal conflicts about longing for closeness with their parents versus competing with them. But they deal with this by burying the intensity and turning away from the more obvious forms of expression of their younger years. They repress, disguise, and divert these forbidden earlier wishes through an increasingly sophisticated array of adaptive defenses that includes intellectualization, humor, identification, and sublimation. They see order as the primary way to control feelings and wishes that are, in developmental time, not so distant. What may look like obsessive interest in collecting action figures, coins, or cards, and in the details of how things work and in the properties of physical phenomena, is only possible because school-age children are developing more sophisticated cognitive processes. These same processes help them order a personal world in which they master and contain their conflicted feelings and impulses.

Curiosity about sexuality does not go completely underground at this stage, but preoccupation with sex, especially thoughts about their parents' intimate life, diminishes. It's hard enough to tolerate the fact that your parents had to have sexual intercourse to create you; the possibility that sexual contact went on *after* you were born is a thought to avoid! When kids aren't being grossed out by incidental exposure to adult intimacy and romance—either in the affection they see between parents or in situations on TV—school-age children's curiosity about sexuality emerges in jokes and private discussions between friends or in fleeting innuendos about the "romances" of boys and girls who show signs of liking each other. Even for those older school-age kids who are eager to identify with adolescents, short-lived experiments of "going steady" or "dating" is usually defined by a statement or rumor that is followed by a burst of discussion among same-sex peers and as little contact between the opposite-sex "couple" as possible. The clever school-age daughter of a friend of mine calls this *virtual dating*.

At the beginning of the school-age stage, this distance is there for a reason. One of the greatest threats to the safety and security of these children is the intrusion of explicit sexual behavior by others, and such exposure to adult sexual behavior is most dangerous if it involves the sexual exploitation of children.

MARTINA'S TERROR

An adult friend of mine, whom I will call Martina, was unfortunately confronted with such explicit sexual behavior when she was a child. She was walking home from school when a man called to her from his car, asking for directions. When she approached the car, she saw that he had exposed himself and was masturbating.

"For several moments, I just stood there paralyzed, transfixed," she recalls. Finally something inside told her to run, and run she did.

But she did not tell her parents. She remembers being so frightened that her thoughts and feelings were "all jumbled up." She also remembers feeling ashamed and guilty. Even though she was not clear about what she had actually seen, she could not push away the experience of being transfixed. "I was not only scared; I was also riveted by a mixture of confusion and curiosity. That's what my shame was about. To tell my parents about what had happened would somehow reveal my fascination or interest, and that made me feel bad. Even though I was terrified and confused, I couldn't disconnect from what I was seeing. I was trapped, and it took a long time to fully escape." Remember the livewire metaphor? Martina knew she was holding on to something dangerous, yet she couldn't let go.

One way of thinking about the intensity of my friend's experience is to consider the shock and immobilization that can happen when something breaches the barrier that is usually maintained between unconscious fantasies and conscious thought. In this case, themes of anatomical differences and adult sexuality that may have been in the background were now thrust into the forefront of Martina's life. The experience was scary enough to cause her to lose control over her thoughts, but there was an additional threat. Not only was she overstimulated, the man's behavior was a radical departure from what she'd come to expect from adults as sources of order and safety.

This grown-up man's behavior was perverse because he exposed his body to a little girl and because he had no self-restraint. He was out of control. Martina's experience was especially disturbing, because it happened just at the time in her development when children are seeking to move from a more obvious and preoccupying excitement about adult sexuality to a more controlled, ordered curiosity. Martina's shame left her alone with her terror. And while assuming some sense of responsibility for what had occurred may have been an attempt to fight her feelings of helplessness, it also left her with the burden of assumed guilt.

Martina was lucky to have parents who noticed her withdrawal and learned what had happened. They were able to comfort her and reassure her that most adults are reliable and would not threaten a young girl. Even so, the experience remains vivid for her today.

OURSELVES AND OTHERS

Think back to when you were between the ages of 6 and 11. What comes to mind? For many of us, it's the memory of a first "best friend." We may also remember competing with others over that friend. We were acutely sensitive to our own feelings of affection and admiration for those kids we thought were the smartest, prettiest, funniest, kindest, or coolest. It was exquisitely painful when they did not reciprocate those feelings. Our intense feelings about best friends sometimes came with nagging uncertainty about these important connections. "Will Alma always be my best friend? What if she likes Annie better than me?"

We may have watched like hawks as other kids made advances on our best friends or directed their attention to someone new. If you've never experienced being ditched or left out as kids made plans that excluded you, consider yourself lucky, your memory is wonderfully selective. Who wants to remember the worst torments of exclusion? School-age kids can be extremely loyal and demonstrative toward best friends—and they also can be extremely cruel to potential rivals.

These dramas are the school-age versions of some of our greatest shared vulnerabilities and fears: losing the love of others and losing the love of ourselves. Similarly, kids' fears about how they do or don't fit in and about how well their bodies and minds do or don't work make this a period rife with fears about bodily damage and control. As a result, differences between their bodies and minds and those of others can feel like dangerous threats that have to be isolated and defeated.

MARCY'S CLASS

Marcy was 10. She had just moved and was having a terrible time in her new fifth-grade class. Marcy had Tourette's syndrome. When it was at its most troublesome, she was plagued by involuntary tics that would spasmodically contort her face and force a series of grunts and snorts that never failed to grab the attention of the class. If that wasn't bad enough, Marcy suffered from multiple fears. In addition to germ phobias that contributed to her isolation from activities that might involve any physical contact with her new classmates, she also became terror-stricken when she heard sirens. There were many days when Marcy would become so agitated she had to leave the classroom and go to the nurse's office until the sirens stopped. Other days, her tearful panic could only be relieved by going home.

On top of all this, Marcy also had to contend with her classmates' fear of her. Some kids simply turned away, protecting themselves from the discomfort aroused by the sight of another 10-year-old's out-of-control body. Other kids tormented her. It was as if Marcy's difficulties in mind and body did not belong to her alone. In their mistreatment of her, her tormentors expressed their hatred of Marcy's symptoms as if they in fact belonged to each of them. The group's fear and loathing of the vulnerability and bodily damage that Marcy represented overrode any compassion they might have felt individually. Identifying with Marcy was way too frightening. The other kids seemed desperate to exorcise their concerns about the integrity and safety of their own bodies and minds and excluded her whenever they could.

Marcy's parents were very concerned about their daughter. Her tics and obsessive-compulsive symptoms and fears had grown worse since their move. They were working closely with a new clinical team to adjust medication and provide psychotherapeutic support, and were fortunate to have good allies within the school as well. They met regularly with Marcy's teacher, the school nurse, and the school social worker. In addition to providing her with an in-school haven when her symptoms were at their worst, this group of dedicated school personnel was also determined to find a way to help Marcy within her new classroom—and to help her classmates too.

At first, Marcy was mortified that there was going to be a class discussion about her and her condition. However, she was equally miserable about what had been happening and increasingly felt so embarrassed that she pleaded to stay home from school.

Marcy and her parents struck a deal: She would attend school long enough to give a new medication some time to take effect and to see if discussion with the class about her condition improved her situation. If there was no change in her classroom experience, Marcy, her parents, and school personnel would talk about an alternative classroom assignment.

Marcy chose not to participate in the first classroom discussion of her Tourette's. Her teacher began by the discussion by describing what she had observed in the class's interactions with Marcy. She said she was concerned about everyone involved. She explained her worries about Marcy's burdens and told the children that none of them could possibly feel proud of their behavior; they were behaving in ways that none of them would ever want to experience themselves. She suggested that often when people don't understand something that is different about someone else, it makes them nervous and fearful.

"So," the teacher continued, "it's time to talk so that the unkind behavior can stop." Did anyone have any questions about what they were seeing in Marcy? Slowly, the questions came. Why does she act so scared? Why does she make those weird sounds?

The teacher spoke in broad terms about Tourette's syndrome and obsessive-compulsive disorder, describing them as illnesses that are not contagious and that can be controlled with medication and help. She explained that sometimes the symptoms would be obvious and at other times not apparent at all. Having received Marcy's permission to talk about her, the teacher told the class that Marcy had had much easier periods in the past but that now her symptoms were particularly bad. She explained that Marcy was hoping a new medication would help and added that feeling supported and less worried about how others were treating her would also improve her condition.

Finally, the teacher added, "If you wish, you may want to talk with me privately about any further questions or concerns you have about Marcy and about your own reactions. What cannot and will not happen anymore is teasing or excluding. You will all feel much better about yourselves when you treat Marcy the way you would hope to be treated if you were struggling with something that created as much difficulty for you as it does for Marcy."

Marcy's new medication and psychotherapeutic support, as well as the natural waxing and waning of her symptoms, went a long way toward improving her life in school. The teacher thought that her first discussion, and later discussions involving Marcy herself, afforded relief to the entire class. They had been able to address their questions and concerns, and the adults had helped put the brakes on the unfair and cruel behaviors that expressed the fears Marcy's condition aroused.

LONGINGS AND RESISTANCE

Marcy and her classmates demonstrated an extreme version of the ways that internal experiences of danger and fear can be shared and played out within a group of peers. Relationships present multiple opportunities and challenges for children in this phase of development. They long for acceptance and closeness while fighting off concerns about personal imperfections and any hint of needs that may run counter to their strivings for increased competence, autonomy, and independence. Over the course of this period, kids are repeatedly faced with a real dilemma: to establish close friendships without experiencing, let alone revealing to anyone else, wishes that may too closely approximate the dependence and neediness they once felt toward their parents. Kids will often prefer to withdraw temporarily or fight with their friends rather than risk displaying what may feel like desperate and therefore "babyish" longings for attention, admiration, and affection.

When all goes well, school-age kids are able to establish close relationships. While they may not last forever, close friendships between 10-to-11-year-olds, for example, are increasingly based on shared

interests and activities as well as the kind of trust that tolerates disagreements and discussions about who likes whom, theories and ideas
about sex, and (less frequently) personal and family troubles.

As school-age kids' needs and interests move beyond preschool concerns, they also shift direction beyond the family. As they get older, kids
welcome autonomy in areas of daily living such as as hygiene, dressing,
and looking after their stuff. This greater independence is also seen at
mealtimes. Breakfast, lunch, and dinner are no longer the battlegrounds
on which struggles about dependence and independence are fought.
School-age kids are too busy telling you about what they did with their
friends to remain eternally vigilant about whether or not they are in
charge of what they eat!

School-age kids' advancing abilities mean they now engage in
joint projects and interests for hours on end, enjoying the give-and-
take of planning and developing shared ideas and activities. Advances
in intellectual, social, and emotional development enrich their interaction with peers, who in addition to being viewed as partners and best
friends are also members of a group with whom the child feels affili-
ated. School-age kids become increasingly interested in organized
activities—academic, athletic, and social—that help bolster and support
a strengthening sense of self.

While friends may be the most important bridge between and beyond the world of the family, adults other than parents also serve important roles in helping school-age children broaden the scope of their
relationships. Teachers, instructors in after-school programs, coaches,
and adolescent babysitters can assume larger-than-life roles in children's
lives. These older figures join parents as additional sources of praise, admiration, confirmation, and control—and your child can try out more
mature behavior with them as well.

Ever been in the midst of one of the those difficult periods with
your school-ager and gotten a phone call from the parent of one of your
child's friends who cannot stop raving about what a super-considerate
and kind kid you've got? It can be cold comfort when, at the most troubling times in your relationships with your kids, teachers and every

other adult who is involved with them has nothing but positive reports about every aspect of their behavior. No, you're not going crazy. The discrepancies between your experiences and theirs are transient, a sure sign that your child is reaching away from you and out to other grown-ups for the needed approval and support that does not any longer come solely from you.

One of the many advantages of this broadening scope of relationships is that the values we hope our children will adopt are reinforced by other adults and introduced as the moral currency of the larger community, nation, and world. As models for identification, teachers and other important adults play a critical role as sources of limits, reality testing, and reassurance. This role is crucial when there is good reason for children to be gripped by apprehension and fear.

THE CANDY MAN

When adult behavior is violent, dangerous, and bizarre, children fear more than the possibility of becoming victims of attack and bodily damage. If it is possible for adults to lose control of *their* most dangerous impulses, how can children continue to lean on grown-ups as guarantors of their own self-control? The world becomes an especially uncertain and frightening place for school-age kids when the adults who are supposed to be ensuring order act in disordered and disturbing ways.

In the same way that Martina was alone with her fear and discomfort in response to perverse adult sexual behavior, I remember the quiet terror I experienced at age 10 when wrapped candies that had been laced with rat poison were found on the playground at my elementary school. It was late October, and there was a great deal of talk in the neighborhood about the incident. All of us kids were on the lookout for pieces of candy lying on the ground wherever we went. We also discussed elaborate versions of our assumptions about the creepy man who must be crazy in his hatred for kids.

The playground was no longer a safe, welcoming place where any of us would happily go after school on our own. There was a certain degree of excitement and a fair amount of ribbing that went on about who was afraid: "You wimp! Why won't you go to the playground?" Of course none of us would own up to our fear directly. We preferred to describe with great bravado the kinds of karate chops or improvised weapons we would use to fend off the horrific and increasingly elaborate attacks we imagined from the crazy candy man.

Our parents did not seem as concerned. They advised us not to pick up candy off the ground and to let them know if we found any. The police were looking into it, and we didn't need to worry.

I never really knew what my friends felt behind their humor and bravado. I knew what *I* was thinking and feeling, and I certainly wasn't telling *them*. In fact, I had a hard time telling anyone. I was plenty scared. For a few weeks, walking home from school included eyeing every unfamiliar car with suspicion. At night, I imagined that the cars I heard slowly driving down my street might belong to the crazy man who was looking for kids to kidnap or hurt. My senses were alert to sights and sounds that could signal trouble. I went to sleep with difficulty as vigilance yielded to the inevitable power of fatigue.

Finally, on a day when there had been a lot of rumors about poison candy sightings and increasingly disturbing portraits of the mad child-hater, I could no longer stand lying in bed with my fear. I went downstairs, looking and feeling not so different than if I had just awakened from a nightmare. But I was fully conscious, fully aware of what was worrying me, and equally determined not to just come out and say, "I'm afraid of the poison-candy guy."

My parents were preoccupied by some house project and were nonchalant and dismissive when I claimed a loud noise had disturbed my sleep. "Probably just heard a branch being blown up against the house in the wind," my dad said. I did everything I could to delay going back to bed. I was both desperate and ashamed for them to know about my fear. Finally, I cracked a feeble joke about how the noise I heard was probably the poison-candy guy making deliveries.

My parents stopped their work. "I guess a lot of your friends have been talking about this candy business, huh?" my dad asked. "What have they been saying?"

"Not a whole lot," I lied. I recognized the concerned look on my parents' faces that said, Something must really be bothering him; we need to pay close attention, and it made me uncomfortable. Yes, I know that's what I wanted, but I didn't want to admit it!

"Are there any questions or ideas you have about the poison candy that was found that you'd like to talk about?" my mother asked. I laughed, kind of. It was one of those short bursts, a mixture of self-conscious anxiety and relief. I went for broke.

"Well, maybe he would try to grab a kid." And then finally I blurted out what was really on my mind. "And then maybe he would really kill him!"

There, I had said it. I had shown that I was scared, even if I was a great big 10-year-old. I looked to them and waited. I think my father spoke next. "That's a terrible thing for *anybody* to have to worry about!"

I was relieved. If "anybody" would be scared by that thought, I was off the hook. I was not a complete and utter wimp. But there was another crucial ingredient to my dawning relief. Somehow the chasm between my terror and their nonchalance about the child-hating poisoner had confirmed how babyish it was for me to feel so frightened and small. But now they got it. Their reactions and their knowledge were different from mine.

My parents explained that they had a number of reasons not to be as concerned as I was about any harm coming to us neighborhood kids. They pointed out that there had been no further discoveries of candy with poison and that there were ways of safeguarding against any possible dangers. "If you see candy on the ground, don't pick it up, tell us or the parents of the friend you are playing with," they told me. They added that, while it was scary to think about, a person who might do something as disturbed as putting poison in candy was not likely to do anything more directly threatening to children. "And," my parents reminded me, "when we know where you are, who you are playing with, and that there are other adults around when we aren't, you will be safe."

My mom and dad asked if I had any other questions or concerns. I'm not sure that I had really heard all that they said, and I wasn't interested in thinking anymore about horrifying fantasies by then. Over the next days, sleeping became easier; I was no longer as hypervigilant or preoccupied with the candy-poisoning bogeyman. When my parents asked how I had slept, we all knew it was face-saving code for, "Are you still afraid?"

That was not the last time I would ever be frightened, but the fear generated by a real threat shrank when I was able to find comfort without humiliation. I was no longer alone.

Experiences that threaten or undermine their most basic sense of competence and independence are most frightening to our school-age children. In this phase of development, fears center around a group of issues: bodily safety, how well and clearly their minds work, and how competent they are at developing close ties with other kids and adults outside of the family. They also fear losing us and the people to whom they are closest. For some children, these fears can become enormous burdens that reopen the door to earlier longings to be protected by us. The difference is that now they don't automatically reach out to us when they are afraid. We are the same parents who swooped to the rescue, whether our toddlers were frightened by sudden loud noises or by monsters under the bed, but we are also the parents from whom our big school-age kids are trying so desperately to feel separate. When their fears inspire the need for us to protect and reassure them, they also may feel humiliated. They revisit oedipal conflicts that involve competition with us at the same time that they are reminded of our relative strength and power.

A host of symptoms may accompany the reemergence of earlier conflicts. These symptoms allow children to express, disown, and disguise the associated longings, wishes, and fears. Not unlike the symptoms they experienced when they were younger, school-age children may develop transient difficulties that include:

- Sleep problems

- More frequent nightmares

- Worries about burglars

- Greater preoccupation with bodily illness or injury

- Increased concerns about parental health and death

- Overt sadness and brief periods of decreased social, academic, or extracurricular interests

- Regression to earlier ways of relating to parents

Increased struggles over food, self-care, schoolwork, and household responsibilities may accompany our school-age children's attempts to defend against and give expression to anxiety and fear.

When our kids engage in these types of struggles, they're trying to tell us something about the nature of their conflicts. We are in the unenviable position of being given a clear invitation once again to pay close attention in areas that have most recently not required our involvement. When we accept the invitation, our kids are, at some unconscious level, lying in wait. We respond and they pounce. The more defiant and provocative they are, the more likely we are to really get into the struggle. Some fights are unavoidable when our kids are so successful in shoving their demands in our faces. And when the fights happen, our kids have achieved an important goal. At these moments, our kids have gotten part of what they need: us, up close and attentive. In this fighting mode they're also able plausibly to deny the possibility that our attention is what they're really after.

The middle of a fight is probably not the best moment to ask your school-age child what he or she is upset or frightened about. When they have calmed down, you might decide to ask more general questions about what's been happening in school, with friends, or at home. It is often particularly hard for school-age kids to open up directly about their worries and fears. Sometimes, listening to complaints about other kids or to your child's observations of other kids may be the easiest, most congenial way for them to talk about their own concerns. "Your friend Jenny seems pretty upset about that little girl who was kidnapped in Colorado," you might say. That opening can give your child a chance to talk about how scared Jenny has been, and to ask questions about the likelihood of such an event happening to a young girl in your neighborhood.

The tendency of school-age children to be critical of themselves and sensitive to the criticism of others may make any discussion a very short one. It might go this way: "Your dad and I have noticed that you haven't seemed very happy the past few days. Anything about stuff at school or home you might want to talk about?" Your child might yell, sounding wounded and irritated, "I didn't do anything! Nothing's bothering me!"

Many times our efforts to help our kids verbalize their problems are not successful. Our children may not yet have the words to describe what they feel. Other times, their need to struggle privately and master the fear outweighs the need for feeling psychologically held by our sympathy and concern.

Respecting your kids' rights and needs for that privacy does not mean you shouldn't offer to listen. In fact, finding the right balance between offering support, backing off, and keeping the door open for later discussion is a challenge. There is no sure-fire strategy for getting school-age kids to open up, but you have to try and try again.

It is also crucial to remember that providing opportunities to talk and listen about worries and fears is not a substitute for the limits you need to set on problematic, infantile, and obnoxious behavior. When, as kids, my brother, sister, or I were at our most unpleasant with our parents, with each other, or with friends, we would hear what became a familiar invocation: "You can either talk about what's bugging you or you can keep it to yourself and work on it. But you don't have any right to take it out on anybody else."

There were, of course, lots of times when those words were maddeningly irritating. They did, however, often cut to the chase. Our most difficult behavior was not always justified by the circumstances. As mine did, parents can and should reestablish the responsibilities that became casualties of kids' regressive retreats from anxiety-producing conflicts and fears. When you don't encourage the good behavior that your kids are capable of, you may unintentionally support their regressive solutions rather than their efforts to achieve mastery and move on.

When children are unable to master fears aroused by the upsetting experiences and normal challenges of this developmental phase, the symptoms listed earlier not only will continue but also will come to overshadow their social and academic success. Kids who are over their heads in internal struggles have ever-more frequent struggles with others or, alternatively, withdraw and appear unhappy and unable to sustain interests, attention, or pleasure in favorite activities. They may become phobic, avoiding places and things they fear, or they may take scary risks, or their schoolwork may suffer.

These worrying behaviors are signs that a child's coping strategies are inadequate to deal with his or her fears. At these times, parents need to move beyond frustration and anxiety to action. First, explore the details of your children's experience of school with their teachers and other relevant school personnel. Don't just ask about their academic performance. Ask how engaged they are in classroom discussions, how interested they seem in their studies. Ask what teachers notice about how your child gets along with others. Have they noticed any changes in behavior and mood?

Parents also must be open to consulting pediatricians, primary health care providers, and mental health-care professionals who specialize in the evaluation and treatment of children. Often, if your pediatrician is someone who has shown interest in your child's emotional development as well as physical health, an initial consultation with such a health-care provider can be a useful place to start getting professional help. After your discussions, the pediatrician or primary health-care provider may want to meet with your child to get a firsthand impression before referring your family to a mental health professional. Parents can also get recommendations for child mental health specialists from friends and from local branches of professional organizations that represent child psychologists, psychiatrists, and clinical social workers.

A consultation is just that, a discussion with a specialist in children's development and mental health about your questions and concerns. If an evaluation is recommended, interviews with parents will include taking a full history of your child's development, current functioning, areas of concern, and descriptions of family life. Direct interviews with the child will involve a mixture of talk about interests and life in general as well as about problems. Playing and talking with your child will give the clinician an opportunity to combine his or her observations with the information that you have provided.

At times, it can be useful to have psychological testing done in order to clarify the nature of your child's difficulties, especially when learning difficulties, problems of attention, and thinking are areas of concern. When an evaluation has been completed, the clinician will discuss the findings and recommendations. Parents often need time to digest and question what they have heard, to be active partners in whatever plan is to be implemented. At times, an evaluation may determine that no further outside help is indicated and that, with additional support from you, your child will be able to negotiate his or her troubles. Talking with the clinician can help parents explore new ways of helping children both at home and school. Some children may require psychotherapy with or without the use of medication. For others, identifying learning and attentional problems, for example, can lead to discussions with school personnel about alterations in the educational program that will maximize your child's capacities and improve his or her feelings of self-worth.

Any of the recommendations you hear should reflect a comprehensive way of thinking about your child. Often, any one type of treatment on its own will not be as helpful as considering a range of approaches. The opportunity to share the burden of your confusion and concerns about your child is the first step to finding the best ways to help free your child from theirs. No one should live in fear.

■

CHAPTER SEVEN

TUMULTUOUS TIMES: ADOLESCENCE (AGES 12 TO 20)

As we walked home from a ninth-grade school dance, my friend Sebastian and I spoke excitedly about the girls we did and didn't talk to. We went into great detail about who we thought were the hottest of our classmates and joked about how much each of them really wanted us instead of the guys they had hung out with all evening. We swapped tales about the bold sexual overtures we had made to any number of girls who inspired us and then, after listening with excitement, amazement, and hope, repeatedly broke into laughter as we shot down each other's fantasies with the usual repertoire of put-downs: "Yeah, right: in your dreams. . . . Not if you were the last guy on earth."

But our own imagined exploits were nothing in comparison to the rumors floating around that night about a small group of kids who were not part of our circle of friends. The story was that the previous weekend three couples had gone to the home of one of the kids whose parents were out of town. They had all gotten drunk and, according to all reports, had "done it."

Sebastian and I weren't close enough to any of the participants to hear the details or confirm the truth of the report. We disguised our awe and envy of these lucky sophisticates with as many deflating and denigrating comments about them as we could possibly muster. This one was a loser delinquent, that one was incredibly stupid, another was a slut, and they were all destined to become alcoholics.

After walking and talking a few minutes more, Sebastian and I grew quiet. Privately, I imagined what might have happened that night, in explicit detail, casting myself as one of the participants. Sebastian mulled over something entirely different. "Um . . . what actually happens . . . you know, when—um, you know—how is it exactly that babies are made?"

I was amazed. This was a guy whose house seemed to have few rules. A collection of his dad's *Playboy* magazines lay right out in the open, and if you were really lucky, you might catch one of his much older sisters dashing semi-clad to her room from the shower. How could he *not* know how babies are made? At first I thought Sebastian wanted to dive into the scientific details of fertilization and cell division. I was wrong. He was not the font of sexual knowledge I had assumed he was. I told him what I knew, dumbfounded by what he did not.

It wasn't until years later in my clinical work with adolescents that I began to appreciate that when fear and anxiety get connected to even the most basic facts, our minds go to great lengths to create a huge gap between what we have been taught and what we actually know. For Sebastian and many other adolescents, bluster and bravado may cover up a multitude of anxieties that are huge enough to interfere with combining facts about other people with images and actions about themselves as sexual beings.

It goes without saying that adolescence is a time of tumult. It is a developmental period chock-full of challenges, for parents as well as for kids. Whether we remember the details of our own teenage years or not, as parents we often anticipate our children's adolescent years with trepidation. Expecting rebellion as a central facet of this phase is only one cause for anticipatory concern. As we think ahead to the shape of our children's adult lives, we alternate between seeing adolescence as a gateway to the future or a precipice over which they will plunge.

Even without worrying about adulthood ahead, the immediate challenges of this period are plenty enough. When parents recognize that their kids' push for independence may involve the risks of experimentation with sex, drugs, alcohol, and driving, the stakes feel very high indeed. It can be difficult to remember much about our own teenage years, not only because there are so many details to remember but also because the tumultuous excitement, pleasure, and pain that accompanied them are feelings that we often wish to forget. Anticipating horrors, we may forget that our children's earlier phases of development sounded the same themes that will emerge in adolescence. But there will be new challenges for them and for us as their bodies mature. It turns out that the supermarket floors of toddlerhood are not the only things that angry fists can pound on as our children now protest their independence. Experimentation with peers will replace doll play and questions to parents as adolescents seek information about sexuality and intimacy. But take heart. Challenges and crises are nothing new in the course of development. Adolescence, like earlier phases, provides yet another chance to address the latest versions of challenges and concerns—and another opportunity to rework earlier ones.

GROWING UP AND AWAY

There are few parental challenges as tricky as helping our adolescent children deal with their fears. If you think back to your teenage years, you will know why. Remember all the stuff that was going on with your body? Teens constantly monitor where they stand in comparison to their friends. At the same time they're trying to cope with the intensity of their sexual feelings and with their relationships with peers and family members. In fact, profound changes in all areas—biological, psychological, and social—make adolescence one of the most dramatic phases in the course of human development.

While there is renewed interest in sexuality in the period between ages 10 and 12, by the early phase of adolescence (12 to 14 years) the endocrinological and biological processes of puberty intensify. Concerns about bodily changes and sexual sensations move front and center. A complicated mixture of pleasure and trepidation go hand in hand with the advent of the primary and secondary sexual characteristics— the growth spurt, voice changes, advent of menstruation, nocturnal emissions, breast development, and body hair—associated with maturity. Exciting sexual sensations and the powerful need for masturbation as a source of relief are accompanied by increased awareness of sexually arousing fantasies. These fantasies may cause conflict and give rise to as much anxiety as excitement for young teenagers.

Teenagers may experience the physical changes that announce their entry into manhood and womanhood as happening too quickly or not quickly enough. One thing is certain: There may never be a time in development when we are as keenly aware of how little control we have over our own bodies. This absence of control is most powerfully demonstrated as young teenagers experience the beginning of menstruation, first nocturnal emissions, or the sexual attraction to others that leads to increased heart rate, spontaneous blushing, and erections. There is also never a time when physical changes feel as public and potentially revealing of our most private longings and fantasies.

IMAGES OF THE BODY

To say that preoccupation with the body is a prominent feature of adolescence is a dramatic understatement. If we have forgotten how much time we spent making sure we were attractive to others, our adolescent children and the time they spend in front of the mirror remind us. The body is the stage for enacting pride or shame and a sense of being beautiful and desirable or deficient and unlovable.

Teenagers' images of their bodies swing dramatically from one extreme to another. At times they treat their bodies with great respect, as objects to be loved and caressed; at other times they seem to regard their physical selves almost as enemies worthy of attack. Normal young adolescent girls devote considerable attention to making themselves attractive to others, taking endless showers and experimenting with hair gel and makeup. Yet the girl who is experiencing turmoil may try to punish and mutilate her body. It is alarming for parents and adolescents alike as the balance between love and hatred for the body, between self-care and self-destruction, shift rapidly, repeatedly, and precipitously.

Psychologically, the young adolescent may experience the rapid changes in his or her body passively, unconsciously recalling earlier humiliating experiences. Adolescents may feel that they are being forced to learn to accept what is not under their control. Some young teenagers deal with this loss of control by trying to deny what is happening. They hold on to the interests, appearance, and interaction style of the preceding phase of development. Other adolescents feel comfortable with their developing bodies and secure with what nature has in store, an attitude consistent with previous pleasurable experiences. Most commonly, adolescents react to changes in the body and mind with a mixture of anxiety and exhilaration. Many kids will push toward mastery and try to take active control by improving upon nature. They adorn their bodies with clothing and makeup and try to change their shape through weight lifting, exercise, and dieting. Distorting the body's appearance with tattoos, unusual clothes, multiple piercings, and wild, sculpted, or no hair is another way to reverse psychologically a physiological process over which they have no control. Through such stage management, adolescents assert a dramatically independent level of care and responsibility for their bodies, all the while reorganizing their ideas about who they "really" are.

The body and the way it looks may preoccupy teenagers who are vulnerable and struggling with concerns about whether their intellectual abilities are good enough and their sexual fantasies healthy and acceptable, and whether they are independent or likable enough. These young people sometimes feel that life is unbearable because various parts of their bodies aren't right: their noses are too long, their penises are too small, their breasts are too flat or too big, or they are too tall or too short. When their bodies become the primary focus of conflict with parents or the battlegrounds on which personal struggles about autonomy are fought, adolescents may be at risk for developing such serious disorders as anorexia, bulimia, self-mutilation, and obesity.

The struggles—both internal and between teenagers and parents— over who owns and controls the body is a reprise of battles from much earlier phases of development. Remember the toddler's battle cry of "I can do it myself!" Your adolescent's disgust at your rules about what's okay to wear to school is a similar declaration of independence. Struggles involving rapid shifts between the longing to remain close and the need for privacy and autonomy may also be played out in a reprise of old and familiar issues. As parents, we may experience a "been there, done that" feeling as our adolescents revisit their early childhood themes with a vengeance. Once again, you're fighting over bodily care and messy rooms.

IT'S PERFECTLY NORMAL

Years ago, I was asked to give a talk to a ninth-grade health class about development and sexuality. After briefly describing some of the matura- tional changes of puberty and introducing some of the challenges that physical changes create psychologically, I suggested that everyone write one question on a piece of paper. I passed around a box to collect these anonymous queries. The questions were wonderfully direct. "Can you get AIDS from blow jobs?" "Can you get pregnant if you have sex dur- ing your period?" But I was surprised by a number of others that clearly indicated that the old myths about sex remain alive and well. "What causes blindness?" or "What causes mental retardation?" were two of the best. What was once called self-abuse was clearly on these students' minds.

I didn't immediately answer the questions, nor did I respond with the stereotypic psychoanalyst's "What do *you* think?" These questions were not just about the practice of masturbation but also about the associated fears and guilt about loss of control, bodily damage, and preoccupation with sexual feelings and fantasies.

I did give factual answers to the questions about the causes of blindness and mental retardation. Earlier I had talked about masturbation as an important part of adolescence. With the chairs in the room scraping from the kids' embarrassed shufflings, I tried to keep these comments brief. I explained that masturbation is a real achievement that represents physical maturation and the capacity for sexual arousal and satisfaction. I added that it's not an easy topic to talk about because the activity itself is private, as are the ideas and fantasies that go along with it. It is an amazing thing that even if we know that everybody does it, it's nevertheless embarrassing.

"So," I said, "people always wonder if it's okay to do and if any serious bad stuff can happen. The answer is yes to the first and no to the second."

Next I went through the shortlist of some common fears: even though it seems hard for people to get sex off of their minds, it doesn't mean they're going crazy; when people have incredibly strong urges it doesn't mean they're permanently losing control of their bodies; the changes that happen to bodies and brains when people get sexually excited in no way means they are damaged.

Maybe the fact that I never spoke in the second person—as in "when *you* get an erection"—helped ease their embarrassment. Maybe it was my matter-of-fact tone. Or maybe it was actually something I said. But after these comments, everyone in the room seemed to breathe easier and laugh with collective relief; they weren't going to go blind or lose their minds after all!

What I didn't go into that day was the fact that one of the other achievements that accompanies adolescent masturbation is the hugely important capacity to imagine and sustain fantasies that can serve as trial runs for the real thing. In fact, when development of adolescent sexuality goes well, masturbation and its accompanying fantasies provide opportunities for rehearsing sexual behavior, expressing and receiving affection, and trying on the different active and passive roles in consensual lovemaking.

Few adolescents are completely without guilt about masturbation. They may experience guilt because they feel their sexual fantasies run counter to their values, or because they feel wild and out of control, or because they believe that when they engage in sex they are somehow appropriating their parents' adult rights.

Adolescents who are too anxious about sexuality or too frightened by aspects of their masturbatory fantasies may try to abstain completely; others may do it compulsively, increasing their guilt and thus the tension that leads to more masturbation. But for most kids, there is ample time over the course of adolescence to use masturbation not only for relief of sexual tension but as a way of gaining control over and getting comfortable with sexual desires. The normal adolescent fears of losing one's mind or of losing control of impulses or losing the love of others diminish over time as teenagers learn that they have the capacity to turn on, delay, and discharge their sexual feelings, more or less at will.

PULLING AND PUSHING

By mid-adolescence (14 to 16 years) the physical changes of maturation begin to level off; girls get monthly periods, boys are able to ejaculate, and both boys and girls are well into attaining their secondary sexual characteristics. These bodily changes fuel the strength of urges that lay dormant in primary-school years. The distant longings of infancy and toddlerhood and the more organized interests and fantasies of the 4-to-6-year-olds are now updated and supercharged. But maturing teenagers are confronted with a crucial difference. They now have bodies capable of carrying out both sexual and aggressive wishes and urges.

As if being revisited by earlier conflicted sexual and aggressive feelings were not momentous enough, young teenagers also need to contend with an intensification of longings for closeness. These may be far too reminiscent for comfort of their dependency on their parents in earlier years. Young adolescents' needs to repudiate these longings are especially pronounced at a time when they feel most uncertain about their maturing bodies and least convinced about their abilities to function on their own. They are in a powerful and inevitable bind. The provocative behavior and battling stance that is so often a central feature of the adolescent relationship with parents can reflect a renewal of the 3-to-6-year-old's rejection of longings for closeness. While struggles about family rules are one aspect of a young teenager's attempt to achieve emotional distance, testing limits may actually serve as implicit invitation for parents to remain involved and to take charge.

"DADDY, HOW *COULD* YOU?"

Around midnight, Diana was sitting by herself on the front steps of her house after the tenth-grade dance. She was thinking about how it had gone. She had danced a lot, including with Andrew, a boy she really liked. Did he like her? she was wondering. It seemed like he might.

This reverie was interrupted when a car zoomed down Diana's quiet street and screeched to a stop in front of her house. Two older boys—juniors, who had recently gotten their driver's licenses—tumbled out of the car and walked over. Diana was both thrilled and horrified. Older boys! She knew one of them pretty well, because he lived in her neighborhood.

"Hi, Tim," she said.

"What's up?" he said, and sat down on the steps beside her. His friend sat on the other side. Diana thought they might have been drinking, but she wasn't sure. Her discomfort warred with the thrill of having older boys show up and seem interested in her.

Everything was okay for a while—until Tim slid closer, put both hands on her arms, and tried to kiss her. Diana was scared. This was getting out of control.

Just as she tried to wriggle away, the porch light blazed on, the door swung open, and Diana's dad looked out.

"Get out of here, *now!*" he shouted at the boys.

They fled.

You might think Diana would have been relieved at her dad's appearance, which rescued her from a difficult situation. Oh, no.

"Daddy, how *could* you?" she said. "I have never been so embarrassed in my *life.*" And she stormed past him up the stairs to her room.

The explicit outrage that greets parental involvement or intervention closes the loop of the adolescent dilemma. With it, they save face. On both internal and external fronts, acknowledging their uncertainty and their continued need for support is an enormous source of danger. Such needs are a humiliating and frightening confirmation of their incompetence and vulnerability.

While our teenagers are attacking us, it can be hard for parents to remember that our kids' battle-ready stances are fraught with these very basic questions and concerns about themselves. Despite their posturing, they feel real regret and remorse about hurting people they still deeply love. At times, it's easier for our adolescents to forget these blowups than it is for us to leave them behind. And quick hugs or pats on the back and breezy discussions about our plans for the evening may be as close as we get to reparation after the battle. Remember, this is their way of reaching out without consciously having to deal with their complicated and deep feelings about their relationship with us.

Parent-adolescent relationships provide a crucial testing ground and launching pad for our children as they integrate new versions of their newly independent selves. They approach us with their worries, then strike out at us for intruding or not understanding them. "I *knew* I shouldn't have told you! I *knew* you wouldn't understand. You *never* understand." This flip-flopping, while crazy-making for us, serves an important function as our adolescents try to gauge how far they have moved toward feeling secure about their own abilities to deal with their impulses and needs.

As they pull us close, only to push us away again, adolescents provoke battles about issues that are of relatively little consequence. In the process of negotiating a curfew or battling about household chores, homework, loud music, or personal appearance, adolescents learn to modulate their rage at their parents and find out whether we can survive their aggression. They become experts at finding our faults. As they trash us, they are attempting to feel less inadequate themselves. They're also trying to justify and support their efforts to separate from us, their previously all-knowing, all-loving protectors. Ironically, when we break down under the pressure of unremitting teenage aggression, our kids do not feel victorious. They feel afraid, even panicked. In their distress, they feel compelled to attack again, demanding we be strong, or they withdraw in an angry, depressive huff.

A TRIP TO THE BEACH

Kate was 16 when she and four other kids were invited for a long weekend at the beach house of her close friend, Lili. She was incredibly excited as she told her parents about the plan. She explained who was going and their travel arrangements. Then, as if warmly, patiently indulging her mom and dad, Kate assured her parents that there was plenty of room in the house and that the two boys who were going would have their own room. "And Lili's parents will be there the whole time!"

Kate conveyed all this information with a delight she was certain her parents would share. She was wrong. Her mother and father looked at each other and then gravely told her that she couldn't go. Kate was incredulous and then enraged. "Why not?" was not her first or loudest salvo. But Kate's mother and father were concerned about boys and girls staying in the same house and about whether there would be supervision adequate to restrain the full force of adolescent libido.

In their daughter's eyes, they were not only being ridiculous but deeply offensive. She protested that these guys were her *friends*. "What? Do you think there is going to be some kind of drug-crazed orgy? Great. I'm glad you know me so well," she muttered sarcastically. Then she yelled, "I don't care what you say, I'm going!"

Kate's parents actually knew and liked all the kids involved, including the boys. They also knew Lili's parents to be responsible and good people. Why the swift and negative response? As they reflected later, they realized that even though Kate had not given them any reason to question her judgment, it seemed that the weekend would unleash a world of abandon and trouble. There had been other times when Kate's parents knew they had been on the stricter side of parenting, but they eventually recognized that their refusal to even consider this request came from concerns that had more to do with them than with Kate.

When Kate returned to do more battle, she was well equipped, and her parents were better able to listen. She had secured an agreement, via Lili, that Lili's parents would be willing to talk with her parents about the arrangements. They listened as Kate calmly challenged their concerns. She told them she was hurt and angry about their disregard for who she was and what they knew about her. "It's like you're accusing me of being someone I'm not, and that's not fair," she said.

Talking to Lili's parents helped. But it was Kate's parents' appreciation of their own strong reactions that allowed them to hear their daughter's reasoned protest this time, and that won Kate the second round.

In relenting, Kate's parents had stepped back and reconsidered the gut responses that had driven their original refusal. They had been afraid that this weekend would be one that involved out-of-control behavior: drinking, drugs, and sex. They were afraid that the mix of boys, girls, and beach would undermine the usual degree of authority and control exercised over their daughter. What was the worst they thought might happen? Out of control meant that anything could happen: their daughter could get drunk and drown in the ocean or become the victim of a drunk-driving accident.

Kate's parents heard how frightened they sounded to each other. They had been teenagers and had done what in retrospect were crazy, dangerous, and irresponsible things with drugs, alcohol, and sex at places other than, but including, the beach!

When you're not in control, it feels like anything can happen. And as our kids are growing up there will many times when the shift from us to them of control and responsibility for actions is scary as hell. It is not easy to remember that when their development is going well, losing control of our adolescents does not mean they lose control of themselves. In fact, our worries about our adolescents' potentially dangerous behavior may have as much to do with our own impulses—both past and present—than it does with theirs. Our battles with our teenagers may be the result of harshly enforced rules that serve as barriers to our own enactment of forbidden wishes. Alternatively, some parents vicariously enjoy the exploits of adolescents, exorcising their rage toward their own overly strict parents by relinquishing the braking function that is a central part of their parental role.

At times, parents may be too understanding of behavior that is at best inappropriate and at worst dangerous. Unless clear limits and expectations are well established and implemented—through both rewards and restrictions—some parents may implicitly encourage their children's promiscuity, drinking, and fast driving while explicitly condemning them once they have gotten into trouble. In these circumstances, when there is such a huge opening for acting on exciting impulses, adolescents may be caught in a dangerous and vicious circle of both enacting and seeking limits on their impulses.

Peers, both same-sex and opposite-sex, offer a shift from intense attachments to parents. Forays into the world of boyfriends and girlfriends and dating are opportunities for experimenting with sexual and emotional intimacy as well as gauging and consolidating a sense of masculinity or femininity. Unlike the fantasies and imaginative play of the younger child, first intimate relationships provide real chances for adolescents to try on and prepare for adult roles. Dating and sexual experimentation also can serve as an active attempt to ward off longings for parents that are not only experienced as infantile but may also feel contaminated by frightening sexual desires. For many adolescents, early dating and sexual experimentation is a reassuring badge of conquest and competence, and these qualities are amplified when exploits are told to and appreciated by an audience of admiring friends.

FROM PARENTS TO PEERS

The complexities of family relationships provide additional incentives for teenagers to engage with the world beyond the home. A broad range of social, intellectual, artistic, athletic, musical, and political opportunities offers kids a refuge from what may feel like the claustrophobic pull of family life, as well as affording settings in which they can operate and express themselves as independent players, truly separate from parental direction and control. They need to be separate and different from us. The child of agnostic parents may become passionately involved in religious observation, the child of Democrats may support Republicans, and so on. An adolescent needs to establish his or her own uniqueness, searching for individual values and not just adhering to ones that originated with the parents.

In their resistance to compromise, our adolescents fear losing the high ground. They are acutely aware of the slippery slope that could lead to losing their hard-won individuality. At this age, they become abstractly conceptual, wondering about how their minds work, about their values, authenticity, and politics. They often feel a responsibility—and have the ability—to make a difference, to reduce the suffering and wrongs of the world. Or they may explain to themselves that, the world being the way it is, there is nothing they can do but simply get by, get even, go along, drop out, have a good time. Whether they choose involvement or disengagement, adolescents are likely to think about their choices philosophically, in categories of value and history, rather than only or consciously in relation to what their parents believe and what they have been taught.

Stronger ties with peers and the accompanying set of social expectations, combined with the push for mastering the world beyond parents and family, lead the adolescent toward real independent functioning. With a great deal of experimentation and no small amount of anxiety and trepidation, adolescents gradually recognize that achieving independence requires relying on their own abilities rather than on their parents.

FITTING IN—OR NOT

It's no surprise that adolescents work on refining who they are in their intense relationship with peers. It's not easy to put ourselves in our children's shoes. We may find it embarrassing and painful to remember how important it was to be acknowledged by a hoped-for friend or group of peers as we arrived at school. That encounter—or lack of it—could set the emotional tone for the rest of the day. When we are able to recall that we too were desperate to belong and be embraced by our peers, we will appreciate our children's excitement, despair, and drama. Negotiating relationships with friends can be all-consuming and feels more important than any longings they may have to be close to us.

If you see that your kids are not able to engage in friendships, you have reason for concern. Something may be getting in the way of a normal shift toward their peers, perhaps especially intense fears about letting go their central relationship with you. Alternatively, when the dramas of social life entirely preoccupy your kids, you should be equally concerned. If adolescents are unable to invest and succeed in school and extracurricular activities and interests, acceptance by the group may be the only way that they feel successful. In this situation, their dependency longings toward you may be so intense and unacceptable that they are displaced onto relationships with peers. Often, their friends will be unable to tolerate this level of neediness. Hungry adolescents in this predicament feel bereft on all fronts—frustrated and hurt by rejection, while loathing themselves for how much they need others in order to feel good about themselves.

RISKY BUSINESS

Kids who are frightened about rejection by peers, about loneliness, dependency, and losing control of impulses, or about their own perceived inadequacies, may turn to other antidotes to allay their fears. These include sexual excitement, self-medicating drug and alcohol use, and other risk-taking, death-defying behaviors. But their strenuous efforts provide them with no opportunities to master the challenges of growing up. The challenges to being independent, successful in academics or other skills and talents, and in intimate relationships with others, become more frightening with each confrontation with failure. In turn, fear requires antidotes, and a destructive cycle begins.

Adolescent sensitivity about fitting in may, in these no-win situations, turn into fear and attendant humiliation that has to be countered at all costs. The adolescent who combines neediness with anger may find he or she fits in with other kids whose antisocial activities—drug and alcohol abuse, delinquency, rejection of school—provide a needed but dangerous way of belonging and feeling whole. Similarly, moving into promiscuous sexual behavior may be a sad as well as dangerous way for kids to fight fears of their own insatiable needs without turning to parents. Some young adolescent girls and boys may engage in oral sex—rarely reciprocal in 13-to-16-year-olds—seeing it as both a badge of maturity and proof of desirability. Yet they experience only the most fleeting glimpse of what they really crave: to be admired, cared for, and assured of their own worth.

When we see our kids engaged in these and other self-destructive behaviors, getting angry and establishing restrictions alone will not solve their real problems of inadequacy and low self-esteem. Doing battle with kids when they are troubled may in fact help them avoid what their behaviors are attempting to disguise: their fear of independence and the terror that there is not enough in them that is worthy of love.

GAY AND LESBIAN TEENAGERS

The issue of fitting in may be an especially sensitive issue for adolescents who are homosexual. All adolescents have complicated feelings about establishing sexual identity, often centered on whether they are masculine or feminine enough. That this uncertainty becomes connected in so many teenagers' minds with homosexuality leads to jokes and comments about who and what is "gay," even among those who might have gay and lesbian family members and friends. These comments and attitudes reflect the adolescents' attempts to distance themselves from their own homoerotic wishes, fantasies, and even experimental same-sex contacts, about which they may feel fear, guilt, and shame.

While many, perhaps most, adolescents experience some degree of sexual interest in individuals of the same sex and may engage in some degree of erotic physical contact, their fantasy lives and the primary focus of sexual arousal are most typically heterosexual. During the usual course of development, heterosexual orientation appears to be based on biological factors that are subsequently reinforced by social experiences in the family and peer group. A sizable number of adolescents, about 10 percent, are primarily involved in thinking about and being aroused by individuals of the same sex. For some, the direction of their attraction became clear during the earlier school years; for others, the intensity and singularity of homosexual attractions and interests become clear only during early adolescence or even later.

As with heterosexual orientation, there are probably a variety of determinants of homosexual orientation in both boys and girls; similarly, biological factors as well as family interactions are involved. A central task for both homosexual adolescents and their friends and families is to recognize that their sexual orientation is as immutable, well integrated, and authentic as heterosexuality is for their straight peers.

The developmental tasks for homosexual adolescents are complicated by both internal and external factors. A young person's realization that he or she is excited by and attracted to individuals of the same sex runs counter to what the adolescent may have expected and is different from the general experiences of his or her peer group. This feeling of being different can compound the usual feelings of estrangement and secrecy of adolescent sexual development. Moreover, the homosexual adolescent often has no peer with whom to share, in locker room or intimate chats, the emerging sense of being a sexual person.

The homosexual adolescent also often lacks socially sanctioned opportunities for sexual experimentation, for finding peer partners with whom to move away from parental ties. In their loneliness, homosexual adolescents may try to deny sexuality altogether and, like heterosexual peers who are in conflict, try to blot out sexual thoughts and feelings as if they didn't exist. Like their heterosexual peers who are painfully conflicted and troubled by erotic feelings and fantasies, they may try to lose themselves completely in the rigors of intellectual and academic pursuits or devote their bodies and minds to athletics or other activities, leaving little room for anything else.

Whether they try to hold on to a sense of belonging to the group by pretending to share heterosexual interests or engage in brief, secretive sexual encounters with same-sex partners, gay and lesbian adolescents without recognition and support from their families may live in the shadows of social and personal isolation. Without the opportunity to engage with other gay and lesbian adolescents and have someone who can listen and help to understand the additional challenges they face, homosexual adolescents may have a especially difficult time mastering independence, autonomy, and intimacy.

THE DANGERS OF DIFFERENCE

Exclusion and ridicule based on difference only compounds an adolescent's deeply personal experience of being different or outside of the mainstream. Along with providing support within our homes, we may also need to provide outside help for our children. This can include support from a mental health professional as well as helping to locate and encourage involvement in groups that are able to offer needed support and friendship from peers. While we cannot enforce or compel schools to find friends and acceptance for our children, we do have a responsibility to step in when discrimination, teasing, or overt threats are making their everyday experience a living hell.

Whether our children are gay or lesbian, belong to a religious, racial, or ethnic minority in an overwhelmingly homogeneous environment, or are struggling with obesity, physical handicaps, or chronic illness, our schools have a responsibility at least to draw the line on offensive behaviors. Often, children are unable to tell teachers about the abuse or pain they experience at the hands of tormentors. Parents often need to confront school personnel directly about their responsibility to protect *all* children in their care.

At best, schools not only establish firm limits on cruelty but also take this behavior as an indication of larger problems. Inattention to the anxiety, values, and ignorance that breed blind hatred will only perpetuate a climate of intolerance and injustice. Schools and parents also need to remember that when a particular teenager or group of teens is involved in cruelty toward others, it may be a sign that they feel insecure, inadequate, and somehow damaged themselves. Their behavior needs to be stopped if we are to protect their targets and help them put brakes on their own fears. Cruel behavior is a warning sign that should prompt questions about the general status of these teen-agers' development. When egregious behavior toward others is some-thing they are unable to stop, we need to act on our concerns and seek consultation and evaluation from mental health providers who spe-cialize in work with adolescents and their families.

SEEKING SUPPORT

Even when by outward appearances life is safe and predictable, adoles-cence can be a tumultuous time, alternately exciting and painful, full both of promise and of periods of fearfulness and despair. Adolescents' rapid physical changes are accompanied by a torrent of new challenges in the realm of defining who they are, how they relate to others, and how they operate in the broader world. As they go through this process, most adolescents experience difficult periods. These so-called develop-mental crises may be accompanied by symptoms of anxiety and depres-sion: moodiness, changes in patterns of sleeping and eating, decreased academic and social activity, increased family struggles. However, these difficult periods are typically short-lived, often ending as quickly as they began when the adolescent has resolved the immediate challenges that introduced the crisis in the first place.

There can also be additional obstacles in the way of adolescent development. The timing of puberty, for example, may mean a child becomes sexually mature before he or she is psychologically ready; delayed puberty may prevent him or her from fully entering into the experiences of the peer group. Sensitivities, conflicts, and poor resolu-tions of earlier phases of development may also present additional burdens in adolescence. Even without extra vulnerabilities, the strength of sexual drives, preoccupation with fantasies, guilt over sexuality and aggression, and troubles coping with the maturing body may at times be burdensome for all adolescent children.

The normal tumult of this period does not automatically lead to the development of psychiatric disorders. Much of their boiling energy is diverted and devoted to intellectual, artistic, physical, and social activities and issues. All these pursuits are socially acceptable and provide the adolescent with a greater sense of mastery and self-esteem. However, with the push toward autonomy and new social expectations, children who have been burdened by preexisting difficulties, such as chronic medical illness, emotional and social difficulties, or cognitive delays, may be especially vulnerable to emerging chronic problems. These psychiatric problems of adolescence may include affective disorders, particularly depression, manic depression, and thoughts of suicide; eating disorders; obsessive-compulsive disorders and ritualistic efforts to be in control; and more complete breaks with reality that can lead to delusional and paranoid ideas and general chaos of thoughts and feelings seen in schizophrenia and other psychotic disorders.

Adolescents can also demonstrate breakdowns that elude categorical diagnosis and include dramatic and life-threatening symptoms, in various combinations: self-destructiveness, brooding despair, complete social withdrawal, sexual promiscuity and perversity, addictions, immobilizing preoccupations, and seeking out and experimenting with such dangerous activities as drug and alcohol abuse, reckless driving, unprotected sex, criminal activity, and physical fights, to name a few. When you have questions and concerns about your adolescents' behavior and functioning at home and at school, don't wait to address them. If you are uncertain about the meaning of your children's behaviors or worried about symptoms that are interfering with their success and happiness, seek help from your primary health-care provider in getting a referral for a consultation with a mental health professional.

While most symptoms of normal adolescent distress do not predict serious or enduring psychiatric difficulties, there is no need for you to worry alone. When you feel your child needs more help than you can offer on your own, a mental health consultation can be the first step to helping him or her return to the path of optimal development. A consultation with a professional who specializes in adolescent mental health can also help to identify when your concerns are an overreaction to the normal ups and downs of this phase. An opportunity to talk with someone outside your family can often help you step back and gain a better understanding of the nature of your teenager's life and concerns.

TOWARD INTIMACY AND THE WORLD BEYOND HOME

By age 17, kids begin to experience real emancipation from the roles and requirements of earlier phases of development. By this time, adolescents have usually established relatively stable peer groups and friendships and engage in increasingly self-motivated academic and extracurricular activities. They're mobile and independent, traveling around the community and beyond. Some achieve at least some degree of financial independence through jobs. They have a more secure sexual identity and a more cohesive sense of self. But in addition to experiencing the joys that come with increasing independence and adult responsibilities, adolescents must battle their own longings to remain dependent on their parents and mourn the passing of their reliance on these powerful figures.

The search for a new and real intimate partnership is one of the most powerful tests of an older adolescent's struggle to break from earlier ties to parents. Young adults are aware of the difference between earlier sexual experimentation, which was about attraction, exciting pleasure, and conquest, and the more complete love of a whole person. Young women who have achieved this level of relating are no longer driven by seductive victory or by the desire to call a partner her own. Young men are no longer singularly guided by the need to prove their masculinity. The full range of longings, once the stuff of fantasy, can now be realized. Longings for physical intimacy, for exclusive attachment, to protect and be protected, to admire and be admired, are played out in the reality of late-adolescent romance.

It is not always easy for parents to appreciate the full range of challenges and vulnerabilities that their late adolescents face in the development of truly intimate relationships, because, as adults, we continue to experience them ourselves. In fact, as parents, our ability to relive the excitement of "being in love" can lead to an overidentification and overinvolvement with our kids' experience.

For the older adolescent, a climate of trust and relative freedom from internal conflict about relationships with parents is essential groundwork for more mature relationships. The depth of his or her new intimate partnerships relies on the young adult's ability to be comfortable with and mobilize components of the earlier attachments to parents, including dependency, exclusivity, jealousy, physical intimacy, empathy, and identification.

Throughout late adolescence into early adulthood and beyond, the journey of discovering and expressing ourselves is played out in shifting interests and ideals, choices about education, careers, and lifestyles. The extent to which these areas mesh with those of a chosen partner will influence the success or failure of the relationship. The amount of emotional energy available for intimate ties with others will fluctuate as older adolescents become increasingly involved in making plans for, and investing their energy in, the future. You only need to recall the intensity of relationships in the senior year of high school, especially as graduation nears, to put yourselves in the shoes of our older children.

For adolescents, the promise of real independence is coupled with the task of negotiating and accepting the disappointment of personal limitations. When your child does not get into the chosen college or is not hired for the preferred job, he or she is confronted with the reality that we are not always equipped to achieve the goals we set ourselves. Of course, it's not always a reflection on us. Social and economic factors that are out of our control can effectively sideline realistic aspirations. This is not such an easy confrontation, when your child's confidence about his or her ability to stand alone is put to the test just as life away from home begins.

The next phase of life involves leaving home and community and significant relationships behind, so it is no wonder that older adolescents often feel emotionally stretched as they place one foot out the door of everything that is familiar and the other into a world that is imagined but not yet fully known. In the last semester of high school and the following summer, these young people aren't the only ones who feel emotionally stretched. You are also anticipating the loss of daily contact with your kids and of your real and imagined control and protection of them.

It is an ambiguous time for kids and parents alike. The separation is coming, but not yet. You have an opportunity during this period to get used to what is to come and gradually relinquish control. As you rely more on their judgment and the hope that they have embraced the best parts of yours, you may actually see a decrease in the frequency of battles. You encourage your children—and they succeed—in gradually assuming more responsibility for themselves. This process is certainly not anxiety-free, but it does prepare you both for the time when they are really on their own. What follows is a greater mutual respect and a greater degree of trust. The decrease in actual dependence and the acceptance of that, though not without pain, paradoxically facilitates freer discussion about what everyone is feeling and strengthens the changing relationship.

As a staging ground for the reorganization and consolidation of earlier experience, adolescence is often described as the last chapter of childhood. However, young people go on weaving multiple strands of development together into adulthood. The ways that they experience and imagine their bodies and sexuality are crucial to how they wind up viewing themselves. Dramatic changes occur over the course of adolescence. While, early in puberty, teenagers may have experienced their bodies and the intensity of their sexual feelings as alien and out of control, by late adolescence—when all goes well—they are able to integrate a very different view. No longer alien, their bodies can now be an enormous source of the excitement, pleasure, and pride that they feel about themselves.

For adolescents, these ways of envisioning and experiencing themselves rests on achievements from earlier phases of development: good physical and cognitive functioning, ongoing support from families and other adults—particularly teachers—and good fortune in finding friends and avoiding irreparable injury and the real dangers that overwhelm and traumatize.

■

CHAPTER EIGHT

WHEN THINGS GO WRONG: TRAUMA AND OUR YOUNGEST CHILDREN

Our children's nightmares are filled with the dangers and fears that span development from infancy into adulthood. These bedrock fears—of losing our lives or the lives of those we love and upon whom we depend, of losing the love of others and the love of ourselves, of damage to our bodies and impairment of functioning, of losing control of our urges, feelings, and rational thought, and of losing the order and structure in our worlds—are also the ones that we try to keep as far away from conscious thought as we possibly can. Even if our efforts are not as successful as we would like, as we get older our capacity to feel and respond to signals of anxiety increases, helping us to watch for, prepare for, and take protective action against danger.

Growing up, unfortunately, does not free us from vulnerability to the fears of previous phases. In fact, we are most acutely and intensely affected and overwhelmed by fundamental fears from the past when they are reawakened and materialize in unexpected events in the present. We are most frightened when internal threats and real external dangers converge. With nightmares, our fear diminishes as we awaken and latch on to our immediate surroundings to counterbalance the dreaded aspects of our imaginations. A very different situation emerges when, in traumatic situations, we are unable to anticipate or avoid real dangerous events. We are clobbered by nightmares that have come true.

For children and adults alike, traumatic situations are similar to earlier times in our lives when we had no words for our worst fears and when our cognitive resources were not yet up to the task of ordering and making sense of complex experiences. Regardless of age and phase of development, psychological trauma can interfere with our established intellectual, emotional, and physiological patterns. At the most acute and intense moments, traumatized children and adults, awash in hard-to-identify feelings and chaotic thoughts, are unable to recognize or explain their experience. In these circumstances, anyone feels confused, disoriented, and terrified.

Traumatized children and adults alike may be unable to control their bodies. They may shake uncontrollably, weep, sweat, or feel nauseated and jumpy. Alternatively, and in exception to many people's expectations, traumatized individuals may look as if they aren't fazed by the horror or danger they have just experienced. In fact, their detachment and emotionally frozen look may be an indication that they are disconnecting or dissociating from their own experiences. This automatic response is one way in which their minds are able to digest the breadth of what has occurred. In truly traumatic events, the capacity to pull together strands of information and experience that are essential for making decisions and protecting ourselves are effectively knocked out of commission.

Well after the traumatic events, children and adults may involuntarily and suddenly reexperience their original loss of control. Their bodies are more vulnerable; they are more apt to be startled and experience rapid changes in heart rate and breathing. These so-called post-traumatic symptoms are especially distressing when we are unable to consciously locate what triggered them or identify the reminders that set such uncomfortable, isolated bodily sensations in motion.

While children and adults share many of the disorganizing effects of trauma, the adult capacity to adapt, figure out defensive strategies, and call on internal resources is vastly different from what is available to our children. Moreover, the self-protective mechanisms that they acquire through normal development are especially vulnerable to traumatic disruptions. A child's experience of helpless surrender to overwhelming circumstances threatens to undermine recently attained developmental capacities. In a regressive slide, traumatized children are apt to return to earlier ways of expressing their needs, fears, conflicts, and anxieties, as well as to previously reliable ways of negotiating them. As a result, young children who have been traumatized show a wide range of symptoms. These include:

- Increased clinginess and difficulties separating from parents

- Disrupted sleep, with increased nightmares, waking, and panic

- Increased worries and hypervigilance

- Avoidance of new or previously identified sources of danger (phobias about animals, noises, monsters under the bed, etc.)

- Toileting problems and physical complaints (headaches, stomachaches, or other aches and pains with no medical cause)

- Eating problems with increased fussiness, lack of interest, or insatiability

- Increased irritability and oppositional behavior with increased aggressiveness, angry outbursts, and inability to be soothed

- Emotional upset with unusual and frequent tearfulness and expressions of sadness

- Withdrawal of interest in pleasurable activities and interactions

- Dramatic changes in or inability to play; playing less creatively; repeatedly reenacting a traumatic event, such as a car crash or a fire

- Blunted emotions with no show of feelings; disconnection, as though going through the motions of regular activities

- Unusual distractibility

- Refusal to engage in previous age-appropriate behaviors (self-feeding, washing, brushing teeth, self-dressing, etc.)

- Return to more babyish speech patterns

While all children may be vulnerable to symptoms of trauma when real dangers converge with their worst fears, it is not surprising that children whose development is already fragile may be at greatest risk for continued long-term effects after sudden overwhelming events. Parents and caregivers fail children when they do not recognize that they have been overwhelmed by trauma and need help.

REAL LOSS

Three-year-old Emma was walking with her trusted babysitter on the way to her preschool program one morning. Out of the blue, Emma announced that Karen, the head teacher of the program, was dead.

The babysitter knew Karen had been out sick the previous day and the kids had been told that she would be back in a few days when she was better, so she was startled but intrigued. She asked Emma, "What does *dead* mean?"

Without skipping a beat, Emma replied earnestly, "Dead means you go away and don't come back. My daddy's dead. He's in Seattle."

In fact, Emma's father was well but divorced from her mom and living several thousand miles away. The babysitter told Emma that Karen wasn't dead; she was sick and would return just as soon as she felt better. She also reminded Emma that she had just talked to her father a couple of days ago. She knew that he wasn't dead!

When Emma's mother and teachers heard about this interchange they recognized that they needed to pay a good deal more attention to the little girl's reactions to what had been a major disruption not only in her living arrangements but also in her ideas and feelings about the most fundamental principles of relationships.

It is indeed hard to trust that the people you love the most will not disappear forever when they go away. For Emma, discussion of her ideas about death and about missing her less-available and much-loved father was only part of the equation of her adjustment to her parents' divorce. It would only be over the course of months and years of enduring, regular, and eventually more frequent contact with her father that Emma could fully appreciate and trust that *gone* was not *gone forever*.

For Emma and so many other children, coming to grips with the undesirable and dreaded aspects of real life is not a process that ends with the initial adjustment to the facts. The most significant, potentially traumatizing events may assume new meaning and significance at different stages of development.

As adults, we can be of greatest help to our children when we recognize the importance of sorting out the confusion of ideas and concepts that disturbing events introduce, comparing our child's very personal concepts to the facts of the events themselves, identifying and labeling our child's emotions and feelings, and establishing the limits of the disturbing event in terms of the time, places, and people involved. But first, we must be able to tolerate listening.

SAMMY'S GRANDMA

Sammy was just 3½ when his maternal grandmother suffered a massive heart attack and died in a bedroom just down the hall from him. She had lived with Sammy—and his mother, father, and 6-year-old sister—all his life and had always helped take care of him. When his mother went back to work when Sammy was about 2, his grandmother provided all of his child care except for the few hours he spent at a preschool program on weekday mornings. Sammy loved his grandmother and she adored him.

His parents described their son as a very sweet and gentle boy who was exceptional in his concerns about other people and tried to help both children and adults when they seemed to be having a hard time. They recalled one poignant example of his sensitivity they observed just a month or so before Grandma's death. She was sitting quietly in the living room, staring off into space, when Sammy went up to her, put his hand on her arm, and asked if she was sad.

Sammy had never met his grandfather but had heard about him from both his mother and his grandmother. They had explained that Grandpa had died before Sammy was born, and Sammy rarely if ever asked questions about him, even when he was mentioned in family conversations.

Sammy's grandmother was at first surprised and perhaps startled from her reverie, but asked why he thought she might be sad. Sammy replied, "Because you were missing your daddy."

When she understood, his grandmother said, "Oh, you mean my husband, the grandfather you didn't know?"

Sammy just nodded. His grandmother took him in her arms and hugged him for a bit longer than usual. His parents, who were on the other side of the room, weren't sure whether her tears were about how moved she was by her grandson's love and concern or a reflection of how accurate Sammy's radar was in reading her mood.

When his grandmother died, it was probably the first time Sammy had seen his parents cry. It was also one of the first times when his mother, in her grief, was unavailable to him. For a couple of weeks after Grandma died, nothing was the same. Schedules were different and lots of relatives and family friends were around the house. Sammy watched grown-ups laugh and then cry as they reminisced about his grandmother. But the biggest change was that she was gone. She had disappeared. She had "died."

Sammy was quiet in those first couple of weeks, staying close to his sister, complying more readily than usual with parental requests, and at times finding his way onto Mother's or Father's lap for longer-than-usual cuddles. It was after life had begun to settle back into its previous rhythms that Sammy began to fall apart. At this point, his parents met with me for a consultation.

Within three weeks of his grandmother's death, Sammy had become irritable, defiant, and incapable of tolerating even minimal amounts of frustration. He dissolved into tears and fell to the floor when asked to engage in any of the typical tasks of daily life: coming to dinner, getting ready for bed, using the toilet. Uncharacteristically, his thumb was now often in his mouth and he was unusually listless. Two months earlier he had not needed diapers during the day. Now he had frequent "accidents" and insisted on going back into diapers.

Sammy's parents tried to talk with him about missing his grandmother and about her death. They told him that she had been very old and that when bodies get very old they stop working. They also tried to talk about how it must have been hard seeing Mommy and Daddy upset and about how life was now back to normal. Sammy countered these wordy explanations by running out of the room or screaming at his parents, "Stop talking!"

Bedtime became a renewed battleground. After finally getting ready for bed and listening to bedtime stories, Sammy now cried when his parents left. This subsided when his parents agreed to keep a light on in his room, but later, almost every night, he appeared in their room in tears and afraid. He had similar difficulties separating from his mother at his preschool group. Teachers were able to help Sammy get involved in activities that seemed to distract him from his anxious goodbye, but they too noted a change. Sammy's play scenarios involved fights between animal and people figures that often ended with figures flying wildly in the toy corner. Then he would retreat to the teacher's lap, seemingly devastated by her reminder to be careful about rough play and the safety of other kids who might be hurt by flying toys. He was equally sensitive about perceived injuries to his body and gave up quickly on many games and physical activities that he complained he was "too little" to do.

His parents and teachers were both concerned and frustrated by Sammy's obvious retreat to the babyish behavior they had all been so pleased to see replaced by big-boy achievements. What no one seemed to recognize was that Sammy was communicating with them in the only way he knew how. His troubling behavior *was* the language that demonstrated his distress. But as they engaged in the struggles that Sammy invited, the adults could only guess at the specifics of his worries.

In our discussions, we expanded the possibilities. Central to these was the idea that the death of Sammy's grandmother had left him frightened about the fact that she could so easily disappear. His parents' explanations had missed the boat. As we tried to take Sammy's perspective, we wondered whether, in addition to being confused by his grandmother's absence and missing her, her death increased his concerns about how easily he might lose one of his parents. We also considered whether Sammy was connecting his normal aggressive feelings to the danger of being left by the people he loved. He might be worried about disappearing himself and, like his grandmother, being gone forever. If this were the case, his behavior could be understood both as an expression of his fears about loss and as a surefire way of securing intense, reassuring closeness with his parents.

By going back to more babyish ways, Sammy could continue to be age-appropriately defiant yet at the same time receive the close attention he demanded. All the while, he could avoid or ignore any awareness of or feelings about his grandmother's death. The problem with his solution was that it did not seem to be helping him to feel more in control or more secure in his connections. Instead, his behavior was robbing him of all the good feelings that had gone along with being a big boy.

The great thing about taking the time to step back and raise questions about our children's behavior is that when it is at its most baffling and frustrating, we cut ourselves enough slack to acknowledge a fact that is as basic as it is hard to acknowledge: *We don't know.* We don't know what exactly is going on inside our children's minds, and we don't know exactly how we can help them. If we try some new approach, we don't know if it's going to work. Paradoxically, when we are able to tolerate these facts, we can reach a much stronger position for figuring out what frightens our children and how we might help them feel safer.

Arriving at the point of embracing our ignorance is easier said than done. It is especially at those times when we feel most worn down and drained by our children's struggles and behavior that we are hardest on ourselves about not coming up with *the* solution to exhausting and worrying problems. With these ideas in mind and as part of our discussions, Sammy's parents were ready to hatch a plan.

Before story time, Sammy's parents asked to sit with him to have a talk. In spite of some initial squirming, Sammy was able to sit quietly between his two parents as they told him that he had seemed unhappy and worried. In a gentle but determined way, they mentioned some of the ways they knew that he wasn't feeling as happy as he used to. They were concerned that Sammy would perceive anything they might say about his troubles as critical or humiliating. So they contrasted each symptom of fear with the pleasurable big-boy feelings that accompanied his behavior before Grandma's death. They pointed out that he used to feel proud of using the toilet, but that now using the toilet seemed so hard. They reminded him that he had felt good about getting his big-kid bed and going to sleep with only the hallway light on, but that now sleeping in his room seemed scary.

Sammy listened. "Sometimes big boys have scared feelings and they don't know what to do with them. . . . Sometimes they don't even know what they are scared of," his dad said. "We want to help you feel like our happy big boy again and not have to feel scared."

They paused.

"Sammy, do you have any ideas about why you have been feeling more scared about things?" A pause and then a slow shake of his head as Sammy looked straight ahead into the middle distance.

"Would you like to hear our idea?"

They were more than willing to interpret his silent "no comment" as an open door and proceeded with what felt like the trickiest part of the conversation. They did not want to impose their preoccupation with Grandma's death onto Sammy if it wasn't relevant. Plus, it was still an upsetting topic, especially for Sammy's mom.

But she pressed on. "We think that it was hard when Grandma died because everything was so different. Mommy and Daddy were upset, and most important, one day Grandma was here with you and then she was gone. It made you sad but maybe it also made you scared that Mommy or Daddy might also go away and not come back."

At that last comment, Sammy looked up at both parents for the first time. He looked at them long and hard before he announced that he wanted to go play with his cars.

Sammy's parents had been prepared for the likelihood that he would not suddenly launch into a full-blown discussion of these complicated feelings. But before he went off to play, his parents told him that they were not old like his grandmother and they were not going to die or go away and never come back. "At night when you go to sleep, at day care when we say goodbye, or when you are doing all the big-kid things that make you feel so proud, we're still here."

Both parents told me that they thought Sammy had smiled a weak smile but acknowledged that perhaps they saw what they wanted to see as he ran off to play with his toys. They repeated their last reassuring comments at troubling moments over the next few days. Increasingly, Sammy's mood and behavior began to shift.

In addition to their private discussions with him, Sammy and his mother had a very abbreviated chat with his day-care teacher about his worries and his behavior. The teacher suggested that sometimes it helped kids to have pictures of their mommy and daddy at the program, especially when they were having such big feelings and worries about them. She pointed out it was good for Sammy and the grownups to try to find words for such big feelings and said she had also been wondering why Sammy might be feeling unhappy and how to help him feel better. Again, the intent of this discussion was to convey to Sammy that he did not need to be alone with his worries and struggles and that the grown-ups would help him in ways that were consistent with his own wishes to feel and act like a big kid.

Sammy went off to play without looking back, until the moment his mother was about to leave. She waved to him and he ran to her with lip trembling. His mom hugged him. His teacher took his hand and suggested that they go together back to the play area, but first asked him if he would like to wave to his mother from the window. He nodded as he reached up to his teacher to be held. He waved and quickly buried his head in her shoulder until she put him down to play. She stayed with him awhile and only spoke after he had built a tall building with blocks. Before she got up to attend to another child, she said simply, "What a wonderful, big building! You must be so proud!"

The changes in Sammy did not occur overnight. His parents felt that their comments about his worry about them disappearing, combined with an emphasis on reminders to the contrary and their attentiveness to the fact that he was struggling, helped contain his fear and served to jump-start his own abundant developmental resources to kick back in.

With an increased appreciation for the indirect ways in which Sammy's behaviors may have given expression to his fear, they were able to replace their own anxiety and frustration (and the accompanying guilt) about his regressed functioning with empathy and sympathy. They were no longer burdened by the imperative to find solutions and an immediate halt to his babyish demands. They were able to be patient, understanding, and genuinely affectionate along with the reminders of their hopes, expectations, and confidence in Sammy's capacity for more mature functioning. While he continued to need his parents' reassuring comments about separations, he no longer panicked at day-care drop-offs or when his parents went out for the evening.

Sammy could not tell us what was most helpful in relieving his distress. It was striking that, at the same time he was able to settle back into his preschool program and return to his bedtime and toileting routines, his spirits brightened and he was able to tolerate and engage in some discussion of his grandmother's life and death. In addition to being able to talk about his memories of her, Sammy was able to join his sister and parents in planting a special tree in their backyard that became known as Grandma's tree.

In the weeks that followed, Sammy took on the big-boy job of watering the tree. His pride in nurturing this living memory of his grandmother seemed to reflect a much broader sense of safety and pleasure that he was able to feel again about his own growth.

A SCHOOL BUS ACCIDENT

For young children in the oedipal phase, issues about competition with same-sex parents, sibling rivalry, power and size, curiosity, struggles between loving and hating, and concerns about bodily integrity provide the context in which they experience events involving real or threatened danger. In chapter 5, we met Mark whose identification with a "cuddly raccoon" set the stage for a frightening scene when it was killed. The impact can be even more complicated when your child identifies with another child who is in danger. For parents and other concerned adults, it's hard to appreciate a child's terror when he witnesses another child being injured.

When such an experience is especially up close and personal, children's reactions may be more than they and their parents can deal with on their own. When real frightening events line up too closely with the concerns, conflicts, and anxieties that are typical parts of development, a child may have great difficulty in untangling overwhelming ideas, fantasies, and feelings from the facts. There are times when, without professional help, these children feel alone and additionally burdened by a host of symptoms that develop in the wake of what amounts to a traumatic situation. Parents are also left feeling helpless as they are unable to fully understand the nature of the difficulties or discover, when they appreciate how upsetting an event has been, that their reassurance is simply not enough to relieve their child's distress.

At midday on a late spring day, a school bus carrying 5- and 6-year-olds was broadsided by a truck that had run a red light. Moments earlier the children had been picked up from their half-day kindergarten program at a school just blocks away from the accident. The bus spun in the middle of the intersection before hitting a utility pole. Even though all eight children aboard were thrown from their seats, only one child was injured. The casualty was a boy who was knocked unconscious and sustained a serious gash across his forehead.

The accident precipitated a massive police and emergency services response. The boy was taken to the hospital by ambulance, where he underwent surgery to relieve pressure created by his closed-head injury. The remaining seven children were checked out and cleared by emergency medical personnel before being taken to a middle school that was just across the street from where the accident occurred. They were greeted by administrators and school counselors and taken to the school gym, the only location that was not in use by middle-school students.

In order to help decrease the trauma that is often associated with exposure to events of violence, danger, and disaster, a partnership has developed in New Haven, Connecticut, and other communities around the country between law enforcement and mental health professionals, who respond together when children are victims and witnesses of scenes of overwhelming terror. As part of this Child Development Community Policing (CD-CP) program, a clinician is on call to the police department 24/7. This mechanism brought two colleagues and me to the scene within minutes of the bus accident.

Police officers, trained in principles of child development and trauma response, were the first to meet the children and contacted members of the CD-CP consultation service to come directly to the school. In addition to dealing with the accident scene itself, officers immediately began coordinating efforts to get the parents of each child to the school. The officers described their central aim as protecting the children from the excitement surrounding the accident—news crews, multiple police personnel, onlookers—and securing the most immediate source of comfort possible by reuniting them with their parents.

When we arrived at the school, my colleagues and I were briefed by police about the details of the accident, the injured boy, and the emotional states of the uninjured children. By the time we entered the school gym, several school personnel had already attempted to en-gage the children in a discussion about what they had seen and how they were feeling. The children had been unresponsive. Expecting us, the school personnel explained that they were concerned about the kids, who now sat quietly on the floor, clutching their knees and star-ing into the middle distance. After introducing us as people who were there to help them with their upset feelings, the school personnel moved into the background.

We soon perceived a pronounced difference between what adults thought would be uppermost in the children's minds and what we learned of their perspectives by following their leads. To bombard children with a hundred questions about what they saw, what they felt, and what they were thinking about is to perpetuate their experi-ence of being out of control. When we do not take the time to watch and listen to the ways in which children experience overwhelming events of danger, we lose the opportunity to observe the true impact on thoughts, feelings, and physical responses. Helping children find a voice for what they have experienced means finding a way to commu-nicate that reaches for age-appropriate cognitive and physical capaci-ties. A statement to young children acknowledging that a scary thing has happened is often the most effective opening offering to children whose thoughts and feelings are chaotic and without words.

At first, we got very little response from these very frightened-looking 5- and 6-year-olds. We had brought paper and markers and sat down with two or three children apiece. We asked if the kids would like to draw pictures, but they quietly declined. When asked if they would like the clinician to draw something, the positive response was unanimous, as was the requested content of the pictures: "Draw a mommy."

Rather than assuming anything, we asked each child what sort of face the mommy picture should have and what words might fill the speech bubble next to the drawing of the face. The instructions for faces fell into two categories: happy and sad. Similarly, the prescribed words were either "I'm so happy to see you" or "I was so sad and worried about you."

After engaging in the drawings, the children grew more verbal and began to ask about where their mommies or daddies were and when they would arrive. All the children were scared that maybe their mothers might not be able to come for them—either because they would be hurt in their own car accidents or get lost. It was wonderfully good timing that the officer who had first met them returned to the gym to let us and the children know that all the parents had been located and were on the way to school.

One of the children asked a clinician to draw a picture of a head. Whose head? "Um, a boy's head . . . that just got hurt." The rest of the children overheard this question and immediately turned their attention to this picture. The clinician requested details in order to complete the picture and asked if any of the children wished to add something. Three children scribbled the same ingredient with a red marker—blood from the head wound—which soon covered much of the page.

Although the children asked some questions about what was happening to the friend who had been hurt, the majority of questions and comments had to do with bodily functions. How much blood does the body have? Can parts of the body fall off? These solemn scientific inquiries quickly turned to a more spirited group discussion about various physical feats each child could perform. The conversation was punctuated by the children's sidelong glances toward the door as parents began to arrive to pick them up.

Each parent was seen briefly by one of my clinical colleagues, who described our impressions of the emotional condition of their child and explained some of the typical concerns and behaviors that children may have after experiencing such a frightening event. The parents were encouraged to monitor changes in their children's behavior and moods. In addition, we suggested that over the next day or two it might be helpful for parents to ask their children if they would like to talk about what had happened and to listen to any questions or ideas that they might have about the accident. We gave them a telephone number to call at any time with questions about their children's experiences and a pamphlet summarizing typical signs and symptoms of distress. We also asked their permission to contact them to check in to see how things were going in the days after the event.

ROSEMARY'S UNFOLDING STORY

Of the seven affected families, five sought consultation from us because of concerns about their children's symptoms, including disruptions in sleeping and eating, separation anxiety, and avoidant behaviors that had not been prominent in any of the children's lives before the accident. Over the course of a few months, the children's problems eased as parents and professionals helped them understand what they had witnessed and separate it from their fantasies. Two of their stories can help us understand the specific, very personal meaning children give to disturbing events. Each example is a condensed version of what happened over the course of two to four months of meetings with the children.

Rosemary, 5½, had been sitting across the aisle from the little boy who was injured. She saw that he was knocked out and saw the large cut and the blood on his head. Until the police officer told her otherwise, she had thought her classmate was dead.

Rosemary had been doing well in school and at home with her mother, father, and 8-month-old baby brother. She had had no first-hand up-close experience of loss, injury, or danger. Her parents sought help for their daughter when, two weeks after the bus accident, Rosemary's difficulties with sleeping and eating, multiple new fears, and an intense need to stay close to her mother had not abated.

With the therapist, Rosemary made drawings and used figures and toy vehicles to reenact the crash. With each version of the accident scene she added an increasing array of details, but the play always ended with Rosemary saying that she felt "scared and bad." Over time, Rosemary revealed that she was scared because she could have been the one whose head got hurt and bloody; she could have been the one who needed to go to the hospital. And she felt bad because her friend had been hurt. At one point, after drawing a picture of a child lying on the ground with what she described as an ambulance nearby, Rosemary grew quiet and looked particularly forlorn. When her therapist suggested that maybe there was a connection between her feelings and the story that the picture told, Rosemary began to reveal a secret that unfolded over several sessions.

The first part of her secret was that, for several days before the accident, Rosemary had been scolded by the driver for bad behavior on the bus. She thought that maybe she was the one who was supposed to be hurt as punishment for having been bad.

What had she done on the bus that was so bad? Well, it turned out that in the days before the accident, she had been teasing and poking the classmate who suffered injuries in the crash. But the plot of Rosemary's story grew even more complex. With great anxiety, she told the therapist that on numerous occasions when her parents weren't around, she teased her baby brother. The other reason she was such a bad girl was because "Sometimes I wish he would just go away, that he'd been somebody else's baby."

With this description, the sources of her worry and guilt became clearer. She was terrified that "bad wishes" could come true, that angry feelings about a rival—either a classmate or a baby brother—could really cause them to be hurt. She was convinced, and perhaps hoped, that her wishes would be discovered and that she would be severely punished. At the same time she was terrified she was no longer lovable.

Rosemary began to feel some relief as her therapist pointed out that she was punishing herself as if she had really had a kind of magical power that could have put the scary bus accident under her control. In the end, a dramatic reduction and final resolution of her symptoms accompanied her telling the details of her deeply personal experience of the bus crash.

There was nothing unusual about Rosemary's hostile wishes toward her rival, her baby brother, nor about the displacement of these feelings onto the classmate whom she had tormented. It was her belief that these wishes had come true that led to overwhelming anxiety and trauma.

Rosemary's conviction that she had magical power was completely consistent with a type of thinking that is prominent in 3-to-6-year-olds. But in Rosemary's situation it was more than a support for pleasurable fantasy and pretend play. She also relied on it as a way of recovering from a frightening real event over which she had absolutely no control. Her belief in her magical power allowed her to reverse her original overwhelming experience of the complete absence of control. In her version, Rosemary wasn't passive and helpless in the face of real danger. However, she had paid a high price. Her reliance on magical thinking would also lead to her tremendous sense of responsibility and guilt about real and imagined events.

ANGEL ON THE RUN

Two weeks after the bus accident, Angel, age 5, had many symptoms of distress. He insisted on sleeping with the light on at night, found leaving his house very upsetting, and began to complain about stomachaches to avoid going to school.

Angel was the youngest in a family of six. Both parents and a 19-year-old brother worked, one sister was in high school, and the other was in middle school. Before the accident, Angel had had no difficulty sleeping, leaving for school, or engaging in activities away from home. When all that changed, Angel's parents requested help.

Over the course of several meetings, Angel revealed both to the therapist and then to his parents that he was terrified that the person who had crashed into his bus would now find him and his family and crash into their car. Being told that the man who had run the red light had felt very badly about the accident did not allay Angel's fears. However, his ability to express this central worry opened the door for further exploration, clarification of his thoughts, and greater mastery over the original frightening experience.

Behind Angel's fear of a subsequent crash and injuries was his attempt to explain to himself why the accident had occurred. It gave him a chance to predict and thus protect himself from similar dangerous events. However, Angel's explanation was limited. While riding in the car with his parents, he had often heard them complain about "crazy drivers." When he asked what they meant, they had explained that sometimes when people are feeling angry they drive in ways that aren't safe.

Angel reconstructed his parents' comments and used them in a scary explanation for what had happened when the truck crashed into his school bus. In his version of the events, the driver was not only crazy and out of control but also angry. When he hit the school bus, he must have been angry at the bus and its occupants. If he was angry with the school kids then, what would stop him from continuing his pursuit? If Angel was a target of this crazy man's rage, the man must still be mad at him, Angel thought.

There was no indication that rage or attacks on children were part of Angel's real-life experiences. However, as a typical 5-year-old, he was struggling with concerns about bodily safety, aggression, and its control. The concept of an "accident" could not hold a candle to the strength of Angel's egocentric, highly personalized experience of real destructive power.

While generating considerable fear, Angel's explanation provided the basis for altering the traumatic episode. His version put him in more control than he had been in the original accident. Instead of being passive in the face of an unavoidable and uncontrollable situation, he could now anticipate the danger and take action. He was on guard at all times. He stayed close to home, avoided travel, and clung to his parents.

Understanding Angel's solution in the context of his developmental phase helped his therapist unravel and clarify the distinction between Angel's fantasies and the facts about the bus accident. As his parents were able to appreciate the thoughts that lay behind Angel's symptoms, their entreaties to stop worrying and their global statements of reassurance were replaced by very specific discussions about Angel's concerns. Discussing the differences between craziness, anger, and accidents helped to reinforce the distinction that Angel was able to make between the real event and his fantasy reconstruction. He was eventually able to give up his reliance on an explanation that, while it gave him some sense of control, also prolonged terror. Instead of fearing an angry driver who was after him, Angel began to tolerate the scary feelings he had had in response to a surprising crash, which not only interrupted his normal daily bus ride but, with the sight of his friend's injuries, his idea that bodies are safe.

WHEN HOME IS A DANGEROUS PLACE

Tragically, some children see, hear, and live with physical and emotional brutality between their parents. In addition to the acute trauma they may experience from witnessing out-of-control or sadistic behavior perpetrated by and directed against adults they love, these children are also at greatest risk for developing longer-term problems. It is very difficult for children from violent homes to recover from their deep sense of insecurity about the safety, reliability, and stability of relationships.

Domestic violence cuts across socioeconomic, racial, and ethnic groups and is one of the most prevalent sources of violent trauma, affecting the lives of millions of women and children in the United States. Youngsters under the age of 5 years are the largest age group of children who witness domestic abuse between parents. These children and their older brothers and sisters are all too often trapped, because the patterns of behavior between their parents can be very difficult to interrupt.

Random explosions of violence and systematic infliction of physical pain, humiliation, and fear are traumatically immobilizing for children. When parents act against each other, demonstrating that there is no difference between feelings, thoughts, and behaviors, children have every reason to be frightened. They come to believe that the dangerous thoughts that lurk in everyone's imagination will come true.

As a result of what they see and hear, young children exposed to domestic violence are far more vulnerable to a range of emotional, behavioral, and cognitive symptoms that result from an exacerbation of the important struggles around aggressive urges that, as we have seen, are a normal part of early development. These children may develop a range of regressive symptoms, including sleep and eating disturbances, loss of newly acquired toileting habits, constant irritability, complaints about bodily pains, increased clinginess, and fears about familiar activities and items that are now sources of imagined dangers. They may also demonstrate the impact of the upsetting and fearful experience of witnessing parental fights by engaging in repetitive play activities that are solely focused on destruction and angry, hurtful fighting.

Most young children are gleeful about their power to both build and crash block towers. But when this is the only activity that holds the interest of a noticeably irritable and unhappy preschooler, we need to help. Without help from adults, this repetitive bashing and crashing play leads not to solutions but rather fuels a level of compulsive excitement from which it is painfully difficult to disengage. Similarly, young children may, at some level, try to exert control over what happens in their home by defying their parents more insistently or behaving in ways that will provoke and redirect their parents' rage toward them instead of at each other. In this lightning-rod function, young kids take charge of when the explosive interactions occur, reversing the terrifying feelings that are connected to the unpredictability of attacks that parents aim at each other.

Alternatively, young children from abusive homes may become extremely tentative in all their interactions, inhibiting their own normal age-appropriate needs and feelings—especially those that might involve their own aggression. These kids may become very passive, withdrawing from typical enthusiastic exploration of the possibilities and limitations of daily life. It is as if these kids are trying to keep their heads down and avoid acting in ways that might rock the boat at home.

For some children, exposure to parental violence and emotional abuse can lead to long-term inability to form close relationships, with other children or with adults. It is especially worrisome that children who see parents battering, intimidating, and humiliating their partner are more likely to engage in antisocial behavior as adolescents and later, as adults, to become involved in abusive relationships themselves.

Withdrawing into fantasy and away from interactions with peers or picking fights with perceived attackers are two examples of the great lengths children will go to avoid the helpless and frightened feelings aroused by witnessing violence and emotional abuse at home. When the young child is burdened by the terror of seeing more hatred than love and when the certainty of affection is so easily shattered by abusive behavior, protecting oneself against feeling frightened and small deflects energy away from exploring the world and mastering concerns about separation, aggression, autonomy, and intimacy. Normal development is derailed.

These issues continue to reverberate for school-age children and, with additional significance, in adolescence when kids once again need parents to serve as the brick walls against which they bounce their own struggles in playing out sexual and aggressive impulses. Additionally, as adolescents are trying on the experience of intimate relationships, the models that parents have or have not provided about reciprocity, mutual respect, and negotiation of competing interests in a relationship come home to roost. When the experience of closeness between adults is uncertain and abusive, the basic trust and confidence required for opening oneself up to another person may be so compromised that the capacity for true healthy intimacy cannot develop fully.

We have come a long way from the days when domestic violence was viewed as a private matter, outside the responsibilities of law enforcement and the courts and outside the recognition of the broader society. However, we have a long way to go if we are to translate our concerns into responsive action. There are no simple solutions. We will only make strides in our efforts to interrupt the cycle of domestic violence when as a broader community we face the facts about its prevalence and recognize the public health problem that it represents for our nation.

When we acknowledge the scope of problems that domestic violence creates, we are in a better position to insist on the development of strategies and training that are needed in order for various systems of care—law enforcement, the courts and legal community, domestic violence advocates, mental health and primary health-care professionals, housing authorities, and others—to work closely together in efforts to identify and respond to the millions of victims who remain its victims. These include:

- Training for medical, legal, child welfare, law enforcement, judges, and legislators to understand and recognize domestic violence and its effects

- Ensuring physical safety

- Supporting economic independence

- Providing options for alternative housing

- Establishing reliable external controls for abusive behavior

All these issues need to be addressed if we are to reverse the helplessness, terror, and trauma that repeatedly rob abused parents and their children of some of the most crucial ingredients necessary for loving oneself and for safely and pleasurably loving others.

VULNERABILITY AND RESILIENCE

Normal concerns about the integrity and safety of the body that are typical of this phase of development intensify when 3-to-6-year-old children experience damage to their own bodies or witness real-life damage to the life and limbs of others. The sense of personal vulnerability that increases when the most frightening ideas about bodily injury come true is compounded by the amount of time and the degree to which a child's own physical functioning or that of a loved one is impaired. When injuries are serious, the impact of the original event is compounded as a child assumes the additional passive role of the injured patient in need of treatment.

Witnessing an injury to someone close, especially a parent, supercharges children's concerns about their own bodies and arouses worries about the strength, competence, and availability of the adults on whom they rely. Real injuries to adults that interfere with daily life contradict the young child's view of parents as omnipotent and omnipresent to care for and protect them. With their tendency to magical thinking, young children may experience injuries to themselves as a consequence of behaviors or wishes that they see as very bad and deserving punishment. Young children may respond with guilt, worry, and shame to injuries suffered by siblings and parents according to these same principles of cause and effect and retaliatory justice.

Although some children rely on their magical thinking to try to regain a sense of control, such thinking also leads them to wrongly conclude that the "bad" thoughts and feelings they secretly harbor are indeed dangerous and powerful and are the root of the "bad" events. When you've been angry with Mommy, and Mommy later gets hurt, you believe that your angry wishes have come dangerously true. For Rosemary after the bus crash, the very efforts she was making to feel safer led to severe and harsh self-evaluation as well as fear of the loss of love of others.

For young children whose level of thinking is still largely concrete or tied to what they can visualize, touch, and hear, more abstract events and concepts such as "death," "heaven," and "God" may be especially confusing. These ideas and concepts, while potentially comforting to older children and adults, may be additional sources of mystification and misapprehension about the world. In trying to make sense of events, especially those involving death or those that arouse the threat and fear of loss, children may generate their own explanations that are based on fragmentary knowledge and frightening memories and fantasies. As a result, children's "understanding" of upsetting events may be fantastic and grotesque, often far scarier or more distressing than what actually occurred. The concept of "heavenly resting places" and of meeting once again with relatives who have died may be central to your beliefs, but for your youngest children, whose sense of time is still so immediate and whose thinking is still so concrete, attempts to reassure with promises of reunions in heaven may fuel frightening ideas about the imminence of their own deaths or fantasies about ghostly visits. These fantasies, and your children's best but flawed efforts to explain death and loss, may be accompanied by increased anxiety and the onset of behaviors such as narrow and repetitive play and ritualistic, avoidant, or regressive behaviors. These behaviors are attempts to restore some sense of order and predictability, yet they ultimately fail to provide relief.

THE POWER OF PLAY

The same developmental factors that contribute to young children's difficulties when they experience trauma can also be the keys to recovery. Their tendency toward magical thinking and their flexible sense of reality allow them to dive into the world of pretend play. When the support and comfort parents have to offer is not enough to help children get over trauma, and when their symptoms of distress don't abate or if they reappear months afterward, consider calling on a professional. Parent and child can benefit from psychotherapeutic guidance and intervention. Professionals can use the play of young traumatized children to shed light on their interpretations of events. Playing gives children the power to write the script and direct the action, focusing on themes aroused by overwhelming, traumatic events. Through fantasy play, they can reverse the original and terrifying loss of control of themselves and their experience of the world.

With information that emerges from play, parents are in a much better position to help their children see the difference between facts and fantasies about frightening events. When we know more about the specifics of the most troubling aspects of our children's experiences, we stand on much firmer ground. We can reassure them by providing facts that offset their most frightening fantasies. When children have undergone a trauma, as the kids on the school bus did, they can untangle the resulting confusion of feelings and thoughts with the help of sensitive parents and professionals. They can, in time, master their worst fears.

Helping our youngest kids find words for their frightening feelings helps them contain unrelenting and uncontrolled fear and helps establish or reinforce their bridges to us. Our youngest children feel our protective embrace when we are able to get as clear as possible in our understanding of the dangers from which they feel the greatest need for protection. The more we can respond to the specific factors that undermine our youngest children's feelings of safety, the less likely we will be to miss the mark and impose responses that are based on *our* reactions. Even if we are unable to recall the language of fear we used as young children, we do know what it is like to be frightened and alone. As we have become much more familiar with our adult versions of terror, it is easy to forget that we once shared their nightmarish fantasies. If we do forget, or if we can't bear to remember and turn away, our children will indeed be left alone in that "affrighted nursery province beyond all succor and comforting."

■

CHAPTER NINE

OUT OF CONTROL: TRAUMA AND OLDER CHILDREN

As children move into the school age and teenage years, they are increasingly able to distinguish their fantasies from real life and are better able to think logically. Yet they remain vulnerable to the trauma that follows overwhelming, terrifying events. Though their capacity for language is greater than younger children's, their responses to trauma can seem as remote and foreign to us as those of our younger children do.

In the wake of traumatic events, older children fall prey to dreaded feelings of helplessness or neediness that threaten to override their normal developmental thrust toward increasing autonomy. When their basic sense of competence and confidence in the navigation of a broader, more complex world is shattered by trauma, their efforts to regain control may lead to a set of seemingly unrelated symptoms. These may, in turn, interrupt the forward movement that is critical to successful development. Following trauma, school-age children and adolescents may demonstrate a range of changes in behavior, including:

• Sudden withdrawal with an accompanying increase in moodiness or feeling numb

- Increasingly provocative behavior that invites frequent and intense conflicts with parents, teachers, and other figures of authority

- Preoccupation that interferes with attention, concentration, and engagement in typical interests and activities

- Sudden changes in academic performance and decreased interest in social and/or extracurricular activities

- Sudden engagement or increase in risk-taking behaviors

- New or increased substance use (alcohol, marijuana, etc.)

- Dramatic changes in appetite, sleeping, and grooming

As distressing as these responses may be, it is important to remember that they can serve enormously important functions. While these symptoms reflect the psychological chaos of dangerous experiences, they may also be the only way that school-age children and adolescents can demonstrate the impact of traumatic events while keeping the associated terrors at bay. Without professional help, they remain in a bind. But when they are able to locate, explore, and understand the feelings that an overwhelming experience has aroused, they need not remain prey to the original traumatic loss of control or to its further erosion. If you observe the symptoms just listed above in your school-age child or teenager, insist that he or she get help.

SCHOOL-AGE TERROR: SUDDEN DEATH UP CLOSE

Ten-and-a-half-year-old Robert was walking home from school when he saw a car slam into a motorcycle. The rider flew in the air and then tumbled and slid across the street, to lie inert against a curb no more than 30 yards from where Robert stood. As the sounds of sirens approached, Robert realized that the motorcycle rider was his 19-year-old neighbor, Jake. The quiet street, only blocks away from Robert's house, became filled with onlookers, who poured from their houses as the police and EMTs arrived.

Robert would later describe being unable to move as he watched the activity around the crumpled body of the young man who had once been his babysitter and was now his idolized and badly hurt friend. Robert didn't see Jake move when they put him into the ambulance.

As the activity cleared, Robert's mother, Grace, spotted him standing very still on the sidewalk. She had come looking for him when he hadn't arrived home at his usual time and had heard about the accident from neighbors along the way. She embraced her son, but his response was uncharacteristically stiff; his face remained blank until they arrived home. "I think Jake was hurt real bad," were the first words out of his mouth. He didn't cry until hours later, when his mother told him that Jake had died.

Robert came to his mother's room several times that night, complaining that he couldn't sleep. He said he didn't feel well but couldn't respond to his mother's questions about his reaction to Jake's death. Grace would later report that it had been a long time since she had needed to sit by her son's bed in order for him to go to sleep. Robert was quiet the next morning and several mornings thereafter as he got ready for school. After much discussion, Robert decided that he did not want to go to Jake's funeral. Instead, at his mother's suggestion, he made a card for Jake's family saying that he was very sad that Jake had died and that he had liked Jake very much.

Over the next weeks, Robert's upset emerged more forcefully. He began having recurring nightmares and was irritable at home and at school. Nothing his mother did was right: her cooking was inedible, and her reminders to wash or get ready for bed were insulting. She was unfair and bossy. He got into more than the usual number of fights with his 7-year-old brother, and for the first time his behavior at school prompted notes from his teacher. He was arguing with classmates and getting into fights on the playground.

The adults in Robert's life knew there must be a connection

between Jake's death and this 10½-year-old's behavior. Grace talked with him. His teacher talked with him. While Robert's parents had divorced when he was 3 and his father, Jim, lived in another city, Robert visited him regularly and they had a good relationship. Jim also tried to talk with his son, but all the discussions were one-sided. Robert wasn't talking. He could only put his feelings into actions. Yet the feelings weren't going away and his actions just served to isolate him.

After several weeks of difficulty, his parents agreed that Robert needed additional help. Grace and Jim met with me before I met with their son. They reported that Robert had been doing well in school, had a range of friends and interests, and that aside from a difficult period following the parents' divorce, his development had proceeded relatively smoothly. Since Jake's death, Grace described herself as being more anxious about Robert's whereabouts. She often met him halfway from his bus stop. She was also aware that since Jake's death she had been preoccupied with fantasies about both of her boys' safety and found herself hovering more than was typical, "fussing about them when they were playing outdoors, on their way to the bus, or out of my sight." She added, "I try to stop myself from having morbid thoughts and from imposing my worries on them, but it's hard."

A few minutes after meeting Robert, I mentioned that I had heard that a very important friend of his had died and he had seen the accident that killed him. Robert remained silent. When I asked him if he liked to draw, Robert picked up a marker and began to find a new way to act on his feelings. He began to draw picture after picture in which a car grew larger and larger as a figure on what looked like a bicycle grew smaller.

Over the course of the next couple of months, Robert's drawings and the accompanying narratives grew more elaborate. In them he revealed the central role that Jake had played in his real life and in his fantasies. Jake had not only been the best babysitter he had had but someone who occasionally tossed a football with him and waved to him whenever he saw him on the street. Jake occupied a place in

Robert's inner life, built on these seemingly brief contacts, as a strong competent man who was interested in Robert and valued him.

As an accompaniment to his drawings, Robert described memories of every detail of his contacts with Jake. He highlighted the ways that Jake's treatment of him contrasted with what he perceived as his mother's nagging and worrying that made him feel like "such a baby." It was in this context—as Robert repeatedly returned to depicting the moment that Jake was struck down—that his sense of disbelief turned to grief and then to rage and guilt.

As he described the enduring image of seeing Jake lying on the ground, Robert was at last able to put into words the essence of his traumatic moment. This figure of strength, competence, and cool, with whom he identified so powerfully and with so much pleasure, was struck down like a helpless baby. Figures in whom you invest strength, power, and love just aren't supposed to topple. They're not supposed to leave you.

I suggested as much to Robert and added that he knew something about feeling disappointed, about not having people he really liked or loved around as much as he would want. "Sometimes, when guys worry that they have those kind of feelings of disappointment, it must mean that they are somehow younger than they really are," I said.

Robert did not jump up and down and scream, Eureka! But he didn't tell me to shut up, either.

Robert's drawing and our discussions continued. His parents and I could begin to make sense of Robert's irritability: It was his way of defying any notions of "being babyish." When he got into rages and fights, he felt powerful *and* was able to push away the feeling of being a little kid that was stirred up by his longings for both his father and his friend who, at some level, he felt had abandoned him. He was alert to those situations in which his sense of competence was under attack. His friends' jokes, his younger brother's taunts, gave rise to angry counterattacks.

Over time, Robert's irritability and fighting diminished and eventually stopped, as did the nightmares that captured his terror and robbed him of the safety of sleep. His parents also recognized that, regardless of their friendly post-divorce relationship and Robert's regular contact with his father, Robert's feelings about the end of his wished-for family had not disappeared. Identifying this elephant in the room opened the door to more direct conversations between Robert and his parents. Individually and together they talked to him about the disappointment and anger he felt toward both of them because of their divorce.

After several months, Robert was getting more comfortable with the existence of these private thoughts. He was able to talk about the genuine sadness he felt about Jake's death and the concerns and fantasies that this loss raised about losing his father. As he described it, the goodbye that ended each of his visits with his father was like a small death, and the accompanying feelings of grief could only be fully repaired when he saw his father again.

By the end of his therapy, Robert was no longer symptomatic. He was living more in the present and was once again happily engaged in school, his friendships, and home life. This would not be the last time that events in the world would reverberate with personal meaning; I hope Robert will not have to witness the horrifying death of anyone again, let alone anyone to whom he feels close. But the impact on Robert of Jake's accident and sudden death would have been far worse if his symptomatic responses had been his only recourse and if he had been left alone with no way of replacing them without intervention by his parents and me.

STRUGGLING FOR CONTROL

When our school-age children have close encounters with overwhelming traumatic events, they may quickly equate their terror and helplessness with earlier feelings of being small and in need of protection. For kids who are strenuously striving for competence and a sense of autonomy, these "babyish" feelings are intolerable. As with nightmares, school-age children who are traumatized attempt to protect themselves from what is both a frightening and a mortifying loss of control. They assume a vigilant stance toward the world. If you are on your guard, they feel, and if you can locate and anticipate danger, you are in a much better position to take action that will avoid a repetition of the frightening experience.

Unfortunately, behaviors aimed at avoiding danger come with their own heavy burdens. As with younger children, school-age children may respond to traumatic events with symptoms that include sleeping difficulties and nightmares, phobias, and preoccupying concerns about bodily injury and death. Traumatized children may be so fixed on thoughts about recurring danger that they're unable to concentrate in school. Or they may withdraw from interactions with friends and from activities that supported their growing sense of competence and independence. In addition, falling back on—or regressing—to earlier modes of relating to parents may reflect both the wish for and the fight against their longing to be protected. Increased struggles over food, self-care, schoolwork, and household responsibilities all involve obvious and perhaps conscious efforts on the part of traumatized kids to insist on their independence; by turning away from us, they flout our rules and expectations.

What is perhaps less obvious to us, and clearly not consciously planned, is that the same behaviors that are supposed to demonstrate autonomy in fact draw our attention. They invite our involvement in a way that compliant behavior does not.

ADOLESCENT TERROR

As if the dangers and threats that derive from the normal biologically and developmentally driven vulnerabilities of adolescence aren't enough, what happens when teenagers are confronted with dangerous and threatening events in the external world? For adolescents, the developmental challenges and tasks facing them are the areas most vulnerable to disruption. Their overarching fear of losing control now has very specific focal points. The stories that follow about Andrea and Jackson illustrate the ways in which these traumatic events can supercharge adolescent fears about losing control over sexual and aggressive impulses, and concern about bodily damage, humiliation, and loss of love.

CORNERED IN A STAIRWELL

Andrea was 15 years old and living with her mother, father, and two younger brothers when she was cornered in a stairwell of her large high school by a group of three older boys. At first they appeared friendly. They said they hadn't seen her around before and asked her name. What class was she headed for? Did she know any of their friends?

At first, Andrea said she was flattered by the attention. But she also recalled being nervous, and not just about being late for class. Whatever excitement she felt quickly changed to fear as the boys created a wall separating her from the stairs. They alternated between eyeing her up and down and trading smirks. Their compliments about her clothes shifted to more explicit comments about her body. Andrea tried to stay calm and cool, laughing nervously at their remarks and saying that she needed to get to class. When the boys began making comments to each other about the various sexual acts they would like to perform with her, imagining out loud what she would like, Andrea wanted to run. Instead, she froze.

Andrea remembers clutching her books to her chest and looking down at the floor, aware that her face was red and her eyes were brimming with tears. When she tried to inch her way around the boys, she felt sick to her stomach and thought she would vomit. Just as the late bell rang, they all heard footsteps and the sounds of two school staff members talking as they came down the stairs toward them.

The boys ran. The two adults found Andrea slumped against the wall, quietly crying. Andrea would later describe feeling surprised that she was able to pull herself together and come up with an excuse for her tears and lateness to class. "I'm sorry, I know I'm late. It's just that I had a fight with my boyfriend, but I'm okay now." She begged not to be sent to the office and went to class.

Over the next week, Andrea complained about various aches and pains and convinced her parents to let her stay home from school for a few days. Her symptoms grew worse as a return to school seemed inevitable. She was unable to sleep through the night, refused outright to go to school, and, perhaps most notably, was unable to go into any of the rooms in her house unaccompanied. Her parents were understandably alarmed and pressed her about what had happened to cause her so much distress. Andrea was able to provide an outline of what had occurred but could not tolerate talking about any of the details. Nor could she remember the appearance, let alone the names, of any of the boys involved.

Andrea's parents were enraged by what they heard and contacted school officials. School staff members wanted to talk with Andrea immediately, but she refused. It was at this point, two weeks afterward, that Andrea saw a psychotherapist.

Before the stairwell event, Andrea had been doing well in school, was well liked by friends, and was involved in a number of extracurricular activities. Both she and her parents described life in their home as normal, including the typical occasional struggles over her messy room, homework, and weekend curfew. In spite of her achievements, Andrea now described herself as feeling like a frightened baby, no longer able to look after herself. Over the course of several meetings with the therapist, both on her own and in joint meetings with her parents, Andrea reported that she continued to feel frightened and jumpy. She and her mother said that, unlike in the past, their bickering was now frequent and usually ended in screaming battles.

Andrea was able to return to school but she was unwilling to discuss the incident with school officials, though she agreed to check in briefly with her counselor for a first few days after her return. For the first weeks, Andrea never went anywhere without at least one friend. She remained frightened and insisted on being taken back and forth to school by her parents. For several more weeks, she was able to have a few select friends come home with her, but she would not engage in after-school or weekend activities outside her house.

In her individual psychotherapy, Andrea began to make a more conscious link between the strength of her increased feelings of dependence, her repudiation of these feelings, and her fights with her mother. Additionally, helping Andrea's mother come to recognize the connection between her own anxiety about the event and a resurgence of the wish to overprotect and control her daughter's activities—as if she were younger—allowed both mother and daughter to disengage from the intensity of their struggles.

Andrea was able to accept the help of a neutral professional listener and use her parents and school personnel for support in ways that were no longer dominated by anxiety, outrage, and drama. As she achieved growing awareness of the deeply personal and most frightening aspects of her stairwell experience with the older boys, her fear diminished. As soon as hiding from scary thoughts was not her only option, her symptoms became increasingly unnecessary. Not surprisingly, ideas about being raped were the most terrifying thoughts from which she sought refuge, but no one could know or predict certain details that connected her fear and her avoidance of school.

Andrea described a budding relationship with a boy at school and said that her thoughts about him had become increasingly romantic. However, since the incident in the stairwell, she had felt especially anxious and somehow ashamed every time she thought of this boy. It became clear that, for Andrea, the normal anxiety associated with burgeoning adolescent sexuality had become contaminated by the intense vulnerability she felt following a real loss of control in a situation fraught with danger, both to her body and to her self-esteem. As a result, Andrea was not only avoiding the boys who had threatened her but also the powerful sexual feelings associated with her potential first boyfriend.

Becoming able to distinguish the difference between feelings involved in two very different experiences of urges and impulses—one out of control, dangerous, and humiliating, the other reciprocal, exciting, and enhancing—helped Andrea let go of her symptomatic behavior. She could see that when faced with three unfamiliar, threatening, and potentially dangerous older boys she had had good reason to feel frightened, immobilized, and helpless; these feelings were ones that any healthy, strong young woman would experience and hate under similar circumstances.

Andrea put it best when she said, "I guess I finally realize that, after what happened, being afraid and feeling like a little kid doesn't mean I am one. But when you're in the middle of something, that's a hard thing to remember!"

Although there were disruptions of Andrea's developmental achievements—in family and peer relationships, school functioning, self-esteem, and emotional regulation—her heightened conflicts and symptoms about autonomy and sexuality did not dominate her adolescence. Her healthy development before the event, family support, and additional help aided her negotiation of and recovery from an experience whose nature, context, and timing made it overwhelming and traumatic. She did not forget the encounter in the stairwell and remained appropriately cautious about situations in which she might find herself vulnerable to predatory behavior. But that awareness didn't interfere with a full range of social situations and interests. As she disentangled the multiple meanings of what she had experienced, Andrea was able to return to school and to more typically adolescent ways of relating to family and friends—including her healthy romantic and sexual interests.

ATTACKED IN AN ALLEY

It was about eight-thirty on a summer evening when 15-year-old Jackson emerged from a movie with four friends, to be picked up outside the theater by one of the group's parents. They waited awhile but their ride was nowhere to be seen. After a series of missed cell phone messages, it was clear that signals had gotten crossed and another set of parents was called into service.

With new arrangements in place, the three boys and two girls decided they had enough time to go for ice cream several blocks away. Jackson trailed behind the group and stopped to look at a window display in a computer store. Later, his friends would say that they assumed that Jackson would show up within a few minutes. But he didn't.

As Jackson neared the ice cream parlor, two men approached him, asked for the time, and then quickly pulled him into a dimly lit alley. Much later, Jackson would explain that "Everything happened so fast, it was like some weird dream, like I was floating . . . like I was watching what was going on with someone else."

One of the men held him from behind and the other put what Jackson described as a huge gun in his face, threatening to shoot him if he made a sound. They demanded his money, his watch, his cell phone, and a prized silver necklace that some of his friends had bought him for his last birthday. After taking his valuables, the assailants fled. Jackson ran to the ice cream parlor, where his friends were growing concerned but figured they would find him as they made their way back to the theater.

Jackson was breathless and shaking uncontrollably when he literally ran into his friends. He was barely able to get out the words "I was robbed" when the parent who would drive them home arrived. On the short drive to Jackson's home, his friends called the police.

As his parents were told what had happened, Jackson ran into his room crying uncontrollably and slammed the door behind him. His parents could not calm him down. He continued to shake and his breathing was rapid, but soon his sobbing was replaced by a blank stare. The police arrived. One of the officers spoke with Jackson's mother outside his room as another entered it to talk with Jackson directly. When he saw the officer, Jackson became agitated.

Both officers had been trained in principles of child development and trauma as part of the Child Development Community Policing program that partners police and mental health professionals in responding to overwhelming events of violence and disaster that affect children and families. One of the officers who entered Jackson's room told him he had heard what had happened and realized that the holdup was a terrifying experience.

Jackson couldn't look at the man but suddenly screamed, "Get out of here!" The officer was about to leave the room when his partner pointed to his gun and utility belt. In response to this signal, the officer removed his holster and weapon and told Jackson that he would leave them outside the room, saying, "The last thing you must want to see is another gun, even if it belongs to a police officer who is here to help you."

Jackson remained agitated but agreed to the officer's suggestion and to his parents' endorsement of the idea of talking with a doctor who could help him get himself together and feel more in control. As the clinician on call with the police–mental-health partnership, I responded to the page.

By the time I arrived, Jackson was in his parents' home office. He was quiet but sat as if frozen to his chair, with a tense face and empty eyes. He looked away as I explained that the police call me when kids and families experience frightening events but finally looked at me directly when I commented that being terrified could make a guy feel small and helpless—not a very desirable feeling for a 15-year-old. Jackson then began to talk about the evening's events.

He described the scene and the assailants' commands to him over and over. This repetitive review is a common response to traumatic events by which the individual tries to take charge and integrate dangerous experiences that have overwhelmed normal capacities to take action through flight or fight. At these moments, both mind and body are immobilized. For some time the victim feels dislocated from the reality of what happened and grapples with attempts to reverse the absolute surprise that left him so vulnerable. One way of understanding the repetitive recounting of events is as an effort to break down or metabolize details that were impossible to chew on at the time, let alone swallow all at once.

People who have not experienced this phenomenon themselves have, unfortunately, had an opportunity to witness it as TV news crews exploit the compulsion to repeat details in their on-the-scene interviews with victims of horrific events. When clinical interviews are guided by the need for a resumption of personal control, simple compulsive repetition is replaced by further elaboration of a personal set of experiences that can be examined, pieced together, and understood. Through this elaboration, traumatized persons can increasingly contain what happened to their minds and bodies, rather than continuing to feel blind-sided and overwhelmed. Now they have time to identify, label, and reflect on the details of their experience.

With no set script, other than being provided with a basic framework and some words for the link between a real frightening event and the profound impact on his thoughts and feelings, Jackson was able to move beyond repetition. The more elaborate account of his experience included slight alterations of the facts—and, for the first time, his anger. He grew intent on reversing what had been his enforced passivity with notions of taking decisive action. "I should have grabbed the gun and kicked each of them in the balls," he growled. As if apologizing to himself, he reiterated to me how large the gun muzzle was and how certain he was that he would be shot dead.

As his shaking, hyperventilating, and sobbing subsided, Jackson began to talk about the earlier part of his evening. He explained that before being robbed he had been hanging back from the other four because they were "sort of, you know, boyfriends-girlfriends" and he wanted to "give them space." Almost as a whispered aside, Jackson shyly told me that he did not have a girlfriend. He then quickly exploded, first with rage and then tears. He wanted to get a gun and kill the guys who messed with him. He did not deserve what had happened to him. He was a good student in school and had just completed an important history paper and they took his favorite necklace!

Jackson clenched his teeth as he again swore revenge. I commented that it must have been humiliating to feel so terrified. Revenge, I said, was an understandable way of getting rid of the idea of being small and helpless that he hated so much. Jackson replied that if he had had a gun or had disarmed his attackers, he would not feel as though he'd wimped out. I agreed that feeling powerful would certainly be the opposite of what he had experienced with a gun in his face.

Jackson's expression brightened and he looked up. He exclaimed that he remembered the gun more clearly. It had not been a huge semiautomatic weapon like the kind he had seen in so many action movies, it was really a BB gun. As the intensity of his terror diminished, Jackson was also able to describe the two men clearly—what they were wearing and in which direction they took off. His revenge fantasies now took a very different shape as Jackson insisted that he wanted to talk to the police, tell them what he remembered, and help them arrest "those two bastards."

Our meeting ended with Jackson still shaken but no longer as disorganized and distraught. His parents were relieved to see their son looking more like himself and were eager to hear the description that I shared with them and Jackson about the effects of terrifying events on the way our minds and bodies respond. I suggested that Jackson might continue to feel a mixture of anger and anxiety for a while. I reviewed several other possible reactions: difficulty sleeping and eating, preoccupying thoughts about the event, irritable or depressed moods, physical symptoms, and being easily startled. I also told them that reminders of events can sometimes make people very nervous even if they don't recognize why they suddenly feel so uncomfortable. I finished this brief lecture with the statement that one of the hardest aspects of the event would be recovering the level of control and sense of safety they had all had before it occurred.

To feel back in control, Jackson and his family needed to acknowledge, even mourn, the fact that certain situations—like having a gun stuck in your face—can make us lose it. And that is difficult.

One of the biggest challenges is to discover that this loss of control is not forever, that it is not a reflection of our ability to take charge of our lives, and that the essentially infantile nature of enforced helplessness is not a confirmation of who we are and who we can be.

I saw Jackson for several follow-up meetings, which focused increasingly on descriptions of his social and academic interests. He told me about some difficulties with sleep and a tendency toward irritability, especially when he thought his parents were being overprotective or bossy. He acknowledged looking over his shoulder, but he quickly added, "not all the time." He was also much more tolerant of the range of his feelings about what had happened to him. His fantasies of what he should have done were eventually mixed with direct talk about his mortification. "You know, the only thing I can think about sometimes is hoping that my friends never realized how much I fell apart—that would be the worst."

Jackson could acknowledge feeling helpless at the business end of a gun, but he did so with an increasing amount of sympathy for himself and recognition that there was nothing he could have done to alter what had occurred. When his sleeping difficulties and hypervigilant feelings abated, Jackson no longer needed to meet with me. This was particularly rewarding for a 15-year-old boy who preferred his autonomy to any need to depend on adults as sources of safety and support, especially when events had made his need for them especially great.

In a last telephone follow-up call, twelve weeks after the incident, Jackson gladly spoke of the latest academic demands at school and in his social life instead of focusing on the rage and terror he had felt after the robbery. His violent revenge fantasies and fearfulness were replaced by a sense of victory and the announcement of important news. "Did you hear? The cops caught those two assholes—sorry, guys—who not only robbed me but had been doing a lot of stickups! They said my good description had been a big help."

I confirmed that I had heard from colleagues in the police department that Jackson's information about the men had been instrumental in their arrest. Jackson reported that the cops thought they had enough on the two men to take them off the street for a long time. In Jackson's words, "That felt really good."

RISK AND RESPONSE

Regardless of their age and phase of development, when our children are traumatized they are unable to turn down the volume on, turn away from, or control their feelings of discomfort and humiliation. When they are confronted with real-life versions of the issues that are closest to normally occurring challenges and concerns, their attention is galvanized in a no-win live-wire situation: too much power to be good for you, yet impossible to let go.

When is a child in a live-wire situation? Many conditions determine the degree of vulnerability to trauma. Knowing about what puts children at greatest risk can help us safeguard their recovery. These factors include:

- Physical proximity: an immediate threat of danger to themselves or to people with whom they are closest

- Degree of the emotional threat (a parent or other family member or a friend's parent has been directly affected by a sudden unanticipated danger)

- Preexisting vulnerabilities in psychological functioning

- Previous traumatic loss or history of exposure to situations of overwhelming danger and distress

- Unremitting dangers and associated threats (in warfare, chronic domestic violence, etc.)

- Degree to which routines and expectations of daily life continue to be disrupted (inability to return to homes that have been damaged or destroyed, closed schools, disrupted transportation, restricted activities, a threat of violence in the community)

- Extent to which parents and other adults involved in the child's life are themselves overwhelmed and demonstrating symptoms of traumatic distress that interrupt their capacity to convey emotional stability, strength, and control

- Degree to which parents and other important adults can recognize that the child has been impacted and can appreciate the connection between the event and changes in the child's behavior and emotional state

When we fail to recognize these risk factors and our children's experiences of traumatic distress, symptoms become chronic adaptations to enduring feelings of helplessness and fear. For example, a child's initial withdrawal into fantasy may lead to academic failure, which then contributes to an already lowered sense of competence and self-esteem. Or when children try to reverse the original feeling of helplessness—especially when they are victims or frightened witnesses of out-of-control anger and violence—they may move from a passive role to an active one, from teasing to bullying to battering. Children increasingly come to see themselves as strong but also bad and unworthy of love.

When we misunderstand the source of our kids' seemingly inappropriate behaviors, we may adopt responses—anxiety, frustration, anger, and withdrawal—that only serve to fuel symptoms and perpetuate feelings of shame and self-loathing. To make matters more complicated, when we get most anxious about our kids they know it. This makes their conflict over their need for us all the more complicated as they may feel that we are treating them like the babies they worry they may be.

STANDING BY OUR CHILDREN

Over the course of their development, children increasingly are able to reassure themselves about frightening ideas. They get better at distinguishing between their fantasies and the safety of ordinary daily life. It's a great accomplishment when children actually begin to believe their own comforting words. When parents are out for the evening and the furnace makes a noise, they can think, Oh, don't be silly, it's not a burglar, it's the heat going on!

But there is no swift reassurance to be had when children experience serious bodily injury, suddenly lose people they love, or find that the world of daily routines has gone crazy. Losing control makes children feel small and humiliated. At these moments, as their most primitive fears and terrors are no longer confined to fantasy but materialize in real life, the distinction between fantasy and reality may become frighteningly blurry.

Our availability to our kids, our ability to recognize that they've been overwhelmed, is a prerequisite to helping them reestablish those essential boundaries. Kids can be helped to distinguish between dangers of the past and present—both real and imagined—as well as between what has just happened and the likelihood of a similar threat emerging in future.

Making the connection between our children's symptoms and the fact that they have been traumatized is the first and most important thing we can do for them. Recognizing these symptoms as signals, as our children's best attempt at expressing their upset, is different from responding with aggravation to behaviors that we'd hoped they had outgrown. When we are able to see that our child's response to traumatic events reflects not only the unique characteristics of the event itself but also his or her particular developmental concerns, we are in a much better position to help. When we understand that symptoms have meaning, our children will not be left to deal alone with their feelings of terror and fear.

When we can't do it alone, we can reach out to others—to our children's pediatricians and to mental health-care providers—for assistance. When we feel trapped by our own traumatic loss of personal control, we need to recognize that *our* symptoms, *our* feelings of helplessness and fear, merit attention as well. If we remain out of control of our own lives and emotions, we will not be able to help our children regain control over theirs.

WHEN TO GET HELP

From the moment they are born, our children's safety and happiness is a central concern and driving force of our lives. Yet in spite of all our efforts, it is not always possible to protect them and secure their happiness. This fact creates problems and induces anxiety for us at various times throughout our children's lives, even when circumstances are at their best. But our hopes for our children, and the limitations on our ability to achieve them, are especially complicated when terrible things happen. It's hard to be calm, listen patiently, and remain concerned and available when what we want to do is rush in and fix things. Our primary protective mission has been thwarted! As we see our children suffering, we feel that we have failed to keep them out of harm's way. And we feel like failures all over again when they turn away from intrusive attempts to help.

How hard it is at this juncture to recognize the need for additional outside help! Asking for it feels like a capitulation to our own helplessness. Yet when our children have high fevers or other physical symptoms that persist in spite of remedies that are immediately available at home, how easily we seek help from their pediatricians! Apply that same thinking to traumatic events if, four weeks after the order of daily life has been reestablished, a child's symptoms of traumatic distress persist. There are times when we all need someone to lean on. We must learn to recognize them when they occur.

■

CHAPTER TEN

WHEN DISASTER STRIKES

WAR

As the shell hits the plane,

And it starts to go down,

He notices they're 'bove water and'll surely go down.

He thinks of his fam'ly and how he loves them

And he looks round the plane at the other men.

Some are yelling and trying to fight,

Some try to assure themselves they'll live through this night,

And the others just sit and close their eyes

And look as if this is no big surprise.

They prob'ly think deep, just like him,

He thinks 'bout his faithful dog, Old Jim.

He thinks 'bout when he signed up to "be a man."

He thinks about his girl and how he should have told her. . . .

One last night through the eyes of a soldier.

—ADAM, AGE 11

In the wake of the attacks on September 11, 2001, we have come much closer as a nation to understanding traumatic experience. As the unanticipated, massive, and violent loss of life breached our most basic sense of safety, security, and control, we were left numb and disbelieving, vulnerable to the fears that all of us share.

For those who lost family members, the consequences of the terrorist attacks will be far more intense and enduring. Those who were closest to the scenes of destruction, injury, and death and those whose family members continue to work in occupations that put their lives on the front lines of defense against potential danger are more likely to feel the uncertainty and fear that terror inspires. For those who were already struggling with loss and the dangers of violence, the attacks exacerbated their existing sense of vulnerability and fear.

We continue to live in the broad dark shadow of terrorist attacks, of the deaths of our soldiers in warfare, of fellow citizens killed by vicious snipers, of the tragic loss of life in uncontrollable fires and natural disasters. Clearly, we are most affected when tragedies strike our close and beloved family members and friends. But the victims could be any of us—our children, mothers, fathers, brothers, sisters, husbands, wives, partners, relatives, friends, and colleagues, even ourselves.

Immobilizing fear does not need to be the only outcome of events that breach our most basic sense of security. When we are able to remember that we not only share what we see and hear but what we feel, when events converge with the most dreaded aspects of our imaginations, and when we do not hide in shame from our own terror, we are better able to recognize and remember what it is for others to feel powerless and frightened. When we remember what we share, we may be better able to listen and attend to each other and to our children. We don't need to be alone with fear.

WHEN ADULTS ARE SCARED

In considering how we are best able to help our children regain as much of a sense of safety and security as possible in these situations, let's first consider the impact that our emotions have on theirs.

Think back to a time in your own life when danger not only was located in the shadows of your bedroom or basement but pervaded the adult world as well, when you saw your parents overwrought with anxiety, whispering to each other about grown-up stuff they meant to protect you from—but the secrecy scared you all the same.

Maybe it wasn't so strange that many of us did not feel really worried as we rehearsed bomb drills in the sixties. Maybe if we had been older, we might have been a little concerned when, within only a few weeks, the now-frequent drills changed from ducking under our desks to going into the hallway and pressing our bodies as closely as we could to the walls. Our teachers seemed to believe that in the real October 1962 shadows of nuclear holocaust, these desk-ducking, wall-hugging strategies would protect us from the blast from an attack on our nation's capital, only a few miles away. Thank you, Mrs. Mitchell, wherever you are, for your calm, cool, almost bored demeanor during those many drills, announced by the blast of a countywide air-raid siren. If you had shown one iota of fear, we would not have been able to enjoy the small scale of our worlds and the boredom and irritation that accompanied our sense that the drills were, at worst, confusing and, more typically, silly interruptions to our predictable days.

What did 9-year-old Americans in suburban Maryland know of Hiroshima? What did we know about the launch-to-impact time from Cuba to the continental United States of a 20-megaton nuclear weapon? Fortunately, for most of us the answer was: not enough.

My friend Luke was not so lucky. He learned more than he would have liked to know. He remembers how anxious his mother was during those days in October 1962. It was hard to hear her talk about the dangers of a "terrible war that will be a bad thing for our entire country." Yes, he remembers it well. It was even more frightening when his mother announced plans to take her boys and join their father in Mexico City, where he had gone on business, in order to avoid the impending disaster of war and destruction.

My friend's recollections are less a reflection of crazy parents than of the degree of terror that their open expression of anxiety and a planned disruption of life as he knew it inspired. I am so grateful that whatever terror my parents felt in those dark days of the Cuban missile crisis, they succeeded in keeping it to themselves!

It wasn't possible to escape the fear that shrouded our lives only a year later. It was the rare adult who was not undone by the Kennedy assassination on November 22, and it would have been a rare kid over 8 years old who didn't feel that something major had shifted in a critical and uncomfortable way. For older school-age kids and beyond, there could be no more visible icon of power and control than the President of the United States of America. What did it mean that this tower of strength, this embodiment of parental order and justice, could be so suddenly and easily struck down? It meant that stability was a relative thing, that the rhythm of our parents' ordered and continuous lives was not as secure as we believed.

In the biography of Anna Freud written by Elizabeth Young-Bruehl (and as I had heard from teachers and colleagues during my training), a story that emerged out of the blitz of London illustrates the huge gulf that can exist between the fears of adults and the experiences of young children. During World War II, children were evacuated from the sections of London that were hardest hit by Nazi bombardment. Some of the youngest children from the East End—a prime target because it was a highly industrialized area, as well as being a hub for river transport and commerce—were evacuated to group homes that were run by Anna Freud, Dorothy Burlingham, and other child analysts in Hampstead, a section of northern London.

However, it was not untypical for German bombers that were either low on fuel or fleeing from British fighters to drop whatever bombs remained in their payloads over Hampstead on the way back from missions in the southern part of the city. On one such occasion, a bomb fell into the backyard of one of the group homes. It didn't detonate, and it was several days before the military could come to defuse it. In the meantime, the staff and children moved to a second group home. In spite of cramped conditions, the child-care staff was intent on maintaining the usual schedules and activities for the 120 children. There was also agreement that, beyond explaining the reasons for their temporary move to this group of 3-to-6-year-old children, there would be no discussion about the bomb unless initiated by the children themselves.

Staff members who regularly met every evening were especially alert to new signs of anxiety and distress among their charges. Some of the staff shared with one another their own anxious reactions to the frightening reminder that, even when out of the line of direct attack, they were still in harm's way.

There was much talk among the staff about their good fortune that the bomb had not detonated, as well as speculation about the damage to their lives, and property if the house had taken a direct hit. There were, however, no observations of symptomatic behaviors—eating or sleeping difficulties, clinginess, tearfulness, increased irritability, new toileting problems, or preoccupation and talk about dangers—in the group of children. They were, however, universally annoyed. They were angry that the "stupid bomb" was in their garden because it meant they couldn't play in their usual backyard—a much bigger and better one than the substitute space behind the second house! When the bomb was defused and removed, the children cheered, rejoicing in the return to the house and the play area that was such an important part of their daily lives. For these kids, the routine of daily care in the group home provided a predictable, loving, and therefore safe part of the world, even in the midst of an adult war.

The experience of Anna Freud and her colleagues during World War II taught us a great deal about the importance of reestablishing order and routine as a way of protecting children from the fearfulness and trauma that is so often associated with the disruptions and chaos of war and terror. Similarly, the war nurseries also demonstrated and supported ideas about the central role that the reactions of adult caregivers play in children's responses. For young children who were already coping with irregular contact with their families, the most powerful predictor of difficulty was the degree of anxiety, fear, and upset expressed by visiting parents. It was also striking that when parents were helped to recognize their own upset about the enforced separations and the impact that their distress might have on their children, they were better able to support their children's efforts to adapt to the situation.

When, at the beginning of each visit, parents were given detailed reports by the child-care staff about how their children were doing, they were much better able to interact with them. They weren't burdened by anxiety about their well-being. Similarly, helping parents to recognize the burdens of separation on their children helped them to develop strategies that reinforced the continuity of their relationships and provided optimal emotional support: engaging in here-and-now activities that were part of their children's daily routines, reminding children of the schedule of contact with them, and tolerating the regressed and needy behavior of children whose own tolerance for separation was being stretched thin.

Unfortunately, since the London war nurseries of the 1940s, we have had almost continual opportunities to observe and learn about the impact of war and disaster on young children's development. In multiple studies that have explored children's and family functioning in the aftermath of earthquakes, floods, and hurricanes, Scud missile attacks on civilian populations, and other forms of warfare and terrorism, risk factors that predict greater difficulties for young children in times of danger and crisis have been identified. In addition to previous developmental and emotional difficulties a child may have had, these risk factors include:

- Separation from parents

- Disruption of the normal predictable routines of daily life

- Overt anxiety and upset (including depressive withdrawal) of parents and other significant caregivers

PROTECTING OUR CHILDREN
FROM OUR BURDENS

Recognizing how much adult responses can affect optimal care and interfere with a child's own regulation of fear and anxiety does not mean that adults are not supposed to have, or allowed to have, emotional responses to overwhelming events themselves. What it does mean is that, in addition to recognizing that our children may be frightened and at their most vulnerable, we need to learn to recognize the signals that we are having a tough time with our own reactions. Ask yourself the following questions:

- Are you preoccupied with thoughts about the traumatic event or new fears about health, death, or loss?

- Do you find yourself more anxious and uncomfortable, wound up, and unable to relax?

- Are you easily distracted and unable to sustain attention to typical activities and goals?

- Do you find yourself feeling unable to enjoy usual pleasures, either more irritable and quick-tempered or down and despairing?

- Are you having difficulty sleeping, either in getting to sleep, staying asleep, or waking earlier than usual?

- Has your appetite changed or are you eating more or less than usual?

- Do you find yourself unable to feel affection or warmth toward your spouse or children, or is there a noticeable decrease in your sexual appetite?

It's not easy to acknowledge our distress. Often, when we are having any of the difficulties described, we may be the last ones to notice. The time when we are experiencing a level of distress that gives rise to problems in daily life may also be the hardest time to hear observations about our difficulties from someone else. At these moments, expressions of concern from others can be hard to bear. We may interpret sympathy as confirmation of our own feelings that vulnerability equals inadequacy.

We may be most successful in offering support to our spouses or partners when we talk to them about our observation of changes in their mood or behavior in an uncritical fashion that specifically states concern but also raises a very straightforward question: "What do you think is going on?" In addition, describing our own experiences of frightening or distressing events and our wish to talk about them may be a helpful way of introducing the discussion with a less communicative spouse.

Even as we try to help each other, we need to remain concerned about whether the level of our distress about catastrophic events means we have less energy to pay attention to the experiences of our children. Our failure to take care of ourselves may not only deprive our kids of the support they need but may also burden them with an unsettled and disquieting new tone we have set for family life.

Being able to acknowledge, when we are having a tough time, that we are scared, sad, or angry about horrible things that happen, requires courage. It may also require a leap of faith. Putting these feelings into words is not a capitulation to helplessness or an infantile bid to be rescued by the listener. Rather, it is an opportunity to take charge. Left unrecognized and unexamined, our reactions will continue to disrupt more than just one life. When we help each other we are better able to help our entire family.

When catastrophic events occur that affect our immediate lives, there are concrete actions to take:

- Carve out private time when you can turn to your partner or close friend to identify and discuss your specific fears and concerns.

- Try to clarify immediate sources of danger and disruption that events have created for you and your children.

- Explore strategies that can ensure the greatest degree of continuity of daily routines with spouse or partner and others engaged in the care of your children.

When you continue to feel burdened by your own anxiety and uncertainty about how to minimize the effects of overwhelming events, turn to professionals who can help clarify the bases for your concerns, identify your children's reactions, and, when necessary, be available to help monitor the adjustment of individual children.

THE STUFF OF CHILDREN'S FEARS

A week after the attacks on the World Trade Center, I received a call from a woman in New York City. She was very concerned about her 4-year-old daughter, Emily, who would repeatedly build two tall block towers and crash a toy airplane into them. Her own explosive sound effects augmented the din of the wooden blocks that clattered noisily to the floor. I asked the mother to describe what her daughter looked like as she enacted this scene six to eight times each hour. She said that Emily was deeply involved in her building activity and seemed determined to get the towers just right. She was pleased when they reached a certain impressive height without falling down.

Emily was equally serious as she lined up the flight path of her plane and sent it crashing into the buildings. After the last block had fallen and the last bit of sprayed spittle exploded into the air as an accompaniment to her sound effects, she would jump up and down, hug herself, and clasp her hands, beaming with delight. Her mother was very worried that her daughter's repeated play was a clear indication that Emily had been traumatized by the attacks that had occurred within miles of their home. She reported that Emily was not interested in invitations to talk about any of her feelings or ideas about "the big accident."

I asked for more details and learned that every time Emily's mom saw or heard the scene played out, she jumped. "I know it's silly, but I keep thinking about the horrible scene . . . all the fire, smoke, and dust . . . all those people who died."

I agreed that it must be hard to be regularly reminded of the horrors of the terrorist attacks, even if the reminders were in miniature form. She agreed, adding that she realized that alongside her concerns about Emily's possible upset, she kept thinking of her child's play as "ghoulish and disturbed." In response to my questions about Emily's pre-9/11 functioning, she told me that she was doing quite well. She had a reasonably good relationship with her 6-year-old brother, adored her father, and enjoyed the preschool program she attended daily. Emily was having no difficulties sleeping, eating, bathing, or toileting. Aside from this new repetitive play, her mood did not seem to have changed dramatically over the past week.

Her mom quickly added, "The one thing we've noticed is how often Emily will stand in front of the TV when the news is on. She never used to be interested. Maybe she doesn't have much choice, given how much we've been following things since the eleventh."

I suggested that Emily could be responding to what she was hearing around her and that the repetitive nature of her play might reflect a mixture of pleasure and worry about a confusing event. She could, I added, be partially mimicking and using it as a focus of play to demonstrate her skills and natural excitement about both constructive and destructive power. I added that one of the things over which Emily had no control was the flood of television coverage and grown-up talk about the terrorist attacks.

In the midst of how caught up her parents were in their own horror and anxiety, Emily's exposure to the images and emotions surrounding the 9/11 events was ungoverned. This, I said, was not likely to be helpful for Emily, especially when she was unable to put any of her ideas into words. Perhaps the repetitive nature of her play reflected her inability to master the facts and understand adult reactions. I advised limiting their own TV news watching and shielding Emily from it altogether. As she was being bombarded by horrible and confusing television images, she was also experiencing her parents' anxiety and the shift in their attention away from her and from the routines of normal family life.

I mentioned that the less disruption there was in the immediate world of her home, school, and neighborhood, the safer Emily would feel. In addition, when she sensed order, routine, and emotional calm in her parents, there would probably be less need for the repetitive building-destroying-building cycle in her play. If she experienced difficulties in daily functioning, behavior, or mood later on, it would be an indication that Emily was unsuccessful in taking charge of and mastering feelings and fears that had been aroused by events in the larger world.

I checked in with the family over the next several weeks. As we had hoped, Emily's repetitive tower building and razing moved from center stage, and there were no further concerns about a traumatized child. Her mother said she didn't know if Emily's repetitive play would simply have faded over time or whether she was able to let go of concerns that fueled the play as a result of changes in the family's behavior. She explained somewhat sheepishly that after our discussion about Emily, she and her husband recognized just how much time and energy had been consumed by their own feelings of fear in the weeks following 9/11.

In addition to all the talk at work and reminders and discussions of the events everywhere they went in the city, Emily's parents had often found themselves uncharacteristically in front of the television, watching the news. "We were news junkies. We couldn't get enough. The more we watched, the more anxious and less satisfied we were and the more we had to see. We weren't even aware of what was happening to us or that our preoccupations had put the children on a back burner."

It was not easy for them to limit their news consumption, but by doing so they had found more private time away from the children to check in with each other—monitoring and discussing how they were feeling, what others were discussing, and their very real concerns about being vulnerable to further attacks.

"I can't say that any of these chats were enjoyable," she reported, "but we think paying attention to the kids also helped us lessen the pressure-cooker feelings between us. Somehow, even though we didn't feel the same, our kids' day-to-day lives returned to normal."

THE IRAQIS ARE COMING

A week into the war in Iraq, friends told me that their 8-year-old daughter, Samantha, was having trouble getting to sleep, was waking frequently with nightmares, and was anxious and clingy during the day. They had asked her about her dreams and about what she thought might be causing her so much worry. She could only reply that she was scared about the war.

Samantha's parents were stymied and she was stuck. When I sat with Samantha and her mother and father, I told her that I understood how worried she was and that I knew a lot of kids who were similarly upset and scared by news about the war in Iraq. She asked me, hopefully, what the other kids were scared about. I said that for many kids it wasn't always so easy to find words for their feelings, but that a lot of them had ideas about people being hurt and killed.

Samantha looked down solemnly and slowly nodded her head. I asked who she might be thinking about getting hurt. "Us," she replied. "My mom and dad and sister and all of our friends." This opening led to Samantha's disclosure of an elaborate fantasy that involved the Iraqi army coming to attack her neighborhood. She said she listened at night for the sound of airplanes or any other signs of an invasion materializing.

As she spoke, Samantha wouldn't look at any of the adults. As her mother began to tell her this would never happen, I quietly waved her off and suggested that it would be important for Samantha to cover all the details of her invasion ideas first so we might compare them with the facts. When her notion about commercial airlines as the mode of delivering the invasion force surfaced, we explained that the airlines and the U.S. government wouldn't ever allow this to happen.

However, the discussion wasn't over. I asked Samantha if she thought her parents or older sister were scared of the Iraqi army landing in her neighborhood. She looked down again and then said in a bare whisper that she wasn't sure. I suggested that maybe she did think her parents were scared and that it would certainly be worrisome if they were. "I think Daddy may be," she said, before adding, "He watches TV about the war all the time. Maybe he thinks they are coming."

By letting me listen carefully and address her fantasies, Samantha was no longer alone with them. She could now compare her ideas with facts. In addition, her parents could alter their behavior and cut down on the amount of time they spent watching TV coverage of the war, which turned out to be the most important collateral support for addressing Samantha's fear: moderating the fearfulness of her parents.

FACING FEAR WITH BRAVADO

A group of six fifth-graders walked back to class from lunch, not aware they were watched by their teacher. They were boisterous, jostling one another as they joked about the meal they had just eaten. Two snipers in the Washington, D.C., area had been arrested several months before, and there were no longer any headlines announcing the immediate threat of anthrax poisoning. But you wouldn't have thought so from what their teacher, a friend of mine, reported.

The teasing seemed to be good-natured. Everyone in the group gave as good as he got, but one comment riveted everyone's attention. "Yeah, Ricky, you better watch out on the way home today. Some crazy person may be hunting for school kids that look just like you!" Everybody laughed, including Ricky.

This loaded comment immediately led to the next from another member of the group. "Well, after the lunch they just gave us, we'll all be dead—it tasted like there was anthrax in that junk!" Again, everyone laughed and commented on how horrible their lunch food was generally. A few of the kids got the biggest laughs as they feigned choking and collapsing to the floor, leading to the hilarity inevitable among 11-year-olds when people start falling over one another.

My teacher friend wasn't surprised by how enduring the thoughts of real-life dangers were in the minds of these middle-class school kids, but he was amazed at how they had been woven into the fabric of everyday interactions. My friend was even more surprised when, as the group split up, he overheard a continuing conversation between two of the boys headed back to his classroom. Their jocularity evaporated as the two boys peeled away from the group and one boy earnestly asked the other, "How do you get anthrax anyway?" The other boy quickly replied, "I don't know, and I don't want to find out!"

My friend was convinced that these boys were revealing both in their jokes and their serious questions the level of uncertainty and fear that now permeated their lives as a result of events that had dominated headlines and preoccupied an entire nation. He was also convinced that to raise these concerns with the entire class would create a burden for kids who weren't consumed by these thoughts already. By approaching the topic, he also ran the risk of humiliating the boys whom he had overheard and driving the discussion further underground.

My friend felt he had somehow missed the boat. When the anthrax scare was the lead news story, he had done little if anything to address the fears that many students in his class may have had about their safety. "If I had it to do over again, I would have raised the subject as an important current events topic. I would also have used it as a way of giving some instruction in science," my friend told me. "I would have talked about how difficult it is to contract anthrax and maybe even said something about psychology. You know, like how when we all get scared, the source of the fear can seem a lot bigger than it is?"

He wished he had talked about the ways in which anthrax can be detected and successfully treated when the public and the health system are alerted to possible infection. "I wouldn't have ignored their fears, but I wouldn't have tried to run a group therapy session either. I'm a teacher and I know how to teach. I just wish I had been able to teach something about what was going on that would have helped some kids feel less afraid."

TERRORISM AND ADOLESCENT ANGST

In the months following the attacks of September 11, 17-year-old Greg and his parents found themselves having increasingly explosive battles over almost every detail of his day-to-day responsibilities. His refusal to take care of household chores and personal commitments invited the very thing that Greg protested: His parents got in his face.

While Greg's parents were intellectually prepared for the struggles of adolescence, these changes in their relationship with their son seemed sudden and extreme. In calmer moments, they attempted to probe what might be giving rise to so much upset. There were no changes academically or socially and no changes in Greg's interaction with his older sister or younger brother, with whom he was close.

His parents consulted with a mental health professional about their concerns. A glimmer of understanding began to emerge after a particularly loud battle about Greg's refusal to help with the after-dinner cleanup. His mother was especially distraught and complained that, given her busy travel schedule, his behavior was both burdensome and unfair.

Greg lashed out in response. "Right, so it's my fault you have to travel so much, just like it's going to be my fault when terrorists bring down the plane you're flying on!" Both parents were stunned. Greg had rebuffed every effort they made to discuss his ideas about terrorism or the world situation. Now, for the first time, he acknowledged that every time his mother packed for a business trip, he was consumed with dread. When his father asked why he had never said anything about this before, Greg replied sheepishly, "Yeah, right . . . and sound like some wimpy little kid?"

This brief retelling cannot do justice to a complex story, but Greg and his parents were eventually able to discuss the specific nature of his fears. They also talked about the increased security measures that were in place at airports, as well as his mother's commitment to keep the family better informed thereafter about her status while traveling. Both parents were able to recognize that their own unacknowledged anxiety of post-9/11 travel may have shortened their fuses in battles with Greg.

In consultation with a mental health professional, the family was also able to recognize the ways in which their fights had served some of their needs. The battles kept them all intensely involved and were an opportunity to express anxiety without acknowledging the elephant in the room—their shared fear of plane travel. By everyone's account, the fighting decreased significantly for several months.

However, when news of continued casualties from Iraq and increased terrorist threats were once more in the news, Greg and his family found themselves again in frequent pitched battles. Their familiarity with the underlying reason now led to speedier acknowledgment and discussion, including everyone's expressed wish for a decrease in Greg's mother's overseas travel time. When she simply had to travel, they discussed safety concerns, monitored State Department advisories, and scheduled telephone calls during her absence.

Greg would at times complain that these measures made them all sound paranoid and that everyone was overreacting. Yet his insistent claims that he was no longer so concerned about his mother becoming a casualty of terrorism were regularly accompanied by a close review before each trip of his mother's itinerary and schedule of calls home.

Greg and the other children described in this chapter are not alone. For the many children whose stories are never heard, symptomatic behaviors are often the only way they can express their most fearful feelings when the horrors of disaster and terror in the world are inescapable. Each child is affected differently by events that impact and interfere with the sense of security of our entire nation. The closer and more personal the damage, injury, and loss, the greater the grief and the dread of more to come will be.

Few kids are completely immune to the tidal wave or the ripple effects that continue after the brutality and terror of violent attacks and overwhelming disaster. Each child may blend what is uppermost in his or her mind in any given phase of development with the individual circumstances of that child's life. For some, the reactions are quiet, fearful, and lonely. For others, vulnerability is expressed in rage and revenge fantasies or in attempts to disown what feel like infantile fears about safety through battles with the very people upon whom they depend. Still others may mask their unease in bravado and jokes about the dangers and fears that may befall their friends. Adolescents may engage in philosophical discussions about the nature of evil, consider thoughtfully what it means to be alive and what it means to suffer loss and death, or pursue heated political debate about the causes of terrorism and war.

TAKING THE TIME TO LISTEN

As adults, we may only be privy to our children's different responses by sheer luck and good timing. However, we don't always need to wait for that perfect moment when our kids are not only able to find words for their feelings but also willing to share them with us. We can watch for signs of struggle in their behavior and their moods and begin conversations that they may not be able to initiate on their own. Questions about what friends and classmates are talking about and feeling in the wake of frightening events or threats are likely to be more productive than asking older children to reach beyond their protective barriers to reveal to us and to themselves how it feels when nightmare fantasies come true.

After the terrible shootings in Jonesboro, Arkansas, the U.S. Department of Justice invited me to visit the traumatized community, where five people had been killed and ten seriously wounded. My goal was to develop recommendations about ways to help communities deal with violent tragedies.

I will never forget the pain, disbelief, and courage of this small community, whose peace had been shattered by the deadly gunfire of two young boys. One of the many poignant moments during my brief visit occurred during a town meeting that had been called 36 hours after the shootings. The local prosecutor and the sheriff, and the mental health professional who had flown in to try to help the community deal with the tragedy, fielded one outraged question after another—about the possible charges and punishments in the case against the alleged 12- and 13-year-old perpetrators, about new security measures that might be needed, and the like.

As an observer and someone who was not part of the fly-in team of experts, I was not asked these questions, nor was I in a position to intervene. I grew more and more uncomfortable when none of the answers addressed or diminished the rage and grief that lay behind the questions that continued to fly. Finally, a 9-year-old girl raised her hand. Plaintively she asked, "But why did they do it?"

The large group fell silent, heads bowed. Tears were shed. The young girl's question and tone seemed to capture the anguish, helplessness, and fear that no one else had seemed able to tolerate or articulate. The mental health professional seemed flustered and, unfortunately, his answer missed the central point of her question. He replied, "We don't know. We just don't know."

Well, we might not have known exactly what triggered the shooters' behavior, but we were able to observe and learn a great deal about the town's reactions and the background for the young girl's questions. The shootings and violent deaths of teachers and children, of wives, mothers, friends, and neighbors, confronted everyone with unanticipated loss and with the absolute danger of out-of-control impulses. The violent events also turned the once predictable daily life of

Jonesboro upside down. The degree of shock, emotional chaos, and dislocation reflected the extent to which these events were a dramatic departure from the relative peace and calm of this southern community. No one would ever have imagined that this elementary, middle, and high school campus, ringed by woods and set on rolling hills, would be the site of a bloodbath, especially one perpetrated by 12- and 13-year-old boys. In a town where faith and family were essential ingredients of shared community values, the killings ran completely counter to all expectations.

I will call the brave 9-year-old girl who challenged all of us Amy. After the meeting, I looked for and introduced myself to her and her parents and then told Amy that I thought she had asked the most important question of the evening. I told her I had some ideas but quickly added that I thought she must have many of her own. I did not have to wait long before Amy elaborated on her question. "How can anyone suddenly do such terrible things? Are we safe? Are we ever going to be safe again?"

In our brief discussion, and later in lengthier discussions with her parents, Amy began to distinguish between the immediate upset of the entire community and the specific fears that the shooting had aroused in her. It had raised questions about her personal safety, about the general safety of the town, and especially about the extraordinarily unusual and disturbed behavior of the boys who committed the tragic crimes.

Our conversation came to an end with the agreement that there was much more for Amy and her family to be thinking and talking about. As we said goodbye, Amy's parents reported that something extraordinary had just happened to them for the first time since the shootings. "In all the upset and concern for our kids, this is the first time that we actually were quiet and listened to what our child had to say."

When we are confronted by horrifying real dangers, it is especially difficult for us to listen to our children. How can we pay attention to what is on our children's minds when events so clearly seem to call for action? It's horrible, and for some intolerable, to take a passive position in the face of the overwhelming realization of our worst fears. We may all become locked into repetitive thinking about what we could, should, and would have done to avert the tragedy.

Unfortunately, this sort of thinking diverts emotional reserves away from clear thinking about what we and our children need in order to recover from the psychological disarray of frightening and catastrophic events. We may also turn to activities and solutions that, while intended to return a sense of control and mastery as quickly as possible, may in fact delay consideration of what we may actually need—as individuals, as families, as communities, and as a nation. Alternatively, we can acknowledge the enormity of our own emotional responses to the realities of loss and loss of control. Only then may we be able to slow down long enough to turn on the lights and identify the specific sources of *our* fears before we assume that our children share them.

WHEN DISASTER STRIKES

In these times, when we are all confronted by the horrors of terror, war, and large-scale disaster, it can be especially useful to have some principles to guide our wishes and efforts to help our children and ourselves.

In 1999, under the auspices of the White House and the U.S. Department of Justice, the U.S. Congress authorized the establishment of the National Center for Children Exposed to Violence (NCCEV) at the Yale Child Study Center. The central goal of the NCCEV is to provide training to communities around the country for collaborative responses to children and families who have been exposed to violent, potentially traumatic events. The NCCEV also provides information to the public about ways of identifying and responding to the impact of such events.

The NCCEV grew out of the work of mental health and law enforcement professionals who have learned to respond together to children and families in their homes, neighborhoods, and schools where violence and other critical incidents have occurred. We have come to understand a great deal about each other's roles. We have also learned that when we share an appreciation for principles of development and human functioning, our actions can also complement each other in ways that support the recovery of children and adults who have been impacted by traumatic events. As a result, police officers and mental health clinicians, educators, social workers, and advocates for those who experience domestic violence have worked closely together over the past decade in thousands of cases that have involved violence and other catastrophic events occurring in homes, neighborhoods, and schools. Through our collaborative response, we have also learned a great deal about the ways that children and families can reclaim the emotional sense of control and order that can be so severely disrupted by such events.

Over the past decade there has been a growing recognition of the short-term and enduring impact that sudden, destructive, and fatal events can have on children's development and on the ways that families and community members are able to support each other. One of the greatest risks to children who are exposed to the horrors and chaos of violence is the failure of adults to recognize how they have been affected. In the aftermath of the Oklahoma City bombing, the school shootings, and the terrorist attacks of September 11, mental health professionals and others have recognized the crucial need to develop a range of approaches that place psychological safety and recovery in the forefront of our national concerns.

TALKING TO OUR CHILDREN ABOUT CATASTROPHE

Along with colleagues from around the country and the world, the National Center for Children Exposed to Violence has been involved in developing guidelines or principles that can inform our responses to children at times when crisis and catastrophic incidents of terror threaten entire communities and countries.

When there is increasing news about war and talk about terrorist threats, a child's sense of certainty and safety can easily be shaken or undermined. At times when school-age children and adolescents may be unable to avoid a steady diet of news and general talk about dangerous threats, it is our job to help them cope. Calmly listening to your children's concerns is one of the most powerful ways of helping them to learn, understand, and feel safe and secure.

The first and most essential source of help for children comes from parents and other adults who are most centrally involved in their lives. Several general principles can help us think about the ways we can support our kids in uncertain times:

- **Know your own reactions first.** Identify personal concerns and take your own emotional temperature with the help of spouse, partner, friends, and colleagues. Recognize that when events threaten our safety and security, arousing fears of loss, losing control, bodily damage, and death, no one is immune to feeling afraid. It's natural to deny or avoid frightening reality. The problem is that it prevents our connecting with one another and with our children at precisely the time when our psychological and emotional presence is so crucial.

- **Recognize the difference between your fears and those of your children.** Remember that the size and scope of the world of children is determined by the phase of development they are in and the specifics of their immediate experience. How close to home are the catastrophic events that occur in the world around them? Has death or injury occurred to someone they know? Has a specific event led to a disruption of their daily routines and activities? How much talk about and exposure to news of the event is pervasive at home and at school? Did your children directly witness the event or were they exposed to it on television? Have your children suffered major losses, injuries, or other traumatic disruptions in their lives that may make them more vulnerable to heightened fearful responses to a catastrophic event in the news? If your children are already struggling in the course of development, is there any increase in symptoms or difficulties since their exposure to this event? Are there new symptoms or difficulties that have emerged in the event's aftermath?

- **Get outside help.** Consult with teachers, pediatricians, clergy, and mental health professionals about the status of your child. Sharing information about upsetting events with teachers and other adults involved in your child's life is a way of circumventing a misunderstanding or an insensitive response to the range of symptomatic behaviors the child might present in settings outside the home.

THE ROLE OF TELEVISION

One of the most concrete examples of the ways that our adult concerns are played out to the disadvantage of our youngest children is the tendency for many of us to become glued to our television sets as part of our response to upsetting events. Turn on any of the 24-hour-a-day news outlets, and you will see that the likelihood of finding news about situations that are disturbing enough for us—but may be very scary or terrifying for younger children—is very high.

I am not suggesting that grown-ups should not be up-to-date on the news, especially when more information serves our efforts to master the anxiety and fear that accompany events that have a bearing on all of us. However, remember that if the television is tuned to hours and hours of disturbing news, our children may have no choice about whether they see or hear too much. Similarly, if we are compulsively watching at times when our children need our attention and thus destroy the regularity of daily routines, we will be depriving them of what they need the most—us. In addition, getting stuck on the news may not serve the aim of mastering feelings aroused by tragic and terrifying events. Instead, as we look for new information that might offer some sense of resolution, watching the repetition of multiple approaches to the same story may only maintain or heighten the levels of overstimulation and fear from which we seek relief.

Adults can help lessen the impact of television news reports on children. To do this:

- Monitor and limit the amount of TV coverage they watch.

- Remember that the more bad news young preschool and school-age children see and hear, the more worried they will be.

- If your school-age and older children are interested in watching reports about terrifying events, watch with them when you can so you can talk about what they have seen and heard.

- Adolescents and adults who are unable to detach themselves from TV news programs may be trying to deal with anxiety in ways that often don't work. Turn off the television long enough to talk with one another about the ideas and concerns that the news arouses.

LEAN ON ME

Countless Hollywood movies and popular novels portray idealized friendships in which one buddy relies on the other to be there with them, through thick and thin. Real life is different. It is often hard for us to tolerate needing someone else's support. Even if we acknowledge intellectually that asking for help takes courage, we frequently go

more easily with the conviction that asking reflects weakness and infantile fear. And when we can admit to our need for the strength of
another, it can be hard to find someone on whom to rely.

The challenges are never more evident than when the dangers of
losing control are not only visited upon one family or one community
but threaten the safety and security of an entire country. When we
feel frightened and overwhelmed as individuals, we turn first for support to one another—to families and friends. As a nation we also hope
that in the wake of the catastrophe, loss, and terror we have all shared,
we can rely on our leadership to help support and steward us through
a process of recovering our strength, order, and resolve.

As adults we turn to our leadership in times of national crisis in the
same way our children turn to us in their most chaotic times. We look
for a kind of calm strength that does not turn away from the pain and
indignation of tragedy and does not crumble into the reactionary rage
of fear. We need to be informed of what has happened in a way that
helps us organize the unbelievable: to order the facts and put words to
unspeakable horror. At times when we are emotionally dislocated and
mute, we need a voice that can jump-start discussions with words that
capture our common pain, fear, and outrage as clearly as they reflect the
courage required to speak them. There is strength in numbers.

This is truest when as individuals and as countries we feel at our
weakest and most wary. This is a time when leadership is about reminding us that our shared values and determination do not disappear in the shadows of catastrophic events. When we can tolerate the
worst of our feelings without hiding from ourselves, we are able to see
that we are not alone. And when we stand together, we are more likely
to mobilize our efforts to recover and avoid the likelihood of being
caught completely unprepared again.

As director of the National Center for Children Exposed to Violence, as a member of the National Commission on Children and
Terrorism, and as part of the National Childhood Traumatic Stress
Initiative, I have had the opportunity to consider issues regarding crisis
response and preparedness with colleagues from around the country.

One of the issues that emerges clearly is the extent to which preparing is not only a necessity, in our efforts to minimize the impact of potential terrorism and mass casualty, but an important way of jettisoning the passivity that follows in the wake of the tragedies of violence, destruction, and loss that have already occurred. We can take charge, as individuals and as a community, when we can anticipate and plan responses to dangers before they overwhelm us.

Let's begin the discussion by asking some of the following questions:

- Does your town or city have a response plan in the event of a disaster or incident involving mass casualties?

- Do emergency management plans coordinate the roles and activities of first responders, medical personnel, schools, mental health providers, public information services, and private response organizations (such as the Red Cross) at the federal, state, and local levels?

- Do your schools have a comprehensive crisis-response plan that considers the short- and long-term emotional impact of catastrophic and crisis events on students, teachers, administrators, and parents?

- Do your local hospitals have mass-casualty-response plans that are coordinated with the emergency management of your municipality, county, and state governments?

- Do mental health professionals in your community have training to provide treatment for acute and longer-term trauma associated with catastrophic events?

- Is adequate funding available to respond to the mobilization of resources (food, shelter, medical care, law enforcement, mental health) in the event of disasters and mass casualties?

- Is adequate information available about the nature of threats and ways of safeguarding against potential dangers?

In times of greatest distress, we all need someone we can lean on and a plan of action to ensure that even in the midst of chaos we are able to turn to established structures and well-trained personnel to help us to recover order. Understanding and appreciating the debilitating impact of danger and fear are the first steps to leading a community and a nation to recover a strength that has been temporarily lost. We don't like to be afraid, but we need to remember that it isn't fear that gets in the way of our moving ahead, it's our attempts to deny the fear. We are best able to turn to our sense of community as a source of strength and resolve when we are able collectively to recognize and tolerate the reality of the threats and dangers we all share. And we all need to remember that both leadership and support begin at home.

ACCEPTING OUR FEARS

There is never a time in life when we are not vulnerable to feeling afraid. To be alive is to be familiar with fear, to learn to live with it, and to overcome and master its sources as they emerge over the course of our lives. Occasionally we will remember with great clarity the most frightening times in our own childhoods. We have regular reminders—both big and small—in our daily lives of the fears that we all share: loss of life, our own and those we love; loss of love of others and ourselves; loss of safety and the wholeness of our bodies and those about whom we care; loss of control of impulses and feelings both those directed toward others and those directed toward us; and loss of control of the world around us, of the predictability that allows us to plan and respond to new challenges.

We go to great lengths to avoid feelings of discomfort when experiences of daily life resonate too closely with fears that make us feel small and helpless. In the course of our lives we develop strategies for confronting rather than crumbling in the face of disappointments and fears that accompany the inevitable challenges of growing up. It is no surprise that all of us would much prefer to go through life without ever experiencing the fear and reality of loss.

When we are confronted by our children's expression of fears, we have a responsibility to protect them from sources that are within our control. When our personal unhappiness and symptoms of psychological distress interfere with the stability and care that our children need, seeking help will be of potential benefit to all of us. When our children are exposed to unrelenting marital discord—with or without the extremes of partner abuse—we need to take steps that will not only protect ourselves but will protect our children from the impact of this climate of uncertainty and fear. Interrupting this cycle and getting professional help can help ensure against the emotional scarring that can interfere with our children's functioning and happiness for many years to come.

When the events in the world around us, the ones over which we have no control, confront our children with a realization of their nightmares, we must remember that we experience our own versions of their worst fears. But if we are to know the difference between the two versions we must be able to listen to our children and relearn their language for the fears that we have all, at some point, shared. Our unhurried presence, our willingness to be the walls against which their feelings, ideas, and behaviors can bounce, means that, even when there is no quick fix to their fears, our children are not alone.

QUESTIONS CHILDREN ASK
ABOUT WAR AND TERRORISM

1. ARE WE SAFE?

When children ask questions about safety, they are often looking for reassurance that their immediate world of family and friends and the other important figures in their lives are safe *now*. Before you decide how detailed you want to be about safety and security information, delve into the specifics of your child's concerns. Finding out that airlines don't deliver invading armies, for example, helped one child to be much less frightened of the Iraq war! It is impossible for us, as adults, to predict how events will develop, but we can tell children our hopes that the war will end quickly and our troops will come home safely and soon and that the violence, destruction, and loss of life that happens in warfare and terrorism will end. We can also reassure them that we are able to stand by and support one another in times of distress.

2. WHOSE FAULT IS IT?

Many adults have very strong feelings about our country going to war, about threats of terrorism, and about our country's response to both. Your children's questions about your views offer a good opportunity to have a conversation about the war and terrorism. The extent to which you want to share details of your own political view is up to you, but do use this opportunity to demonstrate to your kids that having strong feelings such as sadness or anger does not have to lead to actions that run counter to your values and responsibilities. If your children's anger or fear extends to whole groups of people—based on ethnicity, race, or religion—it is important to discuss the factual aspects of war and counterterrorist efforts. For example, with older children, who are most likely to generalize, you might make a simple statement assuring them that everyone who practices Islam is not a terrorist. You might add that that extremism in any group of people can lead to the expression of hatred and to violent and destructive behavior. You might also remind your older children that free countries are built on the ideal of inclusion and have always been at their best when they embrace diversity. We have been proudest as a nation when we fought for the freedom and civil rights of all our citizens and when we were required to help others outside our country fight for theirs.

3. CAN I MAKE A DIFFERENCE?

Some children may want to find ways to help our country at this time of crisis. They can start by taking care of themselves—telling you what's on their minds, expressing their views, their fears, and their hopes. They can also offer help by listening to the views and feelings of others—their friends and classmates, their teachers, and other trusted adults. Over time, they can think about how they, along with others in the community, might be able to do something helpful for members of the armed forces and their families, as well as for children and others who are caught up in and suffer the effects of war and terrorism.

■

QUESTIONS PARENTS ASK ABOUT WAR AND TERRORISM

1. AS A PARENT, HOW DO I TALK TO MY CHILDREN ABOUT WAR AND TERRORISM? I DON'T WANT TO MAKE THINGS WORSE; SHOULD I SAY NOTHING?

Often what children need most is someone whom they trust to listen to their questions, accept their feelings, and be there for them. Don't worry about knowing exactly the right thing to say; there is no answer that will make everything okay. Your silence will not protect your children from what is happening. In fact, it only prevents them from understanding and coping with the situation. Remember that listening, answering, and reassuring should be age-appropriate.

2. WHAT IF THIS DISCUSSION UPSETS THEM?

Talking is an important way to share feelings and learn how to cope with loss. It's okay if your children get upset when talking about disturbing things. Remind them that talking about scary ideas does not make them come true and that it is okay to tell you when they are upset. Remind them that they will feel safer and more secure when they don't try to hide their feelings. When you know what makes them frightened they will no longer feel alone.

3. WHAT IF MY KIDS DON'T ASK ANY QUESTIONS, SHOULD I BRING UP THE SUBJECT? WHAT IF THEY DON'T SEEM TO WANT TO TALK ABOUT IT?

When upsetting things happen, it is a good idea to open the door to discussion about these events with your children, particularly school-age and adolescent kids, who are more likely to consume the same news that you do. Be ready to talk with your children when the scope and weight of events reaches a critical mass. At first, older children may tell you that they don't want or need to discuss it. It is often easier to begin discussions about horrific events by asking your children what their friends and classmates are thinking, feeling, and saying. In most cases it is not a good idea, nor is it possible, to force your children to talk with you. When we are able to remain calm as we introduce the topics of war and terrorism—or more local sources of danger and traumatic distress—and limit our own expectations about the length of our discussions, our kids are much more likely to engage in further talk down the road.

4. WHAT IF MY CHILD DOESN'T SEEM UPSET BY EVENTS THAT UPSET OR HORRIFY THE REST OF US?

Many children may appear uninterested and even irritated by adults' sustained focus on war and terrorism. In fact, during stressful times children may become even more involved in their own immediate day-to-day personal needs and concerns than usual. Deepening their preoccupation with the interests and intrigues of daily life may reflect the normal, developmentally appropriate distribution of emotional investments and provide important insulation from dangerous events that threaten to intrude. Remember, the size and scope of your children's world is smaller than your own, and the situation may not have had a direct impact on them. They may, quite appropriately, be far more concerned about the details of own lives. Young children may not understand what has happened in the world or what it means. Other children may be concerned but afraid to ask questions or share their feelings. Children may visit their concerns briefly but then return to play or involve themselves in schoolwork or other activities rather than letting themselves feel overwhelmed.

5. HOW DO I KNOW IF MY CHILD NEEDS MORE COUNSEL THAN I CAN PROVIDE? WHERE CAN I GO FOR HELP?

The news of war, terrorism, and other catastrophic events evokes a range of upsetting but normal reactions. If your children seem unusually upset for several days—especially if they are upset or worried about many things, or are having trouble in school, at home, or with their friends—it is a good idea to speak with someone outside the family for advice. You may wish to consult your children's teacher or school counseling services, your pediatrician, mental health counselor, or a member of the clergy for advice. Don't wait until your children show signs of being truly troubled. Seek advice whenever you think it would help you be more available, understanding, and comforting to your child.

6. WHERE CAN I FIND ADDITIONAL INFORMATION ABOUT HOW TO HELP CHILDREN EXPOSED TO VIOLENCE?

For further information on what is appropriate to say to children of different ages about violence and its effects, contact the National Center for Children Exposed to Violence at www.nccev.org and click on Developmental Guidelines.

ACKNOWLEDGMENTS

For as long as I can remember, I have been curious about why people act the way they do—especially when their behavior is most disturbing and incomprehensible. As I have struggled to understand, it has been my great good luck to have had wonderful teachers throughout my life. I was especially fortunate to have parents who shared my curiosity and who devoted their professional efforts to studying and treating children and adults who were struggling to understand and increase control of their lives. My father practiced as a pediatrician before training as a psychiatrist, child psychiatrist, and psychoanalyst. My mother trained as a clinical social worker and has practiced psychotherapy with children and adults for over thirty-five years. In addition to being wonderful resources for some of my most basic questions about the mysteries of human motivation and behavior, they taught me how to put my own observations into words and, most important, how to pose questions about what I saw. From my first horrified reactions to scenes of human brutality and suffering in our country's struggles for civil rights, through my own challenges in growing up, to my earliest efforts to help patients, my parents have always been available to listen, to share their wisdom, and to help me to remember that curiosity and compassion are always the best responses to the most confusing and troubling aspects of human behavior. As I wrote this book, my parents were characteristically generous in their reading and consultation as I attempted to articulate experiences and observations that all of us share—as children, as adults, and as parents. I am forever grateful for all that they have given to me. They have been my first and best teachers, and this book is but one outcome of what I have learned from them.

After I graduated from Beloit College in Wisconsin, I met with Dr. Al Solnit, then director of the Yale Child Study Center. When I told him that I wanted to become a psychoanalyst, he suggested that before I pursue graduate studies I should learn about normal development. So I worked for a year at the Edith B. Jackson Day Care Program in New Haven as an aide with children 18 months to 4 years of age, where, by day, Lola Nash and Violet Talbot taught me how to observe and make sense of the lives of normal children. By night I worked at the Yale Psychiatric Institute, where I learned that the most bizarre and seemingly disorganized behavior has meaning and that order and understanding are essential ingredients in helping people who are most estranged from reality to reconnect to others in a world in which they are terrifyingly alone.

Dr. Solnit continued to be a treasured teacher and mentor until his death in 2002. Dr. Robert Evans and Ms. Alice Colonna, who have continued to be valued teachers and friends, joined Al in urging me to embark on my studies in child and adolescent psychoanalysis at the Hampstead Clinic, now the Anna Freud Centre, in London. It wasn't until much later that I would appreciate how the hours I spent observing mothers and infants, toddlers in a nursery school program, and pediatric patients in the Middlesex Hospital contributed to my work conducting intensive psychoanalysis and psychotherapy with patients. My teachers—Anna Freud, Hansi Kennedy, Clifford Yorke, Ilse Helman, Audrey Gavshon, Anneliese Schnurman, Pauline Cohen, Barbara Grant, Rose Edgcumbe, and many others—taught me that the values of embracing uncertainty and listening were the first steps to appreciating, understanding, and untangling the complex mixture of motivations and conflicts that underlie symptoms, suffering, and solutions.

In 1984, it was my greatest fortune to meet Dr. Donald Cohen, the director of the Yale Child Study Center from 1983 until 2001. A brilliant researcher in the neurobiology and psychology of autism and Tourette's syndrome and a gifted child and adult psychoanalyst, he was my mentor and my friend until his death in 2001. He challenged me to apply my training as a psychoanalyst to the challenges of violence and trauma that confront the lives of so many children and families in times of war and in the daily life of neighborhoods throughout our country. In the same way that he steered the Child Study Center in uncovering the biological contributions to serious psychiatric disorders, Donald moved the field of child mental health toward the application of what we could learn in the laboratory and consulting room to benefit the broadest number of children and families at risk. His devotion to improving the lives of many led to the beginning of a pioneering partnership between law enforcement and mental health professionals, with the aim of intervening more quickly with children and families in situations involving violence and trauma. His vision would lead to the development of the National Center for Children Exposed to Violence at the Yale Child Study Center and to the dissemination of what we learned throughout our own country and abroad. In the weeks before his death, Donald helped to shape the Center's response to the new kind of violence that impacted on all of us on September 11, 2001. This book is a just one aspect of his legacy.

Throughout my career as a child, adolescent, and adult psychoanalyst, I have been indebted to the individuals and families who have sought my help. As they placed their trust in me, they have taught me how to listen and learn with them. When we have been most successful, it is because we found words to describe the indescribable and meaning to replace the fear that so often accompanies the unknown. It is my hope that the courage my patients and others have shown in shining light on the sources of their fears and struggles will also benefit those who read this book. So much of what I have learned is the result of their hard work.

During one of my most difficult cases, I sought a consultation with Dr. Sally Provence, a pediatrician and psychoanalyst, a leader in our field, and one of the revered members of the Child Study Center faculty. The child with whom I was working had experienced multiple traumatic events that had contributed to a host of crippling symptoms. Sally listened to my despair about the enormity of what the boy had suffered and offered helpful clinical advice. And then she addressed my emotional response. "You know," she said, in her soft West Texas drawl, "if we can learn just one new thing from a tragedy that can help this child or the next, then whatever occurred is not merely a tragedy."

But first we must be able to listen. Over the last fourteen years in my work with Child Study Center colleagues and colleagues in the New Haven Department of Police Service, I have spent a good deal of time responding to learning from children and families who have had to endure the terror of violence that has occurred in their homes, neighborhoods, and schools and in their nation. I have learned how hard it is to listen. I have also learned how hard it is to take off our blinders to see the emotional impact of violent events that are beyond the control of the children and families who have been witnesses and victims. The challenge and courage needed to confront and struggle with the aftermath of violence is greatest for them. But recognizing and responding, to see their suffering also requires courage and determination. This book is also a testament to my colleagues at the Child Study Center and in the New Haven Police Department, the Connecticut Department of Children and Families, the New Haven Schools, the New Haven juvenile justice system, and domestic violence services, and to colleagues in other Child Development Community Policing programs around the country. They have taught me about courage and about the true meaning of partnership. Working together, we have learned that there is indeed strength in numbers and that when together we take off the blinders, the children and families who are most terrified no longer need to be alone.

I am grateful to my colleagues Drs. Steve Berkowitz and Steve Southwick for their consultation and advice. I am also extremely grateful to Colleen Vadala, whose administrative skills, friendship, and wisdom ensure that children and families who need our help get it. And I am deeply indebted to my dear friends Kay Long and Bruce Benson, who were always willing to read and contribute at crucial moments in my writing, and to my oldest friend, Mark Williams, who has always been there to listen. My wonderful and patient friend Lyn May read and reviewed each chapter as the book progressed, helping me to stay true to my intended audience and to the ideas I hoped to convey. Her warmth and humor and her abiding investment in the lives of children always made even the most difficult editorial suggestions easy to accept. And she was always right! I am also grateful to Josh Horwitz, who thought I might have something to say about listening to fear and helped me to shape what such a book might involve.

I am grateful to my editor at Holt, Lisa Considine, who assiduously read, worried over, and edited every line of text. I am also grateful to Catherine O'Neill Grace, who smoothed out the rough edges and did a masterful job in tuning up the text so that it might reach the broadest possible readership. She was just what the doctor ordered and was a pleasure to work with. I am also grateful to my agent, Gail Ross, without whom *Listening to Fear* would have remained only an idea.

INDEX

gratification. *See also* delayed
gratification
fantasy and, 66
in infants, 45
toddler tantrums and, 76
grooming, 185. *See also* cleaning
group activities, children (ages 3 to 6),
111
growth, children (ages 3 to 6), 93–95
Grubb, Davis, 9
guilt
in child's response to accident,
174–75
internalizing reaction to criticism, 24
masturbation and, 140
seeking punishment and, 27

hair styles, adolescence, 137
hallucinations, 16
health, unrealistic concerns with, 34
health-care providers
parents consulting with, 131–32
role in preventing domestic violence,
180
hearing, infants, 42
heaven, children's concerns with, 182
helplessness, during traumas, 189
heterosexuality, 149
home, adolescents moving out from,
156–57
homosexuality
during adolescence, 149–51
biological and social basis of, 150
peer relationships and, 150–51
hospitals, emergency planning, 229
hostility
ambivalence regarding feelings of, 27
perceiving in others, 24
humiliation
loss of control and, 202
post-traumatic symptoms, 197–98
hygiene, phobias, 20
hypersensitivity, caused by disruptions
in parent-infant relationship, 48

"I can do" attitude, of toddlers, 54–55
imagination
developing in toddlers, 65–68
play and, 84–86, 104
power of, 14

immobilization
of body and mind in trauma, 196
caused by fear, 205
independence
adolescent choices and, 155
adolescent experimentation with
values, 146–47
adolescents pushing for, 135, 138
conflicting needs of adolescents for,
141
infants (birth to 18 months), 37–50.
See also trauma, young children
abandonment or loss, 46
biological building blocks in
developing sense of self, 42–44
challenges to development and, 48
development of self-reliance, 46–47
differentiating me from not me, 45
fears of, 4
objects of comfort, 47–48
overview of, 37–41
parents and caregivers understanding,
41–42
reliance on parents and close
relationships, 49–50
information resources, for helping
children exposed to violence, 237
injury
fears of children (ages 3 to 6), 108
fears of children (ages 7 to 12),
129
response to injury of parent, 181
trauma in young children, 169–70
inner world, of toddlers, 65–68
insanity
adolescent's fears of sexuality and,
139
fear of going crazy, 16
intercourse, 98. *See also* sexuality
intimacy, adolescent longing for, 141
intimate partnership, 154–55
Iraq war, 1, 215–16
irritability
domestic violence and, 178
post-traumatic symptoms, 160, 186,
188

jealousy, children with same-sex parent,
96
Jonesboro shootings, 221–22

ABOUT THE AUTHOR

STEVEN MARANS, PH.D., is the Harris Associate Professor of Child Psychoanalysis and Associate Professor of Psychiatry at the Child Study Center and Department of Psychiatry, Yale University School of Medicine. He is the director of the National Center for Children Exposed to Violence, designated in 1999 by the White House and the U.S. Department of Justice, and is the director of the Childhood Violent Trauma Center, part of the National Childhood Traumatic Stress Network established by the U.S. Department of Health and Human Services. Dr. Marans is also a faculty member at the Western New England Institute of Psychoanalysis. He trained in clinical social work at the Smith College School for Social Work, child and adolescent psychoanalysis at the Anna Freud Centre in London, received his Ph.D. in psychology at University College London, London University, and his training in adult psychoanalysis at the Western New England Institute for Psychoanalysis. He joined the faculty of the Yale Child Study Center in 1984. In New Haven, Dr. Marans developed a pioneering approach to partnerships between law enforcement and mental health professionals known as the Child Development Community Policing Program, which has become a model for similar partnerships around the country. He has worked closely with ranking members of the U.S. Department of Justice, members of Congress, and the White House on issues related to trauma, youth violence, and law enforcement, as well as mental health issues surrounding terrorism and war. Through the National Center for Children Exposed to Violence, he has been deeply involved in responding to the post-9/11 mental health issues of children and families in New York City, Connecticut, and around the country. He lives with his family in New Haven, Connecticut.